Introducing Phonological Awareness and Early Literacy Instruction into Japanese Elementary School English Education
—Its Significance and Feasibility—

Introducing Phonological Awareness and Early Literacy Instruction into Japanese Elementary School English Education

—Its Significance and Feasibility—

Chika Ikeda

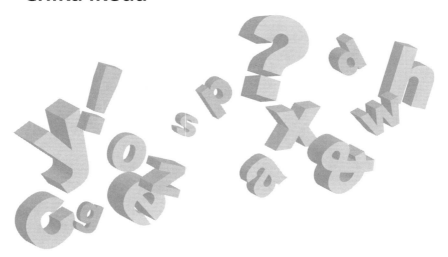

KAITAKUSHA

Kaitakusha Co., Ltd.
5–2, Mukogaoka 1-chome
Bunkyo-ku, Tokyo 113–0023
Japan

Introducing Phonological Awareness and Early Literacy Instruction into Japanese Elementary School English Education
—Its Significance and Feasibility—

Published in Japan
by Kaitakusha Co., Ltd., Tokyo

Copyright © 2015
by Chika Ikeda

All rights reserved. No part of this publication may be reproduced, stored in a retrieval system, or transmitted, in any form or by any means, electronic, mechanical, photocopying, recording, or otherwise, without the prior permission of the copyright owner.

First published 2015

Printed and bound in Japan
by ARM Corporation

Cover design by Shihoko Nakamura

Acknowledgement

This book focuses on the characteristics of phonological awareness that Japanese EFL learners need to develop to learn to read English. I believe that the comprehensive review of earlier research in this area, as well as the results of an exploratory intervention to teach phonological awareness in view of early literacy instruction, will contribute to future research on the introduction of early literacy skills into the English teaching curriculum in Japan.

I would like to take this opportunity to express my immense gratitude to all the people who have provided me with invaluable support and encouragement. This book would not have been possible without their help.

First and foremost, I am profoundly indebted to Dr Annamaria Pinter and Dr Shelagh Rixon, who were very generous with their time and knowledge and assisted me in each step of this study. I have greatly benefitted from their insightful comments and suggestions on my work. They will continue to be my models not only as teachers but also as researchers.

I would like to express my sincere gratitude to Dr Keith Richards, Dr Ema Ushioda, and Dr Seongsook Choi for their insightful advice and warm encouragement. Their guidance helped me throughout the writing process.

I am also grateful to the teachers at M Elementary School who approved my topic and gave support and practical advice during the intervention, and to the children of the target class who patiently participated in the sessions.

I wish to extend my gratitude to Pamela Wilmot for her unstinting moral support and encouragement over the years. Special thanks go to Brett

Cumming for his suggestions and proofreading the ealier versions. I would also like to thank Kaitakusha for agreeing to publish this book.

The publication of this book was supported by Japan Society for the Promotion of Science (JSPS) KAKENHI Grant Number 265072.

Table of Contents

Acknowledgement ·· v
Table of Contents ··· vii
List of Tables ··· xiii
List of Figures ·· xiv
List of Appendices ·· xiv
Abbreviations ·· xv

Chapter 1 Introduction ··· 1
  1.1.   English education in Japanese elementary schools — A historical summary   2
      1.1.1.   Beginning of English education in elementary schools   2
      1.1.2.   'English Conversation Activities' preceding the introduction of FLA   3
      1.1.3.   Introduction of FLA into the elementary school curriculum   4
  1.2.   Aims and objectives   5
  1.3.   Rationale and research questions   6
      1.3.1.   The significance of teaching early English reading at the elementary school level   6
      1.3.2.   Research questions   9
  1.4.   Overview of the book   14

Chapter 2 Phonological Awareness and its Importance for Japanese Children Learning English ... **15**

2.1. Introduction ... 15
2.2. Phonological awareness and its development ... 16
  2.2.1. Definition ... 16
  2.2.2. The levels of phonological awareness ... 17
    2.2.2.1. Rhyme awareness ... 18
    2.2.2.2. Syllable awareness ... 19
    2.2.2.3. Onset-rime awareness as intrasyllabic awareness ... 19
    2.2.2.4. Phonemic awareness ... 20
  2.2.3. The development of phonological awareness ... 21
2.3. Phonological awareness and early reading development in L1 ... 23
  2.3.1. The influence of phonological awareness on learning to read ... 23
    2.3.1.1. The large-unit hypothesis ... 23
    2.3.1.2. The small-unit hypothesis ... 24
    2.3.1.3. Toward a compromise of different conceptualisations — Phonological awareness as a unitary construct ... 25
  2.3.2. The influence of reading development on the sophistication of phonological awareness ... 28
    2.3.2.1. Knowledge of the alphabet ... 28
    2.3.2.2. Reading experience in an alphabetic script ... 30
  2.3.3. Discussion ... 31
2.4. Japanese children's phonological awareness and speech segmentation in L1 ... 32
  2.4.1. Japanese phonological units and the writing system ... 32
  2.4.2. Japanese children's phonological awareness ... 34
    2.4.2.1. Strategies used in counting and deleting syllables and phonemes ... 35
    2.4.2.2. Causes in the development of phonological awareness at the phoneme level ... 38
  2.4.3. The speech segmentation procedure of Japanese children ... 39
    2.4.3.1. Speech segmentation and learning to read in an alphabetic language ... 39
    2.4.3.2. The effect of language rhythm on speech segmentation ... 40
    2.4.3.3. Characteristics of Japanese speakers' speech segmentation ... 41
  2.4.4. Summary ... 44
2.5. Phonological awareness necessary for Japanese children in learning to read in English ... 45

2.5.1.	The effect of orthographic and phonological differences on learning to read	45
2.5.2.	The differences in phonological awareness necessary for early reading across languages	46
2.5.3.	The importance of multi-level phonological awareness in early English reading	48
2.5.4.	Summary	50
2.6.	The necessity of phonological awareness instruction for Japanese children learning English	51
2.6.1.	Cross-linguistic transfer of phonological awareness	51
2.6.1.1.	Evidence of the transfer of phonological awareness	51
2.6.1.2.	The factors affecting the transfer of phonological awareness	52
2.6.1.3.	The effect of L1 phonological awareness on L2 word reading	54
2.6.1.4.	Three questions that need to be answered	55
2.6.2.	The development of phonological awareness of Japanese children learning English	55
2.6.2.1.	The effect of the *Roma-ji* instruction	56
2.6.2.2.	The developmental progression of phonological awareness of Japanese children learning English — A hypothesis	58
2.6.3.	The importance of teaching phonological awareness to Japanese elementary school children	61
2.7.	The instruction of phonological awareness	64
2.7.1.	Features of the effective phonological awareness instruction	65
2.7.2.	The implications for the phonological awareness instruction for Japanese children	67
2.8.	The factors affecting the item difficulty in the phonological awareness assessment	70
2.8.1.	The target levels of phonological awareness	70
2.8.2.	Task differences	71
2.8.3.	The linguistic complexity of target phonological units	72
2.8.3.1.	The number of phonemes in the target stimuli	72
2.8.3.2.	The position of target phonemes	73
2.8.3.3.	The types of target phonemes	74
2.8.4.	Summary	75
2.9.	Chapter summary	76

Chapter 3 Methodology ... 77
- 3.1. Research Design — 77
- 3.2. The intervention — 78
  - 3.2.1. The context — 78
  - 3.2.2. Methods of data collection and the role of the researcher — 79
  - 3.2.3. The content and methods for the instruction — 80
    - 3.2.3.1. Target skills for phonological awareness, sound categories, and spelling rules — 80
    - 3.2.3.2. Session plans — 83
  - 3.2.4. The assessment and questionnaires before and after the intervention — 85
    - 3.2.4.1. Tests for the initial and final assessment of phonological awareness — 87
    - 3.2.4.2. Mini assessment — 92
    - 3.2.4.3. The letter combination in non-word targets — 93
  - 3.2.5. Ethical issues related to the intervention — 94
  - 3.2.6. Data analysis procedures — 95
- 3.3. Chapter summary — 95

Chapter 4 The Results ... 97
- 4.1. Actual sessions — 97
- 4.2. Lower-case letter-name knowledge — 101
- 4.3. Phonological awareness skills — 103
  - 4.3.1. Segmenting and phoneme identification — 103
    - 4.3.1.1. Qualitative observational data — 103
    - 4.3.1.2. Quantitative assessment data — 106
  - 4.3.2. Blending — 115
  - 4.3.3. Deleting — 118
    - 4.3.3.1. Qualitative observational data — 118
    - 4.3.3.2. Quantitative assessment data — 121
  - 4.3.4. Substitution — 123
    - 4.3.4.1. Qualitative observational data — 123
    - 4.3.4.2. Quantitative assessment data — 126
- 4.4. Letter sounds — Short vowels and basic consonants — 130
  - 4.4.1. Qualitative observational data — 130
  - 4.4.2. Quantitative assessment data — 134
- 4.5. Skills and knowledge for early word reading — 135

4.5.1.	Word reading	135
4.5.1.1.	Qualitative observational data	135
4.5.1.2.	Quantitative assessment data	137
4.5.2.	Split-grapheme rule	142
4.5.2.1.	Qualitative observational data	142
4.5.2.2.	Quantitative assessment data	145
4.5.3.	Digraphs — *ch*, *ck*, *sh*, *th*, and *wh*	146
4.5.3.1.	Qualitative observational data	146
4.5.3.2.	Quantitative assessment data	149
4.5.4.	Double vowel-letters — *ee* and *oo*	149
4.5.4.1.	Qualitative observational data	149
4.5.4.2.	Quantitative assessment data	150
4.5.5.	Consonant doubling	151
4.5.6.	Consonant clusters	152
4.6.	The results of children's questionnaires before and after the intervention	153
4.7.	Children's reactions to the reflection sheets	160
4.8.	Summary	162

Chapter 5 Discussion — 163

5.1.	The effectiveness of the phonological awareness instruction in 'Foreign Language Activities'	163
5.1.1.	The outcomes of the instruction and the characteristics of the children's phonological awareness and early English reading — RQ-A	164
5.1.2.	The difficulties in phonological awareness tasks in English for Japanese children — RQ-B	168
5.1.3.	The reaction of children and elementary school teachers to the instruction — RQ-C	170
5.1.4.	Problems related to the instruction — RQ-D	174
5.1.5.	The learnability and teachability of phonological awareness	178
5.2.	Summary	179

Chapter 6　Conclusion **181**
　6.1.　Main findings of this study　　　　　　　　　　　　　181
　6.2.　Theoretical implications　　　　　　　　　　　　　　182
　6.3.　Practical implications　　　　　　　　　　　　　　　183
　6.4.　Limitations and future directions　　　　　　　　　　186
　6.5.　Concluding statement　　　　　　　　　　　　　　　187

References **189**

Appendices **217**

Index **245**

List of Tables

Table 1.1:	The percentage of positive responses to possible objectives and content of instruction in ECA	10
Table 1.2:	The number of public elementary schools which implement 'the activities to familiarise children with English letters' in ECA	11
Table 3.1:	The summary of target sound categories and spelling rules for the instruction and the assessment	84
Table 3.2:	The list of tools for the assessment and information gathering before and after the intervention	86
Table 3.3:	The summary of four conditions in the sound categorisation test	89
Table 3.4:	Target words for the word reading test in the initial and final assessments	91
Table 4.1:	Participating children in the intervention	98
Table 4.2:	Summary of the assessment tasks	100
Table 4.3:	The descriptive statistics of the results of the initial and final assessment	107
Table 4.4:	The results of t-test for the initial and final assessment	108
Table 4.5:	The results of a middle vowel identification test	110
Table 4.6:	The results of a final phoneme identification test	111
Table 4.7:	The results of an initial and final phoneme identification test	112
Table 4.8:	Paired Samples t-tests of children's performance on the oral sound manipulation test in the initial and final assessments	121
Table 4.9:	The average rates of correct responses of each test item of all children	123
Table 4.10:	The results of a recognition and identification of a substituted phoneme test	129
Table 4.11:	The results of a phoneme substitution and identification test	130
Table 4.12:	Children's responses to the revision activity of letter sounds in the reflection sheets	133
Table 4.13:	The correct response rates of all children in the word reading test categorised by the target word characteristics	140
Table 4.14:	Children's responses about their understanding of the sprit-grapheme rule in the reflection sheets	146
Table 4.15:	Children's responses to the initial and final questionnaires (1)	155
Table 4.16:	Children's responses to the initial and final questionnaires (2)	155
Table 4.17:	The results of Pearson's *Chi*-square tests	156
Table 4.18:	Children's responses to the final questionnaires (1)	158
Table 4.19:	Children's responses to the final questionnaires (2)	158

xiv   *Introducing Phonological Awareness and Early Literacy Instruction*

List of Figures

Figure 1.1:	The relationship between ECA in PIS and FLA	4
Figure 2.1:	*Kana* matrix [*50 On Hyou*] with *Roma-ji* letters	36
Figure 2.2:	The model of developmental progression of phonological awareness by Japanese English learners	59
Figure 2.3:	The model of developmental progression of phonological awareness by English speakers	60
Figure 4.1:	The results of the initial and final letter-name recognition tests and the final letter-sound recognition test of all children	102
Figure 4.2:	Sample Elkonin cards	103
Figure 4.3:	The results of the initial phoneme recognition test of all children	108
Figure 4.4:	The results of the phoneme recognition and location test of all children	109
Figure 4.5:	The correct response rates of the sound categorisation test of all children	113
Figure 4.6:	Sample onset-rime slide	116
Figure 4.7:	The results of oral sound manipulation tests	122
Figure 4.8:	Children's reactions to the reflection sheets — General	160
Figure 4.9:	Children's reactions to the reflection sheets — Phonological awareness activities	161

List of Appendices

Appendix 1.1:	The Chapter of 'Foreign Language Activities' in the *Course of Study for Elementary Schools* enacted in the academic year of 2011	217
Appendix 3.1:	The structure of *Eigo Note 1*	220
Appendix 3.2:	The summary of the plans for the information gathering at both the initial and final stages of the intervention	222
Appendix 4.1:	The timetable of the introduction, activities, and tasks for target content	225
Appendix 4.2:	Description of *the new content instruction* and *phonological awareness activities* in each session	228
Appendix 4.3:	The summary of the statistical significance yielded in the written tests of the initial and final assessments	239
Appendix 4.4:	The results of the oral tests in the initial and final assessments — Sound manipulation	241
Appendix 4.5:	The results of the oral tests in the initial and final assessments — Real word and non-word reading	242

Abbreviations

ALT	Assistant Language Teacher
AST	Assistant Student Teacher
D	Designated School(s)
ECA	English Conversation Activities
EFL	English as a Foreign Language
ESL	English as a Second Language
FLA	Foreign Language Activities
HRT	Homeroom Teacher
MEXT	the Japanese Ministry of Education, Culture, Sports, Science and Technology
L1	First Language
L2	Second Language
ND	Non-designated School(s)
P	Pupil (e.g., "P3" is the pupil with an ID 3)
PIS	Period for Integrated Studies
RJ	the instructor's Research Journal (e.g., "RJ18" is the journal about Session 18)
SLA	Second Language Acquisition

Introducing Phonological Awareness and Early Literacy Instruction into Japanese Elementary School English Education

—Its Significance and Feasibility—

Chapter 1

Introduction

In Japanese elementary schools, English education was effectively introduced as the period of 'Foreign Language Activities' (FLA) in Grades 5 and 6 (children at the age of 10 to 12) in 2011. FLA is not a curricular subject in itself, but a required class once a week, 35 classes a year. As the main focus of FLA is to familiarise children with sounds and basic expressions of English, according to the *Course of Study for Elementary Schools*, the use of letters and words are expected to be "supplementary tools for oral communication, in effort not to give too much burden to pupils." From these descriptions, it can at least be understood that FLA does not focus on activities of reading and writing with letters.

However, in *Eigo Note 2* (MEXT, 2009b), which was the first recommended textbook for FLA in Grade 6 and came with *Eigo Note 1* (MEXT, 2009a) for Grade 5, two lessons for learning names and shapes of both upper-case and lower-case letters were included. *Eigo Note 1 & 2* were later replaced by *Hi, friends! 1 & 2* (MEXT, 2012a, 2012b) one year after the introduction of FLA. The content of the new textbooks is mostly the same as the previous one but a lesson for learning upper-case letters is included in *Hi, friends! 1* for Grade 5. Even so, there appears to be no concrete examples of instructional methodology proposed for the use of letters "as supplementary tools for oral communication" in the *Course of Study*. In the *Commentary on the Course of Study for Elementary Schools* (MEXT, 2008a) and the *Guidebook for Teacher Training in Foreign Language Activities in Elementary Schools* (MEXT, 2009c), it is only mentioned that pupils may be taught upper-case and lower-case letters yet should not be unduly exposed to them. Thus, formal introduction of the skills for reading and writing in English is delayed until the instruction of English as a curricular subject in its own right commences at junior-high school. Several simple questions came to the author's mind when the establishment of FLA was announced, such as why only oral aspects of language would be emphasised in its instructional content, why reading and writing should be avoided, and how letters could be used "as supplementary tools for oral communication." These were the starting points of this research.

In this introductory chapter, the contextual background to this book is provided along with aims and objectives. Then, the rationale for the contribution that this research makes to the field of elementary school English education in Japan follows. The chapter will also set out the research questions that this book seeks to address. Finally, a brief overview will be provided.

1.1. English education in Japanese elementary schools — A historical summary

The modern school system of Japan began from the promulgation of the school system in 1872. The Fundamental Law of Education and the School Education Law were enacted in 1947 and the 6-3-3-4-year (elementary school—junior-high school—senior-high school—university) system of school education was established aiming at realising the principle of equal opportunity for education. The National Curriculum Standard is called the *Course of Study* in Japan, revised about once every ten years. The version of the *Course of Study for Elementary Schools* introducing FLA (MEXT, 2008b) was announced in March of 2008 and came into force in the academic year of 2011.

In order to understand the circumstances of how FLA was introduced, it is necessary to have an understanding of the historical background of elementary school English education in Japan. The term *English education* has been used to refer to 'teaching English in the school curriculum' regardless of whether or not it is a curricular subject in itself, and is distinguished from the term *English teaching* which encompasses all other contexts of teaching English including private English schools and in homes.

1.1.1. Beginning of English education in elementary schools

The beginning of English education in Japanese elementary schools can be traced back to the *Meiji* era (1868-1912) (Imura, 2003; Omura, 1980). It is recorded that, under the influence of junior-high schools where English was widely taught as 'education for the elite' in the tide of civilisation and enlightenment after the *Meiji* Restoration, several elementary schools began to teach English. However, due to the directional shift of educational policy to emphasise Japanese language education as well as the outbreak of wars, English education in Japan was forced to change its objectives and forms. Such movement also affected elementary school English education, and finally it was completely abolished except in some private elementary schools (Butler-Goto, 2005).

Then, with the economic growth following the Second World War, learning English as an international language became again in vogue in Japan. In 1986, based on a report from the extraordinary Educational Council stating that the time for starting foreign language education in the educational system should be reconsidered, research into this feasibility officially started. The topic was subsequently proposed by the 'Round-table committee on English Education Reform' in 1991, and in the following year practical research for developing the curriculum of English education commenced in two elementary schools. In 1996 such elementary schools designated for research were located in each of the 47 prefectures throughout Japan. Whereas this inspired other elementary schools to include the instruction of English as a part of 'education for international understanding,' it appeared to be difficult for most public elementary schools to offer a certain number of English classes in their tight curricula unless they were designated schools (Imura, 2003).

1.1.2. 'English Conversation Activities' preceding the introduction of FLA

On the occasion of revising the *Course of Study for Elementary Schools* in 1998, the 'Period for Integrated Studies' (PIS) was established for all grades, and in this period, 'English Conversation Activities' (ECA) was introduced as an option for the purpose of enhancing children's understanding of foreign cultures. The new curriculum, which came into effect in 2002, made it possible to include a class to teach English once a week, and so English education began to spread rapidly in elementary schools throughout Japan. This revision of the *Course of Study* seems to be one of the turning points of English education in Japan, because, in addition to the establishment of ECA in elementary schools, English became a compulsory subject in its own right for the first time at the junior-high school level.

However, it should be emphasised that ECA in PIS was nothing but a part of 'education for international understanding.' In fact, at that time more and more parents were longing for *formal* English instruction in elementary schools. It was shown in the result of 'The survey on the attitudes to English education in elementary schools' carried out by MEXT in 2004, two years after ECA began, that 70.7% of 9,598 parents answered that English should be taught as a mandatory subject (MEXT, 2004).

1.1.3. Introduction of FLA into the elementary school curriculum

In March 2008, the new revision of the *Course of Study for Elementary Schools* was announced. One of the controversial issues behind this amendment that had attracted a great deal of attention among researchers, educators, and parents was whether English would be finally introduced as a curricular subject. Some worried that English learning would delay children's mastery of Japanese (L1). Others claimed that English should be included in compulsory education because Japan had to catch up and be better placed to compete with other Asian countries that had already introduced English as a curricular subject in their educational systems. As a matter of fact, in Thailand for instance, English started to be taught gradually in compulsory education at the elementary school level in 1996, schools in Korea did so in 1997, and in China in 2001.

Figure 1.1: The relationship between ECA in PIS and FLA

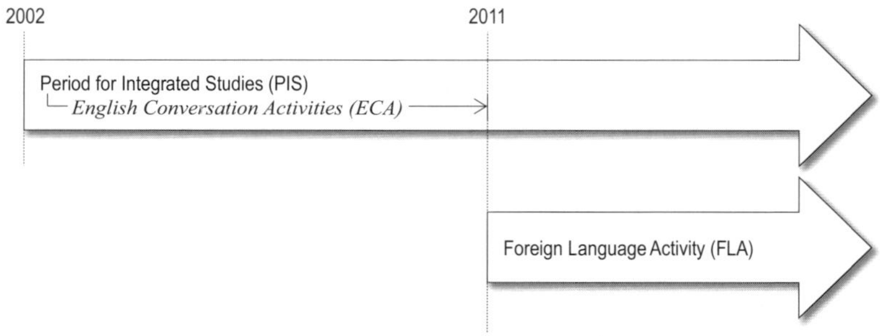

```
2002                              2011
    ┌─────────────────────────────────────────────────┐
    │ Period for Integrated Studies (PIS)             │
    │   └─ English Conversation Activities (ECA) ──►  │
    └─────────────────────────────────────────────────┘
                                  ┌──────────────────┐
                                  │ Foreign Language │
                                  │ Activity (FLA)   │
                                  └──────────────────┘
```

One of the reasons why an increasingly larger number of people became interested in this issue was that in 2002 MEXT formulated 'A strategy to cultivate *Japanese with English abilities*' in a concrete action plan with the aim of drastically improving English language education, as this was expected by the political and business world. The plan *not only* established the attainment goals of English ability for junior-high and senior-high school students and English teachers, *but also* proposed to enhance elementary school ECA which was optionally held in PIS. Since an earlier introduction of English in compulsory education was thought to be one of the essential policies to improve the effect of English education in Japan, people's expectations for it rapidly increased, regardless of whether they agreed to it or not.

Nevertheless, English again failed to acquire the status of a subject in its own right. Instead, English education was decided to be offered in the period of FLA in Grades 5 and 6 (for the chapter of FLA in the *Course of Study*, see Appendix 1.1), which in effect requires schools to teach English. FLA is often considered to be an extension of ECA which was previously taught in PIS in all grades. However, as illustrated in Figure 1.1, PIS is maintained in the new curriculum for all grades with the aim of enhancing children's international understanding, although the activity of 'having a conversation in a foreign language' has been deleted from its content. It does not necessarily mean that English should not be taught in lower grades, but it seems that an attempt has been made to emphasise that English education in the independent period of FLA is fundamentally different from the previous ECA in PIS.

1.2. Aims and objectives

The aim of this book is to discuss and evaluate the significance and the potential of introducing phonological awareness incorporated into the instruction of letters and early reading, which is the beginning stage of literacy teaching, into Japanese elementary school English education where the main focus is placed on oral communication. Hence, in order to fulfil this aim, the following main objectives were established:

1) to discuss the significance of developing phonological awareness for Japanese children learning English as a foreign language (EFL) *as well as* its importance at an early stage of English literacy development
2) to find out whether Japanese children could develop phonological awareness and early reading through the instruction carried out in FLA
3) to investigate the children's reactions as well as the teachers' to the instruction.

In the study reported in this book, the instruction of phonological awareness will be incorporated into the letter instruction, which is considered a part of the initial stage of early reading instruction. Other literacy skills such as spelling or writing may also be considered, but only when necessary, because the acquisition of receptive skills is generally thought to precede the acquisition of productive skills (Carson & Leki, 1993; Krashen, 1989, 2004; Krashen & Terrell, 1983). The outcome of the study will be relevant *not only* to the perspective of establishing the bridge in English education between elementary schools and junior-high schools in Japan by forwarding the introduction of some written aspects of the instructional content in junior-high school to elementary school in order to avoid the sudden change in the instructional mode (i.e., from 'oral only' in elementary schools to 'overwhelmingly written' in junior-high schools), *but also* to the implications for teacher training for future or in-service elementary school teachers. In summary, the primary objective of this book is to investigate and clarify the feasibility of developing Japanese children's *readiness* for receiving formal early reading instruction in elementary school English education through the instruction of phonological awareness integrated with that of the alphabet.

1.3. Rationale and research questions

The importance of early reading instruction in skill-appropriate content has been claimed to be necessary for literacy acquisition in English as L1 (Snow, Burns, & Griffin, 1998). This study is an attempt to apply it to the context of EFL learning in Japan so that children would not fall behind other English-learning counterparts in learning to read in English.

1.3.1. The significance of teaching early English reading at the elementary school level

Considering the status of English education in the curriculum for elementary school in Japan so far, it is clear that the main emphasis of instruction has been placed on developing children's oral communication ability. One of the reasons for *not* teaching letters of the alphabet and reading in elementary school seems to come from the concern that their introduction may become a cause of difficulty for children in the process of learning English. Kageura (1997), who was a member of the editorial committee of *The Guideline for the Practice of Elementary School English Language Activities* (MEXT, 2001), once stated that "introducing English letters together with sounds simultaneously, both of which are new to elementary school children, would cause them to bear an extremely large burden and result in producing children who dislike learning English" (p. 102, my translation).

However, in contrast, some findings from empirical research seem to take a sceptical view of English teaching focusing only on oral communication. For example, the report from an elementary school which had been designated for research states that even lower-grade children appeared to have interest in letters of the alphabet and, when they were used tentatively as supplementary tools, higher-grade children noticeably showed a sign of remembering some English words at the sight of their spellings or trying to remember words with the aid of the alphabet (Naoshima Elementary School, 1996). Similar findings were also reported in other studies (Asai & Mihara, 1999; JASTEC Kanto-Koshinetsu Branch: Second Research Project Team, 1999, 2000; Katagiri, 1985; Kuno, 1996, 1999a; Umemoto, 2000). In addition, after three years of practical research into English teaching, a Japanese elementary school concluded that it might be necessary to construct teaching materials which incorporate letters of the alphabet (Udo Elementary School, 1996). Moreover, many experienced practitioners of early English teaching in Japan have claimed that it would be natural for children to be exposed to the alphabet gradually in the process of familiarising themselves with English sounds (Higuchi, Kanamori, & Kunikata, 2005; Iizuka, 1997; Kuno, 1999b; Nakata, 1993; Naoyama, 2001; Oka & Kanamori, 2009). Thus, later, Kageura (2000) admitted that 'how to deal with letters' would be an issue which ought to be considered in terms of the future of Japanese elementary school English education. In summary, letters and early reading may be able to be taught and play an important role in this field for the following four reasons:

(1) Children are exposed to alphabetic symbols in their daily lives.
(2) Children in Grades 5 and 6 are old and cognitively mature enough to learn the alphabet and early English reading.
(3) Letters of the alphabet can help children in remembering and retaining English words.
(4) Introduction of the alphabet and early reading skills into elementary school English education may help children move on to junior-high school English education more easily and establish the continuity in this field between these different school levels.

First, from the perspective of children's familiarity with alphabetic symbols, they have many opportunities to see the alphabet in their daily lives. For instance, children see and sometimes even recognise these symbols in playing games, using computers, and doing mathematics. In such an environment, there may be no need to protect children from being exposed to the alphabet, and in fact it seems to be unrealistic. Moreover, in Grade 3, children learn the Romanisation of the Japanese language (i.e., *Roma-ji*) which is the way of expressing Japanese syllabaries with the Roman alphabet, and through the experience of learning *Roma-ji*, children may increase an interest not only in the alphabet themselves but also in reading and writing words using them. If so, there should be no reason to delay the introduction of letters and early reading into elementary school English education.

Second, from the perspective of cognitive development, children in Grades 5 and 6 where FLA is taught are around 11 and 12 years old and are in *the formal operational stage* according to the Piaget's theory of cognitive development (Piaget, 1923). They are thought to have the abilities of logical reasoning, abstract thinking, and drawing conclusions deductively. Whereas children in lower grades who are in *the concrete operational stage* would enjoy activities such as singing songs, imitating the teacher's pronunciation in a loud voice, and moving with exaggerated gestures in English classes, higher-grade children might show negative attitudes toward those activities and ask for logical and analytical learning. Thus, as Pinter (2006) discusses, in order to respond to higher-grade children's needs and interests a different teaching approach is required from the one used in teaching lower-grade children. Introduction of letters of the alphabet and reading might in fact be one of the solutions.

Furthermore, from the perspective of the importance of *the alphabet* for Japanese children learning English, the number of opportunities to listen to and speak English outside classes is very limited in Japan where English is taught as a foreign language. With such a limited amount of aural and oral input, letters of the alphabet may be helpful as a means of remembering and retaining English words. Interestingly, some researchers have argued that the relationship between Japanese people and Japanese letters is different from the relationship between English-speaking people and alphabetic symbols in the sense that letters play more essential roles in the Japanese language (Saito, 1996). In other words, since Japanese logographic characters (*kanji*) have visual effects of expressing their meanings, even in oral communication people simultaneously look at the visual image of *kanji* characters being spoken, unconsciously in their mind (Suzuki, 1990). These might imply that Japanese people have a tendency to rely on *letters* not only in using Japanese but also in learning a new language.

Finally, from the perspective of the continuity in English education between elementary school and junior-high school, it has been pointed out that the number of junior-high school students who dislike English learning increases when letters begin to be used in English classes. As mentioned above, it has been the case in Japan that English education as a curricular subject starts at the junior-high school level and includes all of the four macro skills (i.e., speaking, listening, reading, and writing) to be introduced in the early stage of the first year. Therefore it seems natural that many students, even though they enjoyed the previous stage of learning oral English in elementary school, begin to have difficulty in connecting letters with their sounds, i.e., they cannot sound out English words (Kosuga, 1998; Teshima, 1997; Tsuidou, 1996). Moreover, English is thought to be a difficult language to learn to read in terms of its complex grapheme-phoneme correspondence (Adams, 1990; Ehri, 1998; Ehri, Nunes, Willows, Schuster, Yaghoub-Zadeh, & Shanahan, 2001). Especially in the case of the Japanese educational context, this failure in English reading might also be due to the fact that the number of English classes in junior-high schools has been small (i.e., four classes per week after 2012, and three until 2011) and the amount of time available for letter and early reading instruction is insufficient, as well as that the content of most junior-high-school English textbooks are not suitable for the systematic early literacy instruction such as teaching letter-sound correspondence (e.g., Some of the initial letters of words used to introduce the alphabet are pronounced with 'letter names' as in *ice cream* and others are pronounced with 'letter sounds' as in *book* and *driver*.) (Naoyama, 2001; Sasaki, 2004). Therefore, if children have learnt letters and early English reading to a certain extent through FLA in elementary school, they might be able to move on to reading activities in junior-high school more smoothly. Therefore, the introduction of the alphabet and early reading into elementary school English education may be significant in terms of establishing the natural shift to English education in junior-high school.

1.3.2. Research questions

As the *Course of Study* which introduces FLA presupposes, the importance of providing children with a considerable amount of oral input in English before teaching letters of the alphabet seems to be an agreed concept because that is the foundation of literacy development (Terrell, 1982). On the other hand, it is reported that elementary school children's interest in reading and writing English increase when they are in higher grades (Ijima Elementary School, 2003). Moreover, it seems to be problematic that, although relatively large numbers of elementary school children have some knowledge of names and forms of alphabetic symbols, this knowledge is not utilised in English classes. In fact, many elementary school teachers appear to teach children letters of the alphabet, or at least *show* them, in the previous ECA since one of its aims was to enhance children's familiarity with letters of foreign languages. In other words, children seemed to have some experience of reading and writing English letters and words in those classes.

Table 1.1: The percentage of positive responses to possible objectives and content of instruction in ECA

	Positive responses (%)	
	Teachers (N = 2,234)	Parents (N = 9,598)
Objectives of instruction		
To reduce reluctance to English	94.8	94.8
To foster a positive attitude toward communication with foreigners	92.8	87.7
To acquire ability to listen to and speak English	59.6	83.3
To acquire ability to read and write English	20.2	67.0
Content of instruction		
To sing songs and play games in English	96.8	91.5
To learn English rhythm and pronunciation	70.2	87.4
To learn simple conversation such as greetings and self-introduction	92.5	93.4
To communicate foreigners such as ALT (Assistant Language Teacher) and foreign students	87.7	91.1
To read the alphabet and English words	35.7	75.0
To write the alphabet and English words	18.5	67.5
To read and write passages in English	11.5	55.2

(MEXT, 2004, a part of the survey results summarised in a table by the author)

Supporting this idea, the results of the survey on ECA conducted by MEXT revealed that pupils in public elementary schools (N = 10,002) generally have a favourable attitudes toward activities including the use of the alphabet, such as 'activities of writing letters or English words' (38.0%) and 'activities of reading and writing English passages' (39.7%) (MEXT, 2004). Furthermore, out of the pupils who liked ECA (73.9%), 41.1% gave the reason that they enjoyed reading English. On the other hand, out of the pupils who did not like ECA, 50.4% gave the reason that they could not read English well. This percentage was higher than the percentages of other negative reasons such as not being able to communicate with other pupils well in English (39.7%) and that they could not sing English songs nor having the ability to play English games well (35.1%). These findings show that activities using letters of the alphabet, including reading, might have been virtually introduced into classrooms of ECA, and that, unless activities which use the alphabet are introduced and developed in a proper style, some children might have difficulty in dealing with them and even come to dislike English reading activities.

This survey also found that the percentage of elementary school teachers who had positive attitudes toward possible objectives and content of instruction in ECA was remarkably low when these were related to the use of the alphabet (Table 1.1). Additionally, there seems to be a gap between elementary school teachers and parents in their responses to letter-related objectives and content, which might reflect parents' belief that English should begin to be taught as a required subject as early as possible in compulsory education.

Table 1.2: The number of public elementary schools which implement 'the activities to familiarise children with English letters' in ECA

Year	N of schools which participated in the survey	Grade 5		Grade 6	
		N of schools which carry out ECA (%)	N of schools which incorporate activities with letters in ECA (%)	N of schools which carry out ECA (%)	N of schools which incorporate activities with letters in ECA (%)
2005	22,232	19,680 (88.5)	7,781 (39.5)	20,069 (90.1)	8,627 (43.0)
2006	22,031	20,173 (91.6)	8,635 (42.8)	20,576 (93.4)	9,622 (46.8)
2007	21,864	20,404 (93.3)	9,271 (45.4)	20,771 (95.0)	10,050 (48.4)

(MEXT, 2006, 2007, 2008c)

On the other hand, irrespective of the controversy regarding the instruction of English written skills, the results from a series of annual surveys carried out by MEXT (Table 1.2) show that the percentage of public elementary schools which used 'activities to familiarise children with English letters' in ECA increased in both Grades 5 and 6 from 2005 to 2007, although it was still less than half (MEXT, 2006, 2007, 2008c). However, considering that these 'activities to familiarise children with English letters' means the activities which intentionally focus on learning names and forms of the alphabet and excludes natural exposure to letters in other English activities, the actual figure of elementary schools where children had opportunities to see letters could be larger. Unfortunately, this and other surveys on the state of implementation of ECA did not include question items asking for detailed information about how letters of the alphabet were taught or what kind of letter-related activity was used in elementary schools.

Research questions

If the alphabet is taught in most elementary schools and children are attending to a certain form of letter-related activities in FLA, the present instructional methods may be based on conventional practice, not research, as the importance of literacy skills has been underestimated so far in the curriculum not only for elementary school but also for junior-high school in Japan. Indeed, even in the former ECA where letters might have been taught, it was suggested that "the main focus of instruction should be put on oral aspects of language, separating sounds from letters, at the elementary school level" in the *Guideline for the Practice of Elementary School English Language Activities* (MEXT, 2001) [my translation and underlining] based on the report of the Educational Council in 1997 that "letters should not be used in elementary school English education when it is introduced" [my translation]. Further, since letters and words of English are required to play a role only as supplementary tools for oral communication in FLA, the perspective of how to utilise them for written communication has been ignored in earlier studies. However, once children learn to realise the shapes of letters and their sequences (i.e., words), what they will have interest in next might be to read them aloud. Therefore, it seems reasonable to teach the alphabet in view of the subsequent English reading development. In this study, regarding its second aim, the instruction of *phonological awareness* incorporated into the letter instruction will be proposed as a potential way of both making children ready for receiving the formal early English reading instruction and utilising letters effectively in English education at the elementary school level in Japan.

Phonological awareness has been a central issue in L1 early reading research in alphabetic scripts, and is widely recognised that, to achieve reading mastery, it is necessary for children to develop an awareness that spoken words can be segmented into sequences of phonemes as well as to acquire the skills to analyse the internal structure of words on demand to identify individual phonemic constituents (Blachman, 1991; Bradley, 1988; Liberman, Shankweiler, & Liberman, 1989). Furthermore, it is in the course of phonological awareness instruction that it becomes possible and effective to introduce letters and early word reading. Thus, it could be hypothesised that developing phonological awareness might be advantageous to Japanese elementary school children in the sense that it has a facilitative role in subsequent learning to read in English, and a certain amount of it is assumed to be prerequisite to boost the acquisition of literacy in English (Adams, 1990; Perfetti, Beck, Bell, & Hughes, 1987), to be discussed in detail in Section 2.3. A set of research questions for this study follows:

RQ Could phonological awareness and early English reading be effectively taught to Japanese elementary school children?

    A) How much could the children develop phonological awareness and early English reading through the instruction? What are the characteristics of Japanese children's phonological awareness?

    B) What are the difficulties for the children in developing phonological awareness and early English reading?

    C) Would Japanese elementary school children and teachers appreciate the instruction of phonological awareness and early English reading and find it helpful? What are their reactions to the instruction?

    D) Could the instruction be well incorporated into FLA?

These questions will be tackled through the exploratory intervention for teaching phonological awareness and early English reading held in a Japanese elementary school in which the author plays the role of an instructor as well as a researcher. The term *effectively* in RQ does not only mean the effectiveness of the instruction in terms of whether children could achieve the intended outcomes through the instruction, but also signifies whether the children and teachers participating would enjoy and appreciate the instruction, what difficulties children would face in developing phonological awareness, and whether the instruction is well incorporated into the curriculum of FLA.

In contrast to the instruction that focuses only on the acquisition of the alphabet, this perspective of using letters to facilitate children's phonological awareness development in view of the subsequent acquisition of early English reading is new and innovative in the English language teaching research field in Japan. Therefore, this study is expected to make a sound contribution to the future of elementary school English education by claiming the potential significance and the feasibility of introducing phonological awareness, letters, and early English reading to children, as this will be one of the most important issues to be considered in the future revision of the *Course of Study*.

1.4. Overview of the book

This chapter has provided the background to this research and its aims and objectives, in addition to presenting the set of research questions.

Chapter 2 provides a theoretical framework for this research by reviewing earlier studies on phonological awareness and its relationship with learning to read. It first describes the levels of phonological awareness and its causal role in the development of L1 early reading, especially in English, as well as various factors which affect its tasks. Then, from a cross-linguistic point of view, the focus is shifted to the conditions under which phonological awareness may transfer from L1 and L2, and discusses not only the characteristics of Japanese children's phonological awareness and speech processing but also the levels of phonological awareness that they have to develop in order to learn to read in English, considering the differences in phonology and writing systems between Japanese and English. Moreover, the developmental progression of phonological awareness by Japanese children is hypothesised, taking the influence of *Roma-ji* learning into consideration, with the aim of claiming the importance of teaching phonological awareness. Furthermore, literature pertaining to the instructional content and methods for the exploratory intervention is reviewed.

Chapter 3 illustrates methodology for this study; i.e., the exploratory intervention. It describes the intervention sites and context, the content and methods for the instruction, the assessment procedures of children's development, the data analysis methods, as well as the related ethical issues.

Chapter 4 presents the results of the intervention. It reports the results of the participating children's development in phonological awareness and early English reading according to the target instructional content for the intervention. The quantitative data from the assessment tests are complemented with qualitative data such as the instructor's research journal and informal interviews with children. In order to consider children's attitudes toward learning early English reading as well as the intervention itself, the questionnaire data are also analysed. Discussion is provided on the basis of the results obtained.

Chapter 5 summarises the main findings and discusses them with reference to the research questions.

Finally, Chapter 6 draws conclusions from this study and describes some practical implications not only for the future curriculum of elementary school English education in Japan but also for teacher training, in view of the introduction of early reading. Limitations of the study and suggestions for further research in this field are also considered.

Chapter 2

Phonological Awareness and its Importance for Japanese Children Learning English

2.1. Introduction

This chapter aims to claim the necessity of explicit instruction of phonological awareness for Japanese children learning English. After the general introduction of phonological awareness, the reciprocal facilitative relationship between individual levels of phonological awareness and early L1 reading development, especially in English, will be considered, taking the influence of letter knowledge and reading experience into consideration. Next, a detailed description of phonological awareness which Japanese children would develop in the process of L1 literacy acquisition, as well as their speech segmentation affected by *moras* as the basic phonological unit in Japanese, will be given. Moreover, considering not only the orthographic and phonological differences between Japanese and English but also the importance of multiple-level phonological awareness in English reading development, the characteristics of phonological awareness necessary for Japanese children in learning to read in English will be discussed.

Then, suggesting that there is little possibility of phonological awareness transfer between Japanese and English as well as of Japanese children's spontaneous development of phonological awareness for learning to read in English through their cognitive development, the importance of its instruction will be argued. The term 'transfer' in the present research indicates the following type of crosslinguistic influence: A certain level of L1 phonological awareness that has crucial and facilitative roles in developing the awareness of the smaller phonological units and then learning to read in L1 comes to play the same roles in L2 (i.e., 'positive transfer' according to Ellis's (1994) categorisation). This seems to happen under special conditions such as when L1 and L2 share the same level(s) of phonological and orthographic units and characteristics necessary for early reading development, as discussed in Section 2.6.1 in this chapter. On the other hand, the possible negative influence (i.e., 'interference,' or 'negative transfer') of phonological awareness characterised by L1 phonological and orthographic systems will be distinguished from the 'transfer' and considered as the sources of difficulties in developing the specific level(s) of phonological awareness necessary for learning to read in L2.

Finally, the features of effective instruction of phonological awareness and the factors that affect the difficulty of phonological awareness tasks will be summarised based on the findings from earlier research in order to establish a framework for the interventional instruction in a Japanese elementary school carried out later in this study.

Throughout this book, some phonological description of words will be used to illustrate the designs and findings of studies. Each phoneme which comprises a word is represented by phonemic symbols in slant brackets (e.g., /k/ for the beginning phoneme of the word *cat*).

2.2. Phonological awareness and its development

Phonological awareness is thought to be not only one of the phonological processing skills and an aspect of metalinguistic awareness, but also a necessary cognitive substance to apprehend the alphabetic principle underlying the written language system (Fletcher, Shaywitz, Shankweiler, Katz, Liberman, Stuebing, Francis & Fowler, 1994; Liberman, Shankweiler, Liberman, Fischer, & Fowler, 1977; Mann & Liberman 1984; Stanovich, Cunningham, & Feeman, 1984). The alphabetic principle is referred to as an ability to be aware of phonemes as basic sound units of speech and be able to associate individual letters or their sequences with corresponding sounds (Adams, 1990; Liberman, Shankweiler, & Liberman, 1989). Thus, studies on phonological awareness have been mostly carried out in alphabetic languages, especially in English as L1.

2.2.1. Definition

Phonological awareness is sensitivity to the sound structure of language, especially the internal structure of words. It requires multilevel skills and abilities to attend to, think about, and intentionally manipulate phonological aspects of spoken language while temporarily shifting away from its meaning (Gillon, 2004). Being phonologically aware is to have a general understanding that spoken language comprises units of sound; i.e., not only words, syllables (e.g., *mu-sic*), onsets and rimes (e.g., *cl-ear*), but also much smaller phonemes (e.g., /k/ /ɑːr/ /d/ for *card*).

As the phonological structure of spoken language is generally analysed at different levels of linguistic units (i.e., words, syllables, intrasyllabic units such as onset-rime, and phonemes), phonological awareness is also described in terms of all these linguistic units (i.e., rhyme awareness, syllable awareness, onset-rime awareness, and phonemic awareness). In other words, the term *phonological awareness* can be used to refer to the awareness at any or all of these levels of awareness (IRA, 1998).

Phonological awareness and especially a more sophisticated level of phonemic awareness are often confused with *phonics*, but are fundamentally different. Phonics is based on the association of letters and sounds (i.e., grapheme-phoneme correspondence) to read out written symbols (Snider, 1995) and has been developed as a system of teaching reading based on the alphabetic principle (Adams, 1990). More precisely, while phonological awareness involves the ability of manipulating phonemes orally as well as the understanding of the smaller components of spoken words, phonics is a system of teaching correspondence between letters and their pronunciation to sound out words, and advocates of phonics maintain that teaching phonological, orthographic, and morphemic rules should make it easier for children to learn to read. For example, children show their phonological awareness by saying that if the last sound is taken off *cart*, the word *car* is left, and show their phonics knowledge by telling you which letter makes the first sound in *bat* or *dog* or the last sound in *car* or *cart* (IRA, 1998). In fact, in order to decode an alphabetic script and become proficient in phonics, phonological awareness is required (Torgesen, Wagner, & Rashotte, 1994).

2.2.2. The levels of phonological awareness

Many studies on L1 literacy acquisition have investigated the relationship between a certain level of phonological awareness and early reading development (Blachman, 1991, 1997; Brady & Shankweiler, 1991; Liberman, Shankweiler, & Liberman, 1989; Wagner & Torgesen, 1987). It is important to define the term *level* here as there might be two possible interpretations for this. First, it can refer to the extent to which children are aware of phonological processing required in a certain task. Treiman and Zukowski (1991) explains the *level* of phonological awareness as the degree of explicit awareness required in a certain task. For example, a task for manipulating phonemes which asks children to say *sun* backwards seems to be more difficult (i.e., higher in the level) than the task requiring for recognising that *sun* contains phonemes /s/, /ʊ/, and /n/ (Yopp, 1988). Second, the other *level* can refer to the cognitive demand of a task, or the linguistic complexity of a phonological unit focused in it. As children's performance on a task is affected by how challenging the task is for them, the cognitive demand of a task for phonological awareness is determined by which linguistic unit the task is tapping (i.e., larger units such as words and syllables or smaller units such as phonemes). In this book, the latter definition of *level* as the linguistic complexity of a phonological unit is adopted. Thus, levels of phonological awareness reflect a hierarchical structure of phonological constituents of spoken language (Fudge, 1969; MacKay, 1972), and to develop phonological awareness at various levels means having an understanding of different ways of dividing oral language into smaller units. Below, three levels of phonological awareness which appear in the following discussion will be illustrated: From the lowest of rhyme awareness, to syllable awareness, onset-rime awareness, and the highest phonemic awareness.

2.2.2.1. Rhyme awareness

The awareness of rhyme generally means to have some understanding that rhyming words sound the same at the end, and has been explored primarily based on observational data of assessing children's word play (Dowker, 1989; Maclean, Bryant, & Bradley, 1987). The focus of these studies was on the stressed vowels, which specifically are not explained in terms of the syllable structure but in terms of words as units. That is, rhymes necessarily reflect a word-level structure and a word has only one rhyme that may occur within a syllable or extend over several syllables. Thus, while syllable-level *rimes* (i.e., clustering of the vowel and consonants after the initial consonant sounds of a syllable) are found in every syllable regardless of stress, *rhymes* incorporate only the stressed vowel in a word.

The concept of rhyme awareness is important in that it "shows not just that they [children] are aware of rimes, but also that they are able to categorise words on the basis of their sounds" (Goswami & Bryant, 1990, p. 77). Rhyme is often discussed together with alliteration, but the awareness of alliteration might well belong to phonemic awareness since the alliteration is the repetition of the same onsets (i.e., the initial consonant or consonant cluster of a word) and its understanding is usually assessed by the tasks of detecting and categorising phonemes (Gillon, 2004).

2.2.2.2. Syllable awareness

Being phonologically aware at the syllable level means to have a certain understanding that words can be divided into syllables. Syllables are the smallest independently articulated segments of speech which have yet other units of speech segmentation such as vowels and consonants (Wagner & Torgesen, 1987). Syllable awareness has been demonstrated through a realisation of syllabification principles in drawing syllable boundaries such as that a vowel or a vowel sound (e.g., *y* in *lady*) is included in each syllable in a word, that syllable division follows the stress pattern of a word allowing as many consonants as possible to begin a stressed syllable (e.g., *pa-trol*, not *pat-rol*), and that English consonants which cannot be clustered together may not begin or end a syllable (e.g., *on-ly*, not *onl-y* or *o-nly*) (Treiman, 1993, p. 18). However, because it is difficult to determine the precise beginning and end of a syllable (Gipstein, Brady, & Fowler, 2000) and different division of a syllable sometimes seems to be possible due to the lack of general theoretical principles, the tasks for assessing syllable awareness could be confounded with those for other levels of phonological awareness.

2.2.2.3. Onset-rime awareness as intrasyllabic awareness

Phonological awareness at the intrasyllabic level requires an understanding that syllables, including words which are monosyllabic, can be divided into onsets and rimes. The onset is defined as the initial consonant or consonant cluster in individual syllables. Therefore, an onset may comprise a single phoneme (e.g., *s*et) or a phoneme cluster which consists of two or more phonemes (e.g., *str*ike). On the other hand, a rime comprises the vowel and any remaining consonants in each syllable. Although most syllables have the substructure of onset and rime, there are also some words that have a rime but no onset (e.g., *end*) or that have a rime without the final coda (i.e., consonants that come after the vowel in a word) (e.g., *tree*).

Whereas it is a general agreement that syllables have an intrasyllabic structure, there are other theories claiming more probabilistic substructures of syllables by assuming the absolute restrictions (Clements & Keysler, 1983; Fudge, 1969; Kessler & Treiman, 1997; MacCarthy, 1979). However, so far intrasyllabic awareness has been widely assessed through rhyming tasks with monosyllabic words because the awareness of syllable level *rime* is considered to be the foundation for the awareness of larger units such as word-level *rhyme* (Gillon 2004) and, therefore, has been widely adopted as the subcategory of syllable awareness in the early literacy research. Thus, the term *intrasyllabic awareness* is now widely used to refer to *onset-rime awareness.*

2.2.2.4. Phonemic awareness

Phonemic awareness refers to the understanding that words are made up of individual phonemes (e.g., to know that a spoken word *right* consists of three phonemic sounds /r/, /ɑi/, and /t/), and usually it comprises the ability to manipulate these individual smaller sound units to make larger units of spoken language such as syllables and words (Snow, Burns, & Griffin, 1998). In other words, children with phonemic awareness can segment sounds in syllables or words (e.g., pronounce only the initial phoneme heard in a word) and blend a sequence of isolated sounds together to form a recognisable word (IRA, 1998). Typically it is thought that phonemic awareness is the deepest level of understanding of speech that children acquire (Stahl & Murray, 1994).

The phoneme is frequently defined as the smallest unit in phonology which can make a difference in meaning. Originally the phoneme was considered as a psychological reality such as intentions and a mental image with articulatory-acoustic properties (Anderson, 1985). Since the early 20th century, the concept of the phoneme has been described in physical terms mainly with respect to whether it is a 'phonological prime' (i.e., the minimal phonological element which cannot be further decomposed) or the degree of its abstractness (Trask, 1996). Trubetzkoy (1969), a Prague School linguist, formed an autonomous definition of the phoneme (i.e., the autonomous phoneme or classical phoneme), which emphasises the way in which phonemes tend to occur in phonetically identifiable patterns, or phonological oppositions, and regards the phonetic characteristics of a phoneme as fundamental. Furthermore, based on the notion of the phoneme as a system of contrast originally proposed by Saussure who emphasised the significance of the rules that relate sound representations (Anderson, 1985), Jakobson and Halle (1971) described phonemes as a bundle of distinctive features, which can be recognised through the minimal pair test. In addition, under the influence of the Prague School, at around the same time, American structuralism linguists such as Bloomfield (1933) regarded the phoneme "as a structureless object" and "as indivisible and as minimally abstract" (Trask, 1996, p. 265). Thus, the structuralist view considered that a single phoneme may be realised in speech by one or more phonetically distinct phones (i.e., allophones) in varying circumstances.

Then, in the 1960s, the conceptualisation of the phoneme which was fundamentally different from the previous structuralist analysis of phonology developed as generative phonology (Chomsky & Halle, 1968). It proposed a highly abstract definition of the phoneme (i.e., the systematic phoneme), "as opposed to the comparatively non-abstract autonomous phoneme" (Trask, 1996, p. 348). The generative definition of the phoneme was also based on the notion of distinctive features, but they were defined from the articulatory perspective, not from the acoustic perspective as in Jakobson's view. Moreover, in generative phonology, phonemes are described through the analysis of speech in terms of the hierarchies of discrete sound segments, on the premise of universal categorisation of these segments in all languages. In the 21st century, within the generative and systematic tradition, Optimality theory which emerged in the late 1990s and tries to present universal ranked (violable) constraints (i.e., structural conditions) to phonological grammar (Prince & Smolensky, 2004; Archangeli & Langendoen, 1997; Kager, 1999) seems to be most influential on the understanding of the phoneme concept.

However, for the purpose of language learning and teaching, as Ladd (2011) aptly argues, the validity of the recent concept of the systematic phoneme based on generative understanding of phonetics may be doubtful due to its universal assumption of sound segments and abstractness. In developing children's phonemic awareness, minimal pairs and indivisible and contrastive characteristics of phonemes need to be focused on so that children can develop an awareness of their individual sounds as autonomous realities. Thus, in this research, the structuralist view of the phoneme concept is adopted in referring to 'phonemes' and considering 'phonemic awareness.'

2.2.3. The development of phonological awareness

In L1 studies on children's development of phonological awareness, it has been observed that children begin to show their sensitivity to the structure of spoken words at a very early stage of life. The progression in the development of phonological awareness is assumed to be affected by phonological characteristics of a language such as syllabification principles and grapheme-phoneme correspondence (Denton, Hasbrouck, Weaver, & Riccio, 2000; Engen & Høien, 2002; Gonzalez & Garcia, 1995). A common conceptualisation with regard to alphabetic languages such as English is that the awareness of larger phonological units emerges earlier than that of smaller units (Anthony & Lonigan, 2004; Wagner, Torgesen, Laughon, Simmons, & Rashotte, 1993).

The most influential developmental model of phonological awareness seems to be the one proposed in Adams (1990). In this five-level developmental model, the ability clusters of phonological awareness are categorised into five levels of difficulty which corresponds to its developmental sequence. The most primitive level is expressed as "an ear for the sounds of word" (Adams, 1990, p. 80). This is an auditory perceptual ability which is measured by whether and to what extent children have the knowledge of familiar nursery rhymes (Maclean, Bryant & Bradley, 1987). The second level is the analytical perceptual ability of recognising and sorting the components of overall sounds of words according to their similarities and differences. The components to be categorised are often rhymes or alliteration of words which are measured by the oddity tasks (i.e., to decide one word that does not sound the same with others) (Bradley & Bryant, 1983), which can be used with small children as young as three and four year olds. The third level is the ability for blending and syllable-splitting which assumes skills for intrasyllabic analysis and awareness. These tasks require that children have already become comfortably familiar with the notion that words are made of smaller meaningless sounds corresponding to phonemes and the act of producing these sounds by themselves (Perfetti, Beck, Bell, & Hughes, 1987). They are more or less able to be done by kindergarten children because the competence required for tackling them is acquired through the reading-focused instruction by adults and siblings. The fourth level includes comprehensive phonemic analysis skills assessed by phoneme segmentation tasks. These tasks require children to have developed not only a thorough understanding of the word structure as a sequence of phonemes but also the ability to analyse them methodically. Finally, the fifth level requires the skills for phoneme manipulation tasks. This level of phonemic awareness is supported by a sufficient understanding of the phonemic structure of words and proficiency to regenerate words by adding, deleting, inserting, and relocating any designed phoneme (Liberman, Shankweiler, Fischer, & Carter, 1974). These skills for phoneme manipulation as well as phoneme segmentation are thought to be generally unattainable by children unless they have received formal reading instruction.

Like researchers who consider that phonological awareness is "not a unitary capacity, but rather a constellation of abilities" (Koda, 1998, p. 195), this model assumes that phonemic awareness underlies all other levels of phonological awareness (i.e., rhyme, syllable, and onset-rime awareness). One of the most important assumptions drawn from this model seems to be that the differences in tasks and target linguistic units might influence the perceived difficulty of phonological awareness, which needs to be considered in both the instruction and the assessment of phonological awareness as discussed later in Section 2.8.

2.3. Phonological awareness and early reading development in L1

In L1 English reading research, it is now generally agreed that phonological awareness has some influential power of predicting children's later literacy development and it is children's level of phonological awareness on entering school that best predicts their success in early reading development (Adams, 1990; Ehri & Wilce, 1980; Goswami & Bryant, 1990; Liberman et al., 1974; Mann, 1993; Snow, Burns, & Griffin, 1998; Stanovich, 1986). In order to claim the necessity of phonological awareness for Japanese children in learning to read in EFL, it is essential to clarify the specific linguistic levels of phonological awareness which play causal roles in the acquisition of early reading in L1. Moreover, it is important to understand whether the development of phonological awareness plays a facilitative role in enhancing the abilities and skills for reading and/or the reading development promotes the further sophistication of phonological awareness.

2.3.1. The influence of phonological awareness on learning to read

With regard to the effect that a certain level of phonological awareness has on the development of early reading, there are two opposing points of view such as the large-unit hypothesis and the small-unit hypothesis.

2.3.1.1. The large-unit hypothesis

The large-unit hypothesis claims that the ability to perceive larger sound units of spoken language such as rhymes, syllables, and onset-rime units is crucial and even a precursor to early reading development (Bryant, 1998). One early study for this hypothesis is by Bradley and Bryant (1983), which demonstrated that four- and five-year-old children's rhyme awareness assessed with a sound categorisation task was highly correlated to their scores on the standardised reading and spelling tests conducted more than three years later. Moreover, through a further intensive training study, it was found that children who had the training of sound categorisation only were three or four months ahead of those trained in conceptual categorisation only in the standardised tests of reading and spelling. Additionally, children who had the training of sound categorisation combined with alphabetic symbols performed even better than children who did not. Thus, suggesting a causal relationship between the sound categorisation ability and the reading and spelling performance, Bradley and Bryant (1983) concluded that their results supported the hypothesis that rhyme awareness that children acquire in their preschool years has a powerful influence on their later achievement of both reading and spelling.

Following this influential study, adherents of the large-unit view have examined the predictive power of phonological awareness also at the syllable and the onset-rime levels. Some studies have suggested that the word-level rhyme knowledge plays an important role in the progression of phonological awareness development and may predict the literacy acquisition in early school years (Gipstein, Brady, & Fowler, 2000; Goswami & Bryant, 1990; Treiman, 1985; Wood & Terell, 1998), while other studies have claimed that phonological awareness at the onset-rime level is the precursor to developing the awareness at the phoneme level (Goswami, 2002; Seymour & Evans, 1994). In a longitudinal study by Bryant, Bradley, Maclean, and Crossland (1989), it was demonstrated that knowledge of nursery rhymes affects the development of phonological awareness assessed with the rhyme and phoneme detection tasks which in turn enhances one's ability in learning to read. Moreover, adopting the sound categorisation task from Bradley and Bryant (1983), Bryant, Maclean, Bradley, and Crossland (1990) found not only that rhyme awareness leads to phonemic awareness which in turn affects reading, but also that rhyme awareness makes a direct contribution to reading that is independent of the connection between reading and phonemic awareness.

In addition, in terms of *the theory of reading by analogy* hypothesising that readers may access the pronunciation of unknown words by referring to the similar spelling patterns rather than by mapping each individual letter to corresponding phoneme (e.g., to read a word *brick* by knowing how to read *kick*) (Goswami, 1994), it has been demonstrated that the awareness of larger linguistic units plays an important role in learning to read because such awareness in preschool years assists children learn to read unknown words by analogy to familiar words (Baron, 1977; Barron, 1986; Bowey, Vaughan, & Hansen, 1998; Byrne & Fielding-Barnsley, 1991; Ehri & Robbins, 1992; Goswami, 1993, 1994; Walton, 1995).

2.3.1.2. The small-unit hypothesis

The small-unit hypothesis emphasises the primacy of the ability to manipulate more sophisticated spoken word units which are phonemes (Duncan & Johnston, 1999; Savage & Carless, 2005). The findings that support the large-unit theory have been challenged by the advocates of the small-unit hypothesis. For example, Muter and Snowling (1998) indicated that rhyme awareness and phonemic awareness are independent skills. In their study, it was revealed that there was no significant correlation between children's scores on the rhyme discrimination test and those on the reading accuracy test. In addition, early rhyme detection ability assessed together with phoneme deletion ability was found to be a poor long-term predictor of later reading accuracy skills and also failed to predict good versus poor reading accuracy. In contrast, phoneme deletion ability combined with both phonological working memory assessed with a non-word repetition measure and letter knowledge proved to have best predicted future reading accuracy.

A longitudinal study of Muter, Hulme, Snowling, and Taylor (1998) demonstrated that first-graders' rhyme detection ability failed to predict their performance on reading and spelling later in school years, and that phoneme segmentation ability exerted a strong predictive effect on reading and spelling. However, also in this study, by the end of the second year of school, rhyming ability had started to have some predictive influence on spelling but not on reading, and the explanation in terms of the small sample size was given to this finding.

Furthermore, Hulme, Hatcher, Nation, Brown, Adams, and Stuart (2002) reported that the awareness of the initial phoneme assessed with three different tasks (i.e., deletion, oddity, and detection) had the strongest predictive contribution on children's reading ability and that measures of phonemic awareness were generally much stronger simultaneous and longitudinal predictors of children's early reading skills than measures of onset-rime awareness in non-words. Other studies support the claim that phonological awareness at the phoneme level plays a more significant role in the development of reading and spelling than the awareness at the large-unit level such as onset-rime (Hatcher & Hulme, 1999; Høien, Lundberg, Stanovich, & Bjaalid, 1995; Morais, 1991; Nation & Hulme, 1997).

2.3.1.3. Toward a compromise of different conceptualisations — Phonological awareness as a unitary construct

In order to incorporate phonological awareness into the instructional content for early reading, it is necessary to consider how the inconsistent findings on the predictive power of phonological awareness at a certain linguistic level could be interpreted. In fact, some of earlier findings supporting either the large-unit or small-unit hypothesis need careful consideration because there might be confounding of phonological awareness levels tapped. For example, even though Bradley and Bryant (1983) and Bryant et al. (1990) demonstrated the importance of phonological awareness at the large-unit level, there is an argument about the level of phonological awareness evaluated in their sound categorisation task (Macmillan, 2002;

McGuiness, 2004; Morais, 1991). In fact, two of three conditions in their studies might have evaluated children's sensitivity to rhyme (e.g., cot-pot-*hat* and pin-win-*sit*), while the third condition might have required the awareness of alliteration (i.e., the initial consonant of a word) to correctly judge the odd word (e.g., *hill*-pig-pin). Thus, because one score obtained by combining these three conditions was used for analysis, the sound categorisation task might have confounded two levels of phonological awareness (rhyme and phonemic awareness). Moreover, as all stimuli words consisted of three phonemes and were monosyllabic, word-level rhymes equalled syllable-level rimes in their study. Therefore, it is difficult to define whether their task assessed children's phonological awareness at the rhyme level or at the intrasyllabic onset-rime level.

Furthermore, Maclean et al. (1987) may be criticised as they made the direct comparison of children's performance on the large-unit phonological awareness measures with that on the phonemic awareness measures even though these had been administered at different ages (Hulme et al., 2002). In addition, by reanalysing the data of Muter et al. (1998) with different scoring methods, Bryant (1998) reported that children's scores on the rhyme detection task compared favourably with those on the phoneme segmentation task in predicting their later reading skills. Furthermore, whereas the study of Hulme et al. (2002) employed the design with the advantage of directly comparing phonemic and onset-rime awareness, it failed to draw the implication that could be generalised to younger children and this seems contradicting to their earlier findings (Muter et al., 1998). Hulme et al. (2002) even conceded that for younger children, onset-rime awareness may also be the better predictor of later reading than phonemic awareness.

These contradicting results may be explained in terms of the nature of phonological awareness and children's developmental level. As Schatschneider, Francis, Foorman, Fletcher, and Mehta (1999) argue, each task may differ in its ability to provide information about the child's phonological skills and the most sensitive measure of phonological awareness varies according to the developmental level of the child. In other words, the finding that the performance on either rhyme detection or phoneme manipulation yielded more significant correlation with later reading development may be simply due to the fact that the measure was a better predictive construct of phonological awareness at this developmental level.

For example, it was demonstrated that English L1 children at around the age of three could perform competently on rhyme detection tasks (Bradley & Bryant, 1983; Maclean, Bryant, & Bradley, 1987), that even about 25%

of 55 children younger than three years of age answered significantly above chance in rhyme detection tasks (Lonigan, Burgess, Anthony, & Barker, 1998), and that most children have acquired the ability for detecting rhymes by the time they receive formal reading instruction (Stanovich, Cunningham, & Cramer, 1984; Yopp, 1988). In some studies that failed to yield the predictive effect of rhyme tasks on later reading skills, children's rhyme awareness might have been at ceiling by the time of assessment and therefore the awareness of smaller phonological units such as phonemes was claimed to be a better predictor because it was still in the process of development (Muter et al., 1998). Similarly, the floor effect on the phoneme manipulation tasks administered to preschool children or pre-readers may have affected the status of phonemic awareness as a predictor of reading development simply because such tasks require a cognitive capacity beyond their developmental levels (Adams, 1990; Lonigan et al., 1998). Moreover, there are also other researchers who have claimed that different skills for phonological awareness reflect different abilities (Carroll, Snowling, Hulme, & Stevenson, 2003; Høien, Lundberg, Stanovich, & Bjaalid, 1995; Wagner et al., 1993, 1994; Yopp, 1988).

Thus, considering different findings in the relationship between a certain level of phonological awareness and early reading development, it seems reasonable to suppose that phonological awareness is a unitary construct, more precisely a parallel continuum, of various abilities (Anthony, Lonigan, Burgess, Driscoll, Phillips, & Cantor, 2002; Bowey, 2002; Gillon, 2004). That is, as Stanovich (1992) assumes, the phonological awareness may be conceptualised as a continuum from a *shallow* awareness of large phonological units to a *deep* awareness of small phonological units.

Anthony, Lonigan, Driscoll, & Phillips, & Burgess (2003) is the first empirical study that systematically investigated whether the developmental progression of phonological awareness follows a discrete, stage-like pattern or a more continuous one. They argued that the progression toward the awareness of smaller linguistic units might reflect a *quasi-parallel* relationship among phonological awareness skills. In other words, as children improve upon one phonological awareness skill, they also improve upon others. This view of the overlapping acquisition of phonological awareness skills is consistent with the studies that have demonstrated relatively high correlations among phonological awareness skills assessed by the tasks differing in linguistic complexity and necessary cognitive operations (Anthony, Williams, Aghara, Dunkelberger, Novak, & Mukherjee, 2010; Anthony & Francis, 2005; Stahl & Murray, 1994; Stanovich, Cunningham, & Cramer,

1984; Walton, 1995; Yopp, 1998).

2.3.2. The influence of reading development on the sophistication of phonological awareness

In contrast to the causal effect of phonological awareness on learning to read, children's reading experience also seems to facilitate their development of phonological awareness. Below, in view of the phonological awareness instruction for Japanese children whose L1 is orthographically different from English, the influence of letter knowledge and reading experience in an alphabetic language on the phonological awareness development is considered. These factors are important in that, if letter knowledge or reading experience in an alphabetic script underlies the subsequent development of phonological awareness necessary for learning to read in that language, this might be a disadvantage for learners whose L1 is a non-alphabetic language.

2.3.2.1. Knowledge of the alphabet

The importance of letter knowledge which comprises letter-name and letter-sound knowledge in the development of phonological awareness has been suggested by many studies that investigated the relationship between this knowledge and phonological processing at the phoneme level (Ball & Blachman, 1991; Bowey, 1994; Byrne & Fielding-Barnsley, 1989; Ehri, 1979; Hatcher, Hulme, & Ellis 1994; Johnston, Anderson, & Holligan, 1996; Wagner, Torgesen, & Rashotte, 1994). For example, only one of 113 English-speaking kindergarteners and first graders with low letter knowledge could manipulate word onsets in the phonological awareness tasks such as isolation, deletion, segmentation, and blending (Stahl & Murray, 1994). On the other hand, although it was in a German context, children who had limited letter knowledge could perform well in the large-unit phonological awareness tasks such as rhyme detection (Näslund & Shuneider, 1996).

Other studies have demonstrated that the ability of segmenting syllables into constituent phonemes, which is one of the necessary processes in word recognition (Barron, 1986), is dependent on both letter knowledge and phonological awareness at the phoneme level (Morais, Cary, Alegria, & Bertelson, 1979; Perfetti, Beck, Bell, & Hughes, 1987; Wagner, Torgesen, & Rashotte, 1994). Similarly, it has been argued that letter knowledge can be a strong predictor of subsequent reading acquisition (Adams, 1990; Share, Jorm, Maclean, & Matthews, 1984).

Indeed, it seems difficult to assume that the initial level of phonological awareness and early reading abilities such as letter knowledge are developing separately in the process of children's reading acquisition. Literacy acquisition does not start when children can read words, but children develop various pre-reading abilities called *emergent literacy* skills (Teale & Sulzby, 1986) before learning to decode individual words. Since emergent literacy is defined as the knowledge, abilities, skills and attitudes that are considered to be developmental precursors to the acquisition of reading and writing (Sulzby, 1986; Sulzby & Teale, 1991), they are assumed to be predictive of later individual differences in reading and writing abilities (Clay, 1979; Whitehurst & Lonigan, 1998). The level of letter knowledge at school entry, for example, is one of the strongest single predictors of both concurrent and longitudinal reading success (Adams, 1990; Carroll, 2004; Foorman, Chen, Carlson, Moats, David, & Jack, 2003; Stevenson & Newman, 1986).

Furthermore, regarding the nature of the relationship between letter knowledge and phonological awareness, Burgess and Lonigan (1998) demonstrated that preschool children's letter knowledge predicted the development of phonological awareness, and in turn phonological awareness predicted the subsequent growth of letter knowledge when children's age and oral language abilities were controlled. Based on these findings, it was claimed that the relationship between rudimentary reading skills (e.g., letter knowledge) and phonological awareness in preschool children prior to formal reading instruction was reciprocal. However, they also pointed out that letter knowledge and phonological awareness are two separate measures of the same variables underlying the literacy development because they made independently unique contributions to predict subsequent reading achievement.

In contrast to this reciprocal relationship, Johnston et al. (1996) claimed that letter knowledge might be a precursor to phonological awareness among preschool children because some phonological ability develops after at least partial alphabetic knowledge was acquired. However, rather than such a simple linear developmental progression from letter knowledge to phonological awareness, there seems to be an interactive relationship between the development of phonological awareness and letter knowledge. That is, the initial level of letter knowledge may be necessary for phonological awareness to develop (Adams, 1990), and simultaneously rudimentary awareness of phonological structure of spoken language may also be required to learn to be able to use such knowledge in reading (Tunmer, Herriman, & Nesdale, 1988). This view is supported by the results of many interventional studies which demonstrated that the training of phonological awareness was more effective when combined with the letter knowledge instruction than when it occurred in isolation (Ball & Blachman, 1991; Bradley & Bryant, 1983;

Hatcher et al., 1994).

2.3.2.2. Reading experience in an alphabetic script

Reading experience may seem to comprise letter knowledge in that language, but letter knowledge is generally considered to be only one *pre-reading* ability among many (Burgess, 2002). One influential study which demonstrated the relationship between reading background and the higher-level phonemic awareness was Morais et al. (1979). They investigated whether phonemic awareness can develop over time without literacy, and found that although illiterate Portuguese adults were able to respond correctly to some of the target real words and non-words in the addition task, they were generally unable to delete or add a phoneme at the beginning of non-words. On the other hand, people who learnt to read in youth or as adults had little difficulty in both tasks. It was concluded that people become aware of the sounds in words which are not attained spontaneously in the course of general cognitive growth, but the development of such awareness requires some specific training, which, for most people, is probably provided by learning to read in the alphabetic system.

This study inspired other studies, especially from a cross-cultural perspective (Huang & Hanley, 1995, 1997; Read, Zhang, Nie, & Ding, 1986). Read et al. (1986) tested two groups of Chinese in the same method as in Morais et al. (1979) and yielded strikingly similar results to those in the original study: The percentages of correct responses to the phonological tasks (deletion and addition) were significantly higher in the group of people who had learnt not only the logographic system but also pinyin (i.e., an alphabetic phonological representation of Chinese characters) than in the group of people who had learnt the traditional Chinese logographic orthography only for both real words and non-words. Thus, making Morais et al.'s (1979) argument more specific, Read et al. (1986) concluded that "it is not literacy in general which leads to segmentation skill, but alphabetic literacy in particular" (p. 41).

Furthermore, learning to read may facilitate the development of explicit phonemic awareness, especially the ability to manipulate phonemes (Burgess & Lonigan, 1998; Frost, 2001; Johnston, Anderson, & Holligan, 1996). As discussed above, the deepest phonological awareness to manipulate phonemes lies in the last stage of the continuum of phonological awareness development. On the other hand, the awareness of larger phonological units such as rhymes and syllables, which is in the beginning stage of the continuum, may develop prior to the formal instruction of letter knowledge and reading. For example, Wimmer, Landerl, Linortner, and Hummer (1991) found that Austrian six or seven-year-old children exhibited syllable awareness assessed with a counting task but could not score on the vowel substitution task at the beginning of the grade 1. However, after a few months of reading instruction, the majority of children performed almost perfectly on the phoneme task. Muter et al. (1998) also provided evidence that phonemic awareness does not emerge until after formal literacy instruction. It was found that at the age of four, children had great difficulty with phoneme segmentation tasks but found the detection tasks at the onset-rime level the easiest. Moreover, a longitudinal study of Blaiklock (2004) investigated children nine times during their first two years at school. It was demonstrated that they showed rhyme awareness in the oddity task before beginning to read, but they could not score on the phoneme deletion task until they had developed word-reading skills three to four months later.

2.3.3. Discussion

Considering the results from L1 reading research, the relationship between the development of phonological awareness and early reading acquisition seems to be "reciprocal" in nature in the sense that they mutually contribute to each other's development (Stanovich, 1986, p. 395), apart from the influence of other factors such as children's intelligence and memory capacity. Thus, it can be claimed that, in order to facilitate learning to read in English, Japanese children need to develop necessary level of phonological awareness.

Moreover, rudimentary letter knowledge seems to play an important role in the development of phonological awareness. Although both letter knowledge as a facet of pre-reading ability and phonological awareness play facilitative roles in early reading development, they seem to influence it independently as separate variables. Thus, in early English reading instruction, it may be necessary to teach both letter knowledge and phonological awareness as separate content, but *in combination*.

With regard to the significance of reading experience in the development of phonological awareness, the higher-level phonemic awareness develops when children have had a certain length and amount of experience in reading in a target alphabetic language. However, in developing phonological awareness in two languages, different languages may promote different levels of phonological awareness in order to read. Thus, further discussion from a cross-linguistic perspective will be held in Section 2.4, before applying these L1 findings to the case of Japanese children learning English.

2.4. Japanese children's phonological awareness and speech segmentation in L1

In this section, phonological and orthographic properties of the Japanese language which may affect phonological awareness necessary for learning to read in Japanese will be first summarised. Next, based on the findings from earlier studies, the characteristics of Japanese children's phonological awareness will be considered. Furthermore, the differences in the speech segmentation procedures across languages will be discussed, especially with reference to the influence of language rhythm, because this is another factor which may affect Japanese children's learning to read in English. Finally, implications will be drawn for the present study in terms of what should be included in the instructional content for the instruction of phonological awareness and early English reading for Japanese elementary school children.

2.4.1. Japanese phonological units and the writing system

In order to promote the understanding of Japanese children's phonological awareness, characteristics of the Japanese language will be described focusing on 'moras' and its writing system. Moras are the most important phonological units in Japanese which typically have a structure of a simplest syllable consisting of a vowel preceded by a consonant (CV). Since these mono-moraic syllables are at the phonologically lower level than syllables in the prosodic hierarchy, they are considered as subsyllabic units (Inagaki, Hatano, & Otake, 2000; Kubozono, 1989, 1995). In most cases, moras correspond to *kana* characters (Japanese syllabaries), and their boundaries are clear so that they can be counted easily in spoken Japanese. However, in other cases, there are special kinds of 'phonemic moras' which are *sokuon* (the first half of a geminate consonant: Q), *hatsuon* (a nasal coda consonant: N), and *hikion* (the second half of a long vowel: R), and they are thought to require the same amount of time to be pronounced as one mora (Kubozono, 1999, 2006).

Thus, in Japanese, there are 108 distinct moras that are categorised in five types. These are vocalic nucleus (V), nucleus preceded by a syllable onset (CV or CCV), a nasal coda (N) (ん /N/) which is pronounced as the sounds /n/, /m/, and /ŋ/ depending on the following phonetic context (e.g., ほん [*book*] /hoN/), and a geminate consonant (Q) (っ /Q/) which represents a doubling of whichever consonant happens to follow it. Japanese has a very limited set of vowel sounds, consisting of five distinct short vowels (V) (あ /a/, い /i/, う /u/, え /e/, and お /o/) which contrast with corresponding long vowels. Their distinctions "depend entirely on length" (Vance, 2008, p. 56), different from many languages including English whose short and long vowels differ in quality as well as in length. Some CCV moras begin with affricated consonants (e.g., じゃ /jɑ/, じゅ /ju/, and じょ /jo/), while in other CCV moras the second consonant can only be the glide /j/ (i.e., CjV) that may be preceded by only eight consonants and followed by three vowels (e.g., きゃ /kyɑ/, きゅ /kyu/, and きょ /kyo/). It is reported that over 60% of all possible moras have the CV structure (Cutler & Otake, 1994; Inagaki, Hatano, & Otake, 2000; Otaka, 2009; Otake, Hatano, Cutler, & Mehler, 1993).

Modern Japanese is written with a mixture of logographic characters (*kanji*) which are based on a morphology-based system and syllabic symbols (*kana*) which are based on a phonology-based system. While *kanji* characters are derived from Chinese logography and map onto speech at the level of morphemes representing the roots of words without referring to grammatical inflections, *kana* characters are of native origin and comprise two types of syllabaries (i.e., *hiragana* and *katakana*) representing the roots and inflection of words (Mann, 1986; Saito, 2006). Thus, syllabaries are regarded to be phonological in nature but not related to phonemes (Goswami & Bryant, 1990). According to one categorisation of Japanese phonemes (Kazama, Ueno, Matsumura, & Machida, 2004), there are five vowel phonemes and 17 consonant phonemes as follows:

Vowel phonemes: /ɑ/ /i/ /u/ /e/ /o/
Consonant phonemes:
  plosive: /p/ /b/ /t/ /d/ /k/ /g/   nasal: /m/ /n/ /ŋ/
  fricative: /s/ /z/ /h/   semivowel: /j/ /w/
  liquid: /r/   mora phonemes: /N/ /Q/

The processing of *kana* characters is assumed to be different from that of *kanji* characters. For example, it was found that Japanese speakers constantly switch between decoding these two types of scripts. Shafiullah and Monsell (1999) examined the reading process of Japanese adults in naming and semantic categorising tasks in which *kana* and *kanji* characters were continuously switched. The results showed that their performance was significantly slower (13 ms on average) and less accurate on the trials following a change of script between *kana* and *kanji*, whereas no such cost of switching was found within the two equally transparent forms of *kana* characters (*hiragana* and *katakana*). Moreover, Shibahara, Zorzi, Hill, Wydell, and

Butterworth (2003) demonstrated that *kana* stimulus words were pronounced faster than *kanji* stimulus words while *kanji* stimuli produced faster responses in semantic judgement than *kana* stimuli did. These findings support the idea that the processes of decoding *kana* and *kanji* are dependent on somewhat different resources (i.e., phonological and logographic respectively) and require different cognitive procedures (Hatta, 1992; Nakagawa, 1994).

2.4.2. Japanese children's phonological awareness

One of the most important studies that investigated the development of phonological awareness by Japanese children is Mann (1986). Based on the hypothesis that reading experience in the alphabetic code leads to phonemic awareness while syllable awareness develops naturally as children cognitively matured, she predicted that Japanese children, who become aware of moras which are roughly equivalent to syllables, would be aware of syllables but be less sensitive to phonemes than their American counterparts.

It was revealed that Japanese first-graders with no experience in an alphabetic script found both counting and initial-sound deletion tasks at the phoneme level extremely difficult and the scores of these tasks were much lower than those at the syllable level. Moreover, their scores in both phoneme counting and deletion tasks were found to be much lower than those of their American peers reported in Liberman et al. (1974), whereas there was no significant difference in the scores between them in counting and deleting syllables. However, when the same tasks were administered to Japanese children in Grade 4, 5, and 6, fourth graders showed a clear improvement in the phoneme counting task even though their scores were only slightly higher than those of American first-graders. In fact, fourth-graders were tested prior to the instruction of *Roma-ji* (the romanisation of Japanese). Considering that there was not much improvement in the phoneme counting scores between Grade 4 and 5 and then Grades 5 and 6, Japanese children participating seem to have developed the awareness of phonemes before they were tested in Grade 4 regardless of *Roma-ji* learning. Unfortunately, in Mann (1986), no data was given on their performance in Grade 3 or earlier.

In Mann's (1986) further experiment, children in *re-entry* classes in Grade 4, 5, and 6 were also tested. These children had spent some years abroad and learnt to read either the English or German alphabet. Despite the prediction that they would be more aware of phonemes than the children in normal classes because they had learnt letters in either of the two languages, their scores in the phoneme counting task were not superior to those of the children in normal classes, or rather slightly inferior.

Moreover, it was found that the performance of Japanese children in normal classes in the phoneme deletion task was affected by the types of phonemes: the scores of fourth and sixth-graders were significantly higher for /k/ than for /ʃ/ although no such difference could be found in the scores of American children.

2.4.2.1. Strategies used in counting and deleting syllables and phonemes

What should be emphasised in Mann's (1986) study is that the performance of Japanese children on the phonological awareness tasks seems to have been influenced by their knowledge of *kana*.

Generally, Japanese children learn *kana* characters first by reciting each column of the *kana* matrix repeatedly (Figure 2.1). This matrix is organised according to the principles that all the *kana* characters in the same row share the same vowel and that all the characters in the same column share the same consonant except the right end column that consists of single vowels. At the left end, the isolated /n/ character which is a nasal coda mora (N) is located and all characters except this have the CV structure. There are 51 characters in total with some overlaps and inclusion of old scripts for the same sounds.

Mann (1986) reports that, in the syllable counting task, children appeared to deduce the task as counting of orthographic units rather than counting of phonological units. For instance, children gave an extra tap to the test word when it had a mora spelt with two *kana* instead of one, as if they were counting the number of *kana* which are necessary to spell the word (e.g., two taps for ほん [*book*] /hoN/ and きって [*stamp*] /kiQte/). Moreover, the post-test interview revealed that, in the phoneme counting task, many children used a "*kana* plus one" strategy (p. 74) in which they tapped the number of *kana* needed to spell the test word and then added one tap to each *kana* to get to the correct response.

Similarly, with regard to the phoneme deletion task, the interview revealed that some children resorted to a "character substitution" strategy (p. 85) in which they spelt the word in their mind and replaced the initial *kana* character with the *kana* which lies immediately on its right on the *kana* matrix (i.e., /ki-pi/ → replacement of /ki/ with /i/ → /i-pi/), and others used a "phonological" strategy (p. 85) in which they reduplicated the vowel of the first syllable in a word and then deleted the initial consonant-vowel portion (i.e., /ki-pi/ → reduplication of /i/ → /ki-i-pi/ → deletion of /ki/ → /i-pi/).

Figure 2.1: *Kana* matrix [*50 On Hyou*] with *Roma-ji* letters

ん ン n	わ ワ wa	ら ラ ra	や ヤ ya	ま マ ma	は ハ ha	な ナ na	た タ ta	さ サ sa	か カ ka	あ ア a
	(い)(イ)(i)	り リ ri	(い)(イ)(i)	み ミ mi	ひ ヒ hi	に ニ ni	ち チ ti	し シ si	き キ ki	い イ i
	(う)(ウ)(u)	る ル ru	ゆ ユ yu	む ム mu	ふ フ hu	ぬ ヌ nu	つ ツ tu	す ス su	く ク ku	う ウ u
	(え)(エ)(e)	れ レ re	(え)(エ)(e)	め メ me	へ ヘ he	ね ネ ne	て テ te	せ セ se	け ケ ke	え エ e
	(お)(オ)(o)	ろ ロ ro	よ ヨ yo	も モ mo	ほ ホ ho	の ノ no	と ト to	そ ソ so	こ コ ko	お オ o

りゃ リャ rya	みゃ ミャ mya	ひゃ ヒャ hya	にゃ ニャ nya	ちゃ チャ tya	しゃ シャ sya	きゃ キャ kya
りゅ リュ ryu	みゅ ミュ myu	ひゅ ヒュ hyu	にゅ ニュ nyu	ちゅ チュ tyu	しゅ シュ syu	きゅ キュ kyu
りょ リョ ryo	みょ ミョ myo	ひょ ヒョ hyo	にょ ニョ nyo	ちょ チョ tyo	しょ ショ syo	きょ キョ kyo

ぱ パ pa	ば バ ba	だ ダ da	ざ ザ za	が ガ ga
ぴ ピ pi	び ビ bi	(じ)(ジ)(zi)	じ ジ zi	ぎ ギ gi
ぷ プ pu	ぶ ブ bu	(ず)(ズ)(zu)	ず ズ zu	ぐ グ gu
ぺ ペ pe	べ ベ be	で デ de	ぜ ゼ ze	げ ゲ ge
ぽ ポ po	ぼ ボ bo	ど ド do	ぞ ゾ zo	ご ゴ go

ぴゃ ピャ pya	びゃ ビャ bya	(じゃ)(ジャ)(zya)	じゃ ジャ zya	ぎゃ ギャ gya
ぴゅ ピュ pyu	びゅ ビュ byu	(じゅ)(ジュ)(zyu)	じゅ ジュ zyu	ぎゅ ギュ gyu
ぴょ ピョ pyo	びょ ビョ byo	(じょ)(ジョ)(zyo)	じょ ジョ zyo	ぎょ ギョ gyo

Moreover, Mann (1986) explained the advantage of /k/ over /ʃ/ in the phoneme deletion task: On the *kana* matrix, the /k/ column is immediately adjacent to the column of single vowels, meaning that the *kana* character for /kɑ/ is to the immediate left of the *kana* character for /ɑ/, the *kana* for /ki/ is to the immediate left of the *kana* for /i/, the *kana* for /kʊ/ to the *kana* for /ʊ/, /ke/ to /e/, and /ko/ to /o/. On the other hand, most *kana* characters containing /ʃ/ are spelt with a digraph (the character for /ʃi/) which has a subscripted character for /yɑ/, /ye/, /yʊ/, or /yo/ as a second component. Since these characters are located further from the column of single vowels on the matrix, it was argued that children could delete a phoneme /k/ more easily than /ʃ/.

Considering these findings, Mann (1986) interpreted that learning a phonological orthography such as the alphabet facilitated the acquisition of phonemic awareness, yet it takes more time if L1 writing system is the syllabary as in a case of Japanese children who became aware of phonemes by age regardless of whether or not they had received instruction in the alphabetic transcription.

These arguments were further put forward by Spagnoletti, Morais, Alegria, and Dominicy (1989) who tried to assess the possible effect of children's familiarity with the alphabet in learning *kana*. In this study, two groups of Japanese first graders who attended a Japanese school in Brussels were tested between the second and third trimester. It was estimated that all of the children had a fairly good knowledge of *hiragana* because they were taught those characters by the end of the second trimester. One group had very limited knowledge of the alphabet while the other group had formerly attended a Belgian primary school for at least six months and been taught the alphabet. The result showed that the group with previous alphabetic experience was no better than the group without such experience in either task of phoneme counting and phoneme deletion. Moreover, the performance patterns of two groups were quite similar. In the phoneme counting task, although the scores were low, their performance seemed to reflect the *kana* spelling-based strategy as demonstrated in Mann (1986).

Furthermore, in the initial consonant deletion task which was not administered on first-graders in Mann (1986), the children's performance was generally satisfactory with the phonemes /k/, /p/, and /ʃ/. A similar large portion of correct responses was also obtained in the free classification task in which children had to classify a group of three words in either an acceptable way according to a shared vowel or a consonant. Based on these findings, it was argued that children with the knowledge of the alphabet may respond according to their knowledge of *kana* and did not think of using their experience of another language system because the instruction and materials were in Japanese. Therefore, Spagnoletti et al. (1989) concluded that their findings supported the hypothesis that the written characters used to represent a language tend to dominate the conscious perceptual representation of the phonology of this language, as children spontaneously resort to their knowledge of the writing system when they are tested on the phonological constituents of speech without any explicit reference to written representations.

2.4.2.2. Causes in the development of phonological awareness at the phoneme level

The most unexpected result in Mann's (1986) study was the fact that, although Japanese first graders could manipulate syllables but not phonemes, the majority of Japanese children came to be able to manipulate both syllable and phonemes by the age of nine regardless of their experience in alphabetic writing. Spagnoletti et al. (1989) proposed two possible explanations for this based on the characteristic of Japanese children's literacy acquisition in Japanese. First, in *kana* there is a character for a nasal consonant /n/ whose phonetic realisation varies according to the following segment (e.g., When added to a nasal consonant initiated syllable, it indicates consonant lengthening.), and there are diacritic signs to distinguish voiced consonants from their unvoiced counterparts. Second, a large number of *kana* characters used to represent syllables in words of foreign origin may require segmenting the word at the phonemic level. For example, the syllable "ディ" for /di/ in the word *disc* is spelt with a *kana* character "デ" for /de/ and a small character "ィ" for /i/. It can be assumed that Japanese children come to treat the written form of /di/ as including the consonant /d/ exactly in the same way as in the alphabetic writing system children have to ignore the vocalic sound associated with the consonant. The familiarity with such phonemic manipulation was thought to be a cause of the development of phonemic awareness demonstrated with fourth graders in Mann's (1986) study.

Later, considering the findings in both Mann (1986) and Spagnoletti et al. (1989), Morais (1991) came to speculate that "the whole system need not be alphabetic for phonemic awareness to develop" (p. 18). This could be regarded as a broader view of the causal relationship between the development of phonological sensitivity and reading experience than the specific view proposed by Morais et al. (1979) and Read et al. (1986) that phonological awareness is not attained spontaneously but most likely provided by learning to read in the alphabetic system. However, it seems more prudent to assume that "experience in manipulating the internal structure of words" (Mann, 1991, p. 62) would be causally related to the development of phonological awareness in that language because this leaves the possibility that whatever special experiences might enable a language to be learnt.

Here, it needs to be mentioned that there is a feature in the phonological processing of Japanese speakers also made noticeable by the presence of loan words. As Japanese has an extremely simple syllable structure and prohibits consonant clusters, a phenomenon called 'vowel epenthesis' generally occurs when foreign words are adapted to fit the phonological structure of Japanese (e.g., /s(u)t(o)rɑik(u)/ for *strike*). The relationship between the epenthetic vowel and the preceding consonant is unique because vowel sounds inserted in Japanese loan words are /i/, /u/, or /o/ and the choice of an appropriate epenthetic vowel depends on the consonant that precedes it in the output (Kubozono, 2006). Therefore, by considering the phonological differences between Japanese and English as well as the influence English has on Japanese, it becomes clear what aspects of the phonological structure and writing system of English should be focused in early English reading instruction for Japanese children.

2.4.3. The speech segmentation procedure of Japanese children

As children develop and become more sophisticated in their awareness of phonological units, they come to be able to consciously segment spoken language into smaller units (Bradley, 1988; Lundberg, Olofsson, & Wall, 1980). Children who lack this skill would have a disadvantage in word reading because it depends on the awareness of the phonological structure of spoken language and in turn this awareness is required to "crack the code" of the language system (Mann & Liberman, 1984, p. 592). In other words, the segmentation skill is regarded as a strong precursor to being able to decode in reading before the mastery of letter-sound correspondence (Adams, 1990). In this section, the influence of language rhythm on speech segmentation (especially at the word level) as well as the relationship between segmentation and reading acquisition will be discussed. Then, the characteristics of speech segmentation by Japanese children will be considered in terms of the effect of Japanese moraic rhythm.

2.4.3.1. Speech segmentation and learning to read in an alphabetic language

With relation to the relationship between the segmentation skill and L1 reading acquisition in English, Tunmer and Nesdale (1985) found six-year-olds' phonemic segmentation skills measured by the tapping task were strongly and directly related to their decoding abilities, and in turn the decoding abilities were related to reading abilities. Moreover, Treiman and Baron (1983) demonstrated that the training focused on phonemic analysis with tasks of segmentation and blending altered children's patterns of word reading.

Thus, an essential step in learning to read alphabetically is learning to perceive speech as a sequence of discrete segments and then to use this awareness to segment speech on demand. The skill for segmenting words into their phonological constituents is related to phonological awareness at the syllable and phoneme levels, and therefore seems to be more complex for learners than the skill for segmenting speech into words. In fact, Liberman (1983) discussed reading and reading disability based on the premise that "the reader and writer must be something of a linguist— able, at the very least, quite deliberately to divide utterances into the constituent segments that are represented by the characters of the orthography" (p. 85). However, this would be difficult for some language learners, especially learners who first encounter an alphabetic writing system in the second or foreign language learning, such as Japanese learners of English.

2.4.3.2. The effect of language rhythm on speech segmentation

One of the common phonological distinctions of languages is that their rhythms are categorised into either syllable-timed or stress-timed (Abercrombie, 1967; Roach, 1982). In a syllable-timed language such as French and Spanish the length of time each syllable takes to be pronounced is roughly the same, whereas in a stress-timed language such as English, Russian, and Arabic, stressed syllables tend to be produced at consistent intervals regardless of the number of unstressed syllables between the stressed syllables. Recently it has been demonstrated that language-specific rhythms may affect how speech is segmented by listeners (Cutler, Mehler, Norris, & Segui, 1986; Wood & Terrell, 1998; Wood, 2006).

Mehler, Dommergues, Frauenfelder, and Segui (1981) found that in listening to French, speakers of French rely on the syllabic segmentation procedure which is characterised by its syllable-timed rhythm. On the other hand, Cutler, and Norris (1988) demonstrated that English speakers used a procedure of segmenting English speech corresponding to its stress-timed rhythm. Thus, the hypothesis that, in segmenting speech, listeners may use the procedure which is dependent on the rhythm of their L1 has been widely supported (Cutler & Batterfield, 1992; Cutler & Carter, 1987; McQueen,

Norris, & Cutler, 1994).

Moreover, developing this hypothesis further, the segmentation procedures based on the L1 rhythm have been observed in segmenting speech in a foreign language. Otake et al. (1993) demonstrated that speakers of French, in which syllabic segmentation would be effective, showed the similar pattern of syllabic segmentation in a detection task with Japanese materials. Combining this result with earlier findings that French listeners also used the syllabic segmentation procedure in the detection task with English materials (Cutler et al., 1986), Otake et al. (1993) argued that listeners would apply the segmentation procedure specific to their native language even to the speech of foreign languages regardless of whether or not it produced the appropriate segmentation.

2.4.3.3. Characteristics of Japanese speakers' speech segmentation

In considering the segmentation procedure of Japanese speakers, it should be noted that Japanese is regarded as a mora-timed language in which moras occur at equal intervals (Kubozono, 1989, 1995; Kubozono & Homma, 2002), playing an important role as regular timing units (Trubetzkoy, 1969).

It is generally believed that Japanese speakers use the unit of mora for auditory perception and speech segmentation (Cutler & Otake, 1994; Kubozono, 1989, 1995; Otake, Hatano, Cutler, & Mehler, 1993; Otake, Hatano, & Yoneyama, 1996; Tamaoka & Makioka, 2009). In addition to the observational fact that Japanese *kana* characters represent moraic units, some aspects of Japanese culture and children's play seem to affect this reliance on moras. For example, in a cultural aspect, *haiku* (i.e., traditional Japanese poetic) is composed of 17 moras to make a form of three metrical phrases of 5-7-5 moras respectively, which implies that the basic unit for Japanese phonetic counting is the moraic unit. On the other hand, from a developmental point of view, it was suggested that Japanese children develop the sensitivity to moras. Katada (1990) demonstrated that the mora constitutes a phonological representation in Japanese based on the evidence drawn from a word-chain language game *shiritori*. In this game players take turns giving a word that begins with the last sound unit of a word given by a previous player. The game is over when a player gives a word that ends with the mora phoneme /N/ and the game cannot be continued because there is no word that begins with /N/ in Japanese. Thus, this game respects phonological constraints in Japanese.

Katada (1990) also explained that moras are fundamental units in the segmentation procedure of Japanese speakers showing that the matching unit in this game is neither a syllable nor a segment, but a mora. That is, in the following example, the first word /bʊdo:/ ends with a syllable /do:/. However, since this /do:/ has a long vowel and is treated as two separate units as /do+o/, the second word /origami/ begins with /o/ not with rather /doo/ or /do/. It should be noted that a discrepancy between the mora sound and the *kana* writing system in Japanese can be found when a word has a long vowel as in this case. The word /bʊdo:/ is spelt with *kana* characters for /bʊ.do.ʊ/ (ぶどう) not with the characters for /bʊ.do.o/ (ぶどお). Such mistakes are commonly found in children's writing. Then, similarly, the third word /miNkʊ/ begins with /mi/ because the previous word ends with /mi/. The onset of the last moraic position of the syllable in the previous word plays a role unless the mora includes a long vowel.

e.g., ぶどう /bʊ.do:/ (grape), おりがみ /o.ri.ga.mi/ (paper-folding),
みんく /mi.N.kʊ/ (mink), くうき /kʊ.ʊ.ki/ (air),
きりん /ki.ri.N/ (giraffe) [game over]   (Katada, 1990, p. 642)

Thus, in this game the mora seems to operate as an essential unit that is associated with both the onset and the nucleus of a word at the phoneme level. Since Japanese pre-literate children widely play this game, it is assumed that in the process they improve awareness of moras as important units for Japanese speech segmentation and phonemic assembly.

Several studies have demonstrated that Japanese speakers use the moraic segmentation procedure in speech perception. In Otake et al. (1993), a target task was used to extend the rhythmic segmentation hypothesis from French and English to Japanese. The subjects were 48 Japanese undergraduate university students who were asked to listen to sequences of stimulus words and detect a word beginning with the target sound. The target was visually presented by the Roman characters immediately prior to the beginning of a sequence. The result showed that the mean response times for detecting a CV target (e.g., *ka*) in stimulus words beginning with a CV initial (e.g., CVCVCV words such as *kanoko*) and in those with a CVN initial (e.g., CVNCV words such as *kanko*) were not significantly different, but both are equally shorter than the response times for a CVN target (e.g., *kan*). It was assumed that Japanese listeners detected two-phoneme targets equally quickly and accurately by identifying the first mora (i.e., CV) from both CV initial words and CVN initial words in the same way. However, they found it much more difficult to detect a CVN target (e.g., *mon*) in stimulus words with a CVNV initial (e.g., CVNVCV words such as *monaka*). Otake et al. (1993) revealed that three-phoneme targets were detected accurately when they corresponded with two moras in stimulus words with a CVN initial (e.g., CVNCV words such as *monka*), and predicted the use of moraic segmentation procedure among Japanese listeners. Cutler and Otake (1994) also revealed that in a phoneme deletion task Japanese listeners could delete moraic targets more rapidly and accurately than non-moraic targets. These findings suggest that, if efficient perception of speech depends on the approximately equal duration of moras in Japanese, the moraic segmentation procedure may work much more effectively than other procedures including the syllabic segmentation procedure irrespective of the notion that most moras comprise syllables in Japanese (Inagaki et al., 2000).

It was also demonstrated that, as the acquisition of *kana* literacy improves, Japanese children's segmentation changes from the mixture of mora-based and syllable-based procedures to the exclusive use of the mora-based procedure. Inagaki et al. (2000) administered a modified version of the vocal-motor word segmentation task, which was originally designed for assessing whether children were using the syllable or the mora as their segmentation unit in Amano (1986), on Japanese four to six-year old kindergarteners who had had no systematic instruction of letters and numbers. The results showed that children's segmentation of words containing a nasal coda (e.g., CVN as in kure*yon* or VN) or words containing a long vowel (e.g., CVR as in hi*ko:*ki or VR) seemed to change from being a mixture of syllable-based and mora-based to being predominantly mora-based, as children's levels of *kana* literacy skills became higher, whereas such change for the words containing a geminate stop (e.g., CVQ as in *rapp*a or VQ) was not clear. Moreover, it was found that the shift to the mora-based segmentation was associated more strongly with the *kana* reading level than with the chronological age.

However, in addition to the causal relationship in which learning to read *kana* facilitates the mora-based segmentation, Inagaki et al. (2000) also pointed out that segmenting speech based on the unit of mora might promote the acquisition of *kana* literacy, because Japanese children's development of moraic segmentation could be hardly discussed separately from their experience in phonological processing of Japanese. That is, since mora and syllable overlap to a considerable extent in Japanese, young children might rely at least partly on syllables in segmentation at the earlier stages of literacy acquisition. Then, as children become phonologically mature enough to rely on the Japanese language-specific rhythm (i.e., the mora-timed rhythm), they may learn to recognise mora as the basic unit in segmentation and this may facilitate the acquisition of *kana* characters which are moraic. Thus, there might be a *bidirectional* facilitating relationship between the moraic segmentation and the *kana* literacy development.

With a closer look, these arguments are of interest in a stricter sense. The moraic segmentation procedure and mora awareness is thought to be conceptually very different. As Inagaki et al. (2000) describes, the moraic segmentation is "preferred reliance on moras as basic units in prelexical processing" (p. 89), while mora awareness implies the ability to segment a word into moras on demand and reflects how the word is represented in the mental lexicon (Metsala, 1999). Generally it is between phonological awareness and literacy development that a reciprocal relationship exists, and it has been argued that learning to read some *kana* characters enhances children's mora awareness because *kana* characters represent moras, which in turn facilitate learning to read other *kana* characters (Akita & Hatano, 1999) However, in the interpretation of Inagaki et al. (2000), it was assumed that there is a mutually enhancing relationship between learning to read *kana* characters and both the moraic segmentation and mora awareness. One caveat is that, even if segmenting Japanese speech on the basis of the unit of mora facilitates Japanese children's acquisition of *kana* literacy, it cannot be presumed that this also promotes learning to read English. Rather, it may have a negative effect on the literacy development in English whose speech appears to be segmented efficiently based on its stress-timed rhythm.

2.4.4. Summary

From what has been discussed so far, two assumptions could be made regarding the development of early English reading and phonological awareness by Japanese elementary school children learning English. First, they may develop some phonological awareness at around the phoneme level naturally in their cognitive development, as Japanese fourth graders with little experience of reading in an alphabetical script had developed it up to the level which was slightly higher than that of English-speaking first graders (Mann, 1986). It is still not clear whether such a level of phonemic awareness is ample for Japanese children to benefit from the formal early English reading instruction. However, if this is the case, it could be presumed that at least Japanese children in Grades 5 and 6, to which English teaching is introduced have some *readiness* for early reading in English. Second, in segmenting English speech, Japanese children may come to use the moraic segmentation procedure which depends on the mora-timed rhythm specific to Japanese, as listeners would adopt the procedure which is specific to their native language in segmenting speech even in a foreign language (Cutler et al., 1986; Otake et al., 1993). Thus, it may be necessary to explicitly teach children phonological awareness required for English reading development in order to avoid the negative influence of their L1-specific segmentation procedure.

2.5. Phonological awareness necessary for Japanese children in learning to read in English

Just as the segmentation procedure is affected by the rhythm, or the basic phonological unit, of a language and it is different across languages, the levels of phonological awareness necessary for decoding words in a language may differ according to its phonological properties. In order to teach phonological awareness to Japanese children so that it could promote early reading development in English which is phonologically and orthographically different from Japanese, it is important to understand what level or levels of phonological awareness are needed for learning to read in English, as well as its difference from the case of learning to read in their L1.

In this section, the effect of the difference in orthographic and phonological units on reading acquisition will be first discussed. Then, based on earlier studies that investigated the characteristics of phonological awareness that English speakers develop, what the instruction of phonological awareness for Japanese children learning English should aim for will be considered.

2.5.1. The effect of orthographic and phonological differences on learning to read

The way in which phonology (i.e., speech) is represented in orthography seems to have an influence on learning to read in that script. Wydell and Butterworth (1999) and Wydell and Kondo (2003) investigated the case of a 16-year-old English-Japanese bilingual boy who had reading difficulties in English but not in Japanese.

In order to argue that there was a clear dissociation between his ability to read in English and Japanese, Wydell and Butterworth (1999) proposed *the hypothesis of granularity and transparency*, which maintains that orthographies can be described in two dimensions: *transparency* and *granularity* (i.e., relative size of the smallest orthographic unit that represents word sounds). As to the transparency dimension, it is assumed that any orthography whose print-to-sound mapping is one-to-one or transparent will have a very low possibility of producing phonological dyslexia regardless of the level of mapping (phoneme, syllable, or character). As to the granularity dimension, it is assumed that any orthography whose smallest orthographic unit representing sound is at the coarse level (i.e., a whole character or a whole word) will not produce a high incidence of phonological dyslexia. This hypothesis implies that phonological and orthographical processing plays distinct roles in learning to read across languages. Based on this hypothesis, both *kana* and *kanji* orthographies of Japanese belong to the category of languages that show the lower possibility of phonological dyslexia. In the *kana* writing system, the orthography-to-phonology mapping is one-to-one at the syllable (more precisely, syllabary) level, and the granularity of the smallest orthographic unit that represents phonology is more sophisticated than the whole word, but coarser than each grapheme. On the other hand, in the *kanji* writing system, the orthography-to-phonology mapping is very opaque, and the unit of granularity is much coarser. In contrast, in the English alphabetic writing system, the unit of granularity is fine, but the orthography-to-phonology mapping is not transparent and not always one-to-one. On the basis of these differences, Wydell and Butterworth concluded that it might be possible for an English-Japanese bilingual speaker to become dyslexic in English but not in Japanese.

Furthermore, according to *the psycholinguistic grain size theory* proposed by Ziegler and Goswami (2005), beginning readers need to develop efficient strategies for mapping symbol to sound (i.e., recording), but these strategies "may need to differ in terms of grain size [orthographic units] to meet the requirements of the orthography that is being read" (p. 20). In other words, phonological awareness of different linguistic units may vary in its importance for word reading across different orthographies.

2.5.2. The differences in phonological awareness necessary for early reading across languages

Whereas it was assumed earlier in this chapter (Section 2.3.1.3) that the developmental progression of phonological awareness could be better described by representing it as a unitary construct (Anthony & Lonigan, 2004), the reference to its distinct *levels* becomes necessary here, in order to discuss specific units of phonological awareness needed for literacy acquisition. This is not only because most spoken languages including both alphabetic and non-alphabetic languages have at least common phonological units such as syllable, phonemes, and rhyme, but because awareness of all such units are positively related to word reading abilities across orthographies (Cheung,

1999; Jusczyk, Goodman, & Baumann, 1999; Keung & Ho, 2009; McBride-Chang, Tong, Shu, Wong, Leung, & Tardif, 2008). That is, just as Castles and Coltheart (2004) failed to explain literacy development only in terms of its relationship with phonological awareness of smaller linguistic units (i.e., phonemic awareness), different orthographies (writing systems) might require different psycholinguistic sizes of phonological awareness in order to read. Thus, especially for the present purpose, the conceptualisation of phonological awareness as a single component is insufficient because it underestimates the possibility of cross-linguistic transfer of phonological awareness at multiple linguistic levels.

Wang, Perfetti, and Liu (2005) demonstrated that the Mandarin (a dialect of Chinese) onset matching skill of Mandarin-speaking children learning English was significantly correlated with their English onset-rime matching skill, suggesting a cross-linguistic transfer of phonological awareness from L1 to L2. Moreover, children's tone processing skill contributed significantly to predicting English pseudoword reading with their phonemic awareness statistically controlled. Lexical tone is a salient feature in Chinese but not in English. Thus, it was assumed that bilingual reading acquisition might be a joint function of shared phonological processing skills and orthography-specific skills. However, it should be noted that Mandarin and English share the phonological components of onset-rime and consonant cluster, and therefore Mandarin-speaking children might develop more sensitivity to word-initial consonants than speakers of other languages whose phonological system is very different from that of English. This might lead to Wang et al.'s (2005) success to find the significant correlation between Mandarin onset awareness and English onset-rime awareness, while there was no such relationship between Chinese rime matching skill and English phonological skills.

Then, McBride-Chang et al. (2008) proposed more persuasive evidence for general cross-linguistic transfer of phonological awareness from Cantonese as L1 to English as L2 than in Wang et al. (2005). Cantonese is not only very different from English in writing systems, but it virtually does not share the phonological unit of consonant cluster with English (Chan, 2006). They investigated the association between Cantonese-speaking English-learning children's awareness of three phonological units (i.e., syllable, phoneme, and tone) and word reading in Cantonese and English. The results showed that all three phonological variables were significantly correlated with word recognition in both Cantonese and English after statistically controlling age, although the strength of correlation of some associations was small. More specifically, it was found that, in contrast to the shared importance of syllable awareness for early reading in both English and Cantonese, tone discrimination awareness might be strongly salient for reading in Cantonese where tone is integral to character recognition, and phonemic awareness might be more specialised for reading in English where grapheme-phoneme correspondences are more complex at the phoneme level. Thus, it was argued that, irrespective of some evidence of cross-linguistic transfer, the linguistic unit of phonological awareness specifically significant for word reading in English was different from that in Cantonese. This study is crucial in that such differences in linguistic units of phonological awareness necessary for word reading between two orthographically different languages were demonstrated in the same group of bilingual children.

Likewise, Mishra and Stainthorp (2007) compared phonological awareness and word reading between Oriya-English and English-Oriya bilingual fifth-graders. Oriya is the official language of Orissa, an eastern part of India, and its writing system is an alphasyllabary (i.e., Graphemes represent consonants and vowels like the alphabets, and orthographic representations are mainly consonant-vowel combinations as in Japanese). It was revealed that awareness of the smallest unit (phoneme) achieved through literacy development in English as L1 could facilitate reading in a script with a more intermediate grain size (Oriya as L2). However, the effect was not reciprocal. Awareness of larger phonological units in Oriya as L1 might facilitate reading in an intermediate grain-size script (e.g., onset-rime in English as L2), but further awareness of the smaller units was necessary for reading English with a small grain size. Because Oriya is a very similar language to Japanese in terms of the phonological and orthographic properties, these results are insightful in considering phonological awareness necessary for Japanese children in order to learn to read in English.

2.5.3. The importance of multi-level phonological awareness in early English reading

In relation to the shared importance of syllable awareness across languages with different orthographies demonstrated in McBride-Chang et al. (2008), the syllable is generally thought to be the fundamental psycholinguistic unit for reading acquisition in diverse languages (Ziegler & Goswami, 2005). As discussed above, in L1 reading research, syllable awareness was assumed to be a precursor to the subsequent development of phonological awareness of smaller linguistic units (Treiman & Zukowski, 1991; Wagner & Torgesen, 1987). Moreover, it has been demonstrated in L1 reading research that syllable awareness is uniquely related to reading acquisition in Greek

(Adins & Nunes, 2001) and in Norwegian (Høien, Lundberg, Stanovich, & Bjaalid, 1995), and that syllable awareness predicted subsequent L1 character acquisition better than phoneme onset awareness in Cantonese and Mandarin (McBride-Chang, Bialystok, Chong, & Li, 2004) and in Koran Hangul (Cho & McBride-Chang, 2005).

However, it is also claimed that the phonological complexity of a language is reflected in phonological awareness developed in the process of literacy acquisition in that language (Caravolas & Bruck, 1993). In this light, in order to learn to read in English, phonological awareness of at least more than one linguistic level (i.e., awareness of both larger and smaller phonological units) seems to be needed. Kim (2009) found that both onset-rime and phoneme awareness in Korean were positively related to children's English reading skills, but only Korean phoneme awareness was related to word reading skills in Korean. Ziegler and Goswami (2005) argue that in learning to read in relatively consistent (i.e., transparent) languages, children can rely exclusively on smaller linguistic units of phonemes without making many errors. On the other hand, when "small grain-size correspondences are inconsistent (e.g., English) or not available (e.g., Chinese), beginning readers have to learn additional correspondences for larger orthographic units, such as syllable, rimes, or whole words" (Ziegler & Goswami, 2005, p. 19). Moreover, as inconsistent orthographies such as English "appear to push readers into developing both small unit and large unit recoding strategies in parallel" (Ziegler & Goswami, 2005, p. 19), a strategy of mapping symbol to sound by analogy becomes developmentally important (i.e., using an orthographic chunk -*ate* corresponding to a rhyme /eit/ in *late* to read *gate*) (Goswami, 1994, Goswami, Porpodas, & Wheelwright, 1997), and even skilled English readers are thought to use a flexible metaphonological approach that permits speech to be analysed into units that are not exclusively phonemes (Scarborough, Ehri, Olson, & Fowler, 1998). This seems to explain partly why learning to read in English is more cognitively demanding and takes longer (Brown & Deavers, 1999).

Furthermore, for Japanese children learning English reading, this *multilevel* phonological awareness might not necessarily mean only a simple pair of syllable awareness and phonemic awareness. Japanese children develop awareness at the phonological level of 'mora' whose structure is a more systematic combination of a consonant and a vowel (CV) than that of 'syllable' in Japanese (L1) reading acquisition, and a mora consistently corresponds to a *kana* character (Inagaki et al., 2000). Since they learn how to read *kana* characters by rote learning of one-to-one correspondence between a character and a sound, they tend to consider a mora as one sound, not as a combination of two sounds (C+V). This may cause them to pay little attention to the intrastructure of moras, and therefore it cannot be presumed that they develop phonological awareness of intrasyllabic units spontaneously. The intrasyllabic onset-rime unit is one of the unique phonological characteristics in English speech, and awareness of it makes the foundation of developing phonemic awareness skills as, for example, analysing onsets with clusters requires the ability of segmenting consonant phonemes.

Finally, it should be mentioned that recent studies have proposed the conceptualisation that moras and syllables may coexist in a single hierarchical phonological structure, in which the lowest level is *phoneme* (consonants and vowels), the next higher level is *mora*, and the highest level is *syllable* (Haraguchi, 1996; Kubozono, 1989, 1995, 1999; Kubozono & Ota, 1998; Otake, 2006; Otake & Imai, 2001; Otake & Yoneyama, 2000). This is based on the findings that Japanese speakers may use moraic units for segmentation but they use the syllabic units for vocalising a visually presented word. For example, as Tamaoka and Terao (2004) illustrate, when pronouncing the word カレンダー which is a loan word from English *calendar* and segmented into five *kana* characters (moras), it would seem inefficient to use the moraic units (/kɑ/ - /re/ - /N/ - /dɑ/ - /R/). Rather, it is easier for Japanese speakers to pronounce it by using the syllabic units (/kɑ/ - /reN/ - /dɑR/). Although this is not directly related to the above discussion, the idea that moras and syllables need not be treated separately might assure that the shared importance of syllable awareness in learning to read across languages is also applicable to Japanese.

2.5.4. Summary

Previous studies have demonstrated that linguistic units of phonological awareness necessary for learning to read vary across languages, whereas syllable awareness is assumed to be important in early reading commonly in many alphabetic and non-alphabetic languages.

It was highlighted that, in order to learn to read in English, Japanese speakers have to develop not only this shared syllable awareness but also phonemic awareness because English is an orthographically deep language and requires flexible use of multiple phonological units of awareness in speech processing. In addition, they need to enhance intrasyllabic awareness of onset-rime because it is one of the unique phonological characteristics in English and cannot be found in Japanese whose basic segmentation unit is mora.

2.6. The necessity of phonological awareness instruction for Japanese children learning English

In this section, why explicit instruction of phonological awareness should be needed for Japanese children to learn to read in English will be discussed. According to the aforementioned linguistic interdependence hypothesis, the development of L2 competence is partially a function of the type of competence already developed in L1 at the time when intensive exposure to L2 begins (Cummins, 1978, 1979). The transfer of abilities and skills is assumed to occur not so much at a linguistic level, but rather at a metalinguistic level of competence (Verhoeven, 1994). If so, phonological awareness as a facet of metalinguistic awareness could be an underlying ability across languages. However, this assumption does not seem to apply to the case of Japanese children learning English, or the extent of it might be lower than in other combinations of languages.

2.6.1. Cross-linguistic transfer of phonological awareness

To date, the development of phonological awareness and its relationship with L1 early reading has been examined mostly with English monolingual children (Adams, 1990) in terms of its facilitative role in acquiring word reading skills (Goswami & Bryant, 1990) and predicting subsequent reading development (Muter, Hulme, Snowling, & Stevenson, 2004). On the other hand, phonological awareness has also been found to influence L1 reading development not only in other alphabetic languages (Lundberg, Frost, & Peterson, 1988; Lundberg et al., 1980; Näslund & Shuneider, 1996) but also in non-alphabetic languages (Ho & Bryant, 1997; Siok & Fletcher, 2001).

2.6.1.1. Evidence of the transfer of phonological awareness

In SLA research, attempts have been made to verify the prediction that phonological awareness may be transferrable from L1 to L2 (Geva & Wang, 2001). For example, Durgunoğlu, Nagy, and Hancin-Bhatt (1993) demonstrated that Spanish-speaking children who performed better in Spanish phonological awareness tasks at both onset-rime and phoneme levels could read more English words and pseudowords than children who performed poorly in phonological tasks. Furthermore, children's performance on English word and pseudoword recognition tests was predicted by their levels of both Spanish phonological awareness and Spanish word recognition. Similar evidence of cross-linguistic transfer of phonological awareness between Spanish and English, which share fundamental alphabetic principles, has been reported in other longitudinal studies (Cisero & Royer, 1995; Lindsey, Manis, & Bailey, 2003).

The correlations of phonological awareness in L1 with that in L2 and word reading in L2 have been demonstrated also in other *alphabetic* language combinations; English-speaking French-learning children (Bruck & Genesee, 1995; Comeau, Cormier, Grandmaison, & Lacroix, 1999), Italian-speaking English learners (Campbell & Sais, 1995; D'Angiulli, Siegel, & Serra, 2001), and Hebrew-speaking English learners (Geva & Siegel, 2000). Gottardo, Yan, Siegel, and Wade-Woolley (2001) is one of the limited studies that demonstrated the transfer of a particular level of phonological awareness from *non-alphabetic* L1 (Chinese) to *alphabetic* L2 (English). Their results showed that children's rhyme detection ability in L1 was significantly correlated with their phoneme deletion ability in L2, and that phonological awareness in L1 and in L2 contributed uniquely to L2 word reading ability.

2.6.1.2. The factors affecting the transfer of phonological awareness

If phonological awareness transfers from L1 to L2, especially in consideration of the developmental progression of phonological awareness in English among Japanese children learning English, it is necessary to have a general understanding of conditions under which such cross-linguistic transfer occurs; i.e., the factors which affect the occurrence of transfer. This topic has been investigated mostly in studies on heightened phonological awareness of bilingual children (Rubin & Turner, 1989; Rubin, Turner, & Kantor, 1991), and two factors are now recognised: differences (1) in the phonological complexity and (2) in the orthographic transparency (grapheme-phoneme consistency) between L1 and L2.

With regard to the phonological complexity of languages involved, earlier findings are contradictory (Kuo & Anderson, 2008). For example, it has been claimed that the transfer of phonological awareness occurs when L1 has a more regular and simpler phonological structure such as Italian which has only five vowels and no diphthongs (Campbell & Sais, 1995) or when segmentation units in L1 are distinctive as in French which has more salient syllables compared to English as L2 (Bruck & Genesee, 1995). Bialystok, Majumder, and Martin (2003) revealed enhanced phonological awareness in Spanish-English bilingual children over English monolingual children, whereas they failed to find such advantage in English as L2 for Chinese (Cantonese)-English bilingual children. These results can be attributed to the facts that phonological structure of English and Spanish are more similar than those of English and Chinese, and that phonological awareness in Spanish with a simple phonetic structure may transfer more easily to that in L2 (Dodd, So, & Lam, 2008).

In contrast, other researchers argue that it is phonological awareness in L1 with a more phonologically complex structure that may transfer to another language. Chen, Anderson, Li, Hao, Wu, and Shu (2004) found that Cantonese-Mandarin bilingual children had the advantage in onset-rime awareness over monolingual Mandarin speaking children, and this was attributed to their exposure to phonologically more complex L1 (Cantonese which has a greater number of lexical tone contrasts and syllables) than L2 (Mandarin). Supporting this result, Dodd et al. (2008) demonstrated that Cantonese-Putonghua (standard Mandarin) bilingual kindergarteners had more enhanced phonological awareness than both of two matched monolingual control groups. Furthermore, using the same pair of languages, Loizou and Stuart (2003) compared phonological awareness between English-Greek and Greek-English bilingual children, and found that English-Greek bilinguals performed significantly better than Greek-English counterparts, especially on phonological awareness tasks of smaller units (phonemes).

Then, regarding the influence of orthographic transparency, it has been demonstrated that bilingual children who are literate in L1 with more orthographic transparency tend to show more phonological awareness in L2 (Cunningham & Stanovich, 1990; Liow & Poon, 1998; Mumtaz & Humphreys, 2001). Liow and Poon (1998) compared phonological awareness in English across three L1 groups of multilingual Singaporean children. Children learnt English in the same school, but their L1 was different (i.e., English, Mandarin, and Bahasa Indonesian that had a very shallow, or regular, alphabetic orthography). The result showed that the performance on phonological awareness tasks were best with Bahasa Indonesian speaking children, followed by English speaking and Mandarin speaking children. It was argued that a relationship between L1 script exposure and phonological awareness develops in line with the orthographic depth hypothesis (Frost, Katz, & Bentin, 1987; Frost & Katz, 1992) which states that the use of phonology is determined by the orthographic properties of a language. In relation to this orthographic factor, bilingual children had the advantage of enhanced phonological awareness when they were tested in the language in which literacy instruction occurred (Bialystok et al., 2003), and children who cannot read and write in L1 are not likely to show such an advantage (Bruck & Genesee, 1995).

2.6.1.3. The effect of L1 phonological awareness on L2 word reading

Regarding the role of transferred L1 phonological awareness in L2 early reading development, it has been argued that degrees of similarity (linguistic and orthographic distances) between L1 and L2 should have a significant influence not only on the *process* of phonological transfer but also on the *rate* at which L1 phonological awareness affect the development of L2 phonological awareness and reading across diverse languages (Geva, Wade-Woolley, & Shany, 1997). Koda (2008) hypothesised that in early stages of L2 acquisition, transferred facets of L1 metalinguistic awareness reflect dominant L1 properties, but they are gradually adjusted to those unique to L2. The necessary degree of adjustment and the amount of L2 input and experience needed for it are determined essentially by how closely the two languages are structurally related, and orthographic distance between L1 and L2 such as alphabetic and non-alphabetic is considered to be one of the factors (Goswami, Gombert, & de Barrera, 1998; Green & Meara, 1987; Koda, 1989, 2000; Muljani, Koda, & Moates, 1998).

While there has been only limited number of studies that empirically investigated the mediating role of L1 phonological awareness between orthographic distance and the efficiency of L2 word reading, the study of Muljani et al. (1998) is informative. They compared the performance on the lexical decision task among Indonesian and Chinese-speaking university students who were learning English as L2. Indonesian uses Roman-alphabet orthography related to English, but Chinese is logographic and unrelated. The results showed that only Indonesian participants benefitted from the congruity of the stimulus word structure (spelling-pattern consistency) between L1 and L2. It was also found that the spelling patterns in English stimuli affected the performance of Indonesian participants: The facilitative effect of the congruity was larger when intraword structures of the stimulus words were similar to those in Indonesian, not those unique to English. Thus, it was suggested that related orthographic backgrounds induced general facilitation in lexical processing, and also the effect might become larger when more orthographic properties were shared between the two languages making processing demands posed to learners identical.

Moreover, since facilitation of the development of phonological awareness in L2 may be accelerated if the two languages involved are more linguistically and orthographically similar (cf., Section 2.6.1.2), the emerging awareness in L2 can reflect properties of both L1 and L2 properties and vary systematically according to learners' L1 backgrounds (Koda, 1998, 1999, 2000, 2008; Wang, Koda, & Perfetti, 2003). For instance, Wang et al. (2003) found that Chinese ESL learners relied more on (ortho)graphic information while Korean ESL learners more on phonological information in English lexical processing. In other words, ESL learners' preferences of lexical processing were strongly affected by their own L1 orthographic experience. Conversely, Koda (1999) revealed that ESL learners were sensitised, to a similar degree, to the internal structure of English words irrespective of whether their L1 is alphabetic or non-alphabetic, showing that the nature of target orthography plays a role in learning to read in L2. Thus, as phonological awareness in L2 is a result of sustained assimilation of processing experiences in both L1 and L2, it should reflect major characteristics of phonological awareness in both languages at least in the early stage of L2 development.

2.6.1.4. Three questions that need to be answered

If phonological awareness which Japanese children develop in learning to read in English should have characteristics of both Japanese and English as discussed in Section 2.6.1.3, the instruction of phonological awareness for them needs to be based on the understanding of the following:

(1) What are the characteristics in Japanese children's phonological awareness which reflect phonological and orthographic properties of the Japanese language?
(2) What are the characteristics of phonological awareness necessary for learning to read in English which reflect phonological and orthographic properties of the English language?
(3) In terms of the differences in phonological and orthographic properties between Japanese and English, what are the characteristics of the phonological awareness development by Japanese children in learning to read in English?

These questions will be considered in the following sections.

2.6.2. The development of phonological awareness of Japanese children learning English

In the process of Japanese children's acquisition of early EFL reading skills, positive and negative effects of the differences of phonological structures and writing systems between Japanese and English seem to be entangled in a complicated manner. Some L1 reading research has investigated Japanese children's development of phonological awareness at the levels of syllable and mora which are important for learning to read in Japanese (Akita & Hatano, 1999; Amano, 1986; Cutler & Otake, 1994; Otake et al., 1993; Otake, Hatano, & Yoneyama, 1996; Tamaoka & Makioka, 2009). On the other hand, to the author's knowledge, there is a very limited number of studies that have examined the development of phonological awareness of smaller linguistic units such as phonemes by Japanese children (Goetry, Urbain, Morais, & Kolinsky, 2005; Mann, 1986; Spagnoletti et al., 1989). This may be partly due to a common notion that the basic units of Japanese phonology (i.e., moras) are larger than phonemes and focusing on phonemic awareness is not so practical in L1 reading research in Japanese.

Hence, in this section, based on what has been discussed so far in this chapter, an attempt will be made to hypothesise the possible shape of the development of phonological awareness in English by Japanese elementary school children, taking both the effect of *Roma-ji* instruction and the cross-linguistic transfer of phonological awareness into consideration. This discussion will make an important foundation for the methodology of the intervention to teach phonological awareness in Japanese elementary schools.

2.6.2.1. The effect of the *Roma-ji* instruction

In the 2011 curriculum reform under the new version of the *Course of Study for Elementary Schools*, the grade in which *Roma-ji* is taught was shifted from Grade 4 to Grade 3 "considering the necessity of the knowledge of *Roma-ji* in the use of ICT and in other learning activities" (*The Guidelines for the National Curriculum for Elementary Schools*, 2008, my translation). Whereas the knowledge of *Roma-ji* seems to influence Japanese children's literacy development not only in Japanese but also in English, there may be even pitfalls in expecting that learning *Roma-ji* will automatically facilitate children's understanding of the English phonological system.

As described earlier, two writing systems are used in Japanese in a mixed manner; i.e., logographic *kanji* and syllabic *kana*. In addition, Japanese children are taught the *Roma-ji* writing system that *converts* the *kana* script into the alphabetic code. However, in Japanese the relationship between a *kana* character and its pronunciation (sound) is one-to-one, and in the *Roma-ji* system most of the syllabaries are spelt with pairs of a consonant letter and a following vowel letter (CV), except a nasal (N) and some geminates (Q). Thus, it can be argued that, once Japanese is written with the alphabet according to the Romanisation rules, it falls into the category of alphabetic shallow orthography whose spelling is transparent. This view may be supported by Wydell and Butterworth (1999) that considered Japanese as a less dyslexic language whose letter-sound correspondences are consistent at a coarse level according to *the hypothesis of granularity and transparency*. Therefore, the easiness of reading aloud *Roma-ji* may cause Japanese children to adopt its pronunciation rules (i.e., letter-sound correspondence) to reading loud English words only because both are written with the letters of the alphabet.

Japanese children may develop some awareness of smaller phonological units like phonemes spontaneously as they cognitively mature or as they develop *kana* literacy (Mann, 1986; Spagnoletti et al., 1989). The knowledge of *Roma-ji* may also play a facilitative role in this development of phonemic awareness, because it is in *Roma-ji* learning where Japanese children are explicitly taught that each *kana* character consists of a combination of smaller constituents (i.e., consonant and vowel phonemes). However, phonological awareness of smaller *grain size* units is essential in learning to read in phonologically inconsistent languages like English (Ziegler & Goswami, 2005; McBride-Chang et al., 2008). If *Roma-ji* has properties as a phonologically consistent language, the awareness of smaller phonological units would not be required so much in learning to read its script, and the development of phonemic awareness which might be observed in the process of *kana* learning may not be promoted as expected.

Moreover, an alternative explanation is also possible to Japanese children's development of phonemic awareness demonstrated in earlier studies (Mann, 1986; Spagnoletti et al., 1989). As a facet of metalinguistic awareness, phonological awareness is defined as the ability to *consciously analyse* the phonological structure of spoken words (Dowker, 1989; Gillon, 2004). Whereas Japanese children might become able to recognise and manipulate phonemic sounds in any way, they do not generally have to use this ability in reading Japanese and *Roma-ji* because these are phonologically consistent and orthographically transparent and, therefore, do not require the awareness of smaller phonological units in order to read. In other words, children do not have to analyse the phonological structure of Japanese speech *consciously* at smaller linguistic levels. Therefore, Japanese children's 'phonemic awareness,' if they have any, might be an *implicit* level of awareness induced by means of tasks that explicitly forced them to manipulate phonemes, and might not be identical to the implicit ability that is related to learning to read and might not be transferable.

Furthermore, since Japanese children learn to use the moraic segmentation procedure in speech perception, their developing phonemic awareness, if any, may help Japanese children to insert a vowel within a consonant cluster or add a vowel after the final consonant (i.e., vowel epenthesis) more 'skilfully and efficiently' in reading aloud English words. This, in turn, may lead to segmenting English in a more mora-based way, trying to maintain a sequence of CV pairs in English speech and preventing its natural segmentation. Moreover, mora awareness developed through learning to read *kana* characters might also be improved by reading and writing CV pairs dominantly found in *Roma-ji*, and this might become another facilitator of mora-based segmentation. In summary, although again there are few studies that empirically examined the relationship between the knowledge of *Roma-ji* and English literacy development among Japanese children, *Roma-ji* learning seems to affect Japanese children's English acquisition both positively and negatively. What is important is to make sure that children do not begin to learn English without the full realisation of the fact that *Roma-ji* is one of the Japanese writing systems. They need to become *explicitly* aware of how English phonological structure is different from that of Japanese. That is, children should have the *rudimentary* phonological awareness in English before early English reading instruction is introduced.

2.6.2.2. The developmental progression of phonological awareness of Japanese children learning English — A hypothesis

Insofar as what has been discussed, the developmental progression of Japanese children's phonological awareness in Japanese as L1 and then in English as L2 around when FLA begins in Grade 5 may be hypothesised in the following way (Figure 2.2) compared to that of English speakers (Figure 2.3).

First, through early exposure to Japanese oral input and pre-reading experience in its orthography, Japanese children begin to become aware of its phonological structure. Theoretically, the development of phonological awareness is assumed to start from the level of larger phonological units such as word-level rhymes and syllables (Adams, 1990; Anthony & Lonigan, 2004).

When formal early reading instruction in Japanese begins in Grade 1, they are taught how to read and write both scripts of *kana* characters (*hiragana* and *katakana*), although the majority of children master reading *hiragana* prior to *katakana* (Tamaoka & Terao, 2004). In this early stage of literacy development, their segmentation procedure of spoken language might be a mixture of syllable-based and mora-based procedures.

However, the more children improve *kana* literacy through experience in the Japanese traditional poetry such as *haiku* and *tanka* and in the games with *kana* characters, the more aware they may become of moras as fundamental phonological units and their speech segmentation may become dominantly moraic (Inagaki et al., 2000).

Figure 2.2: The model of developmental progression of phonological awareness by Japanese English learners

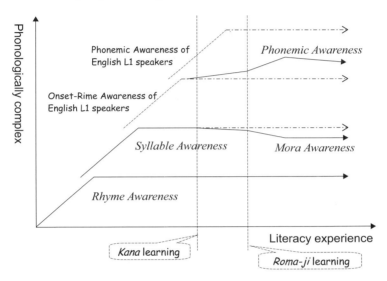

1. Phonemic awareness begins to develop later and more slowly than that of English L1 speakers.
2. The development of phonemic awareness may be facilitated by *Roma-ji* learning. Then, as mora awareness (moraic segmentation) develops, it may be decreased because phonological analysis at the phoneme level is not required to learn to read in Japanese.
3. Since the intrasyllabic structure such as onset and rime is not recognisable in Japanese phonology, it seems unlikely that onset-rime awareness develops spontaneously along with literacy development.
4. Syllable awareness as a fundamental level of awareness across languages may develop naturally with Japanese L1 speakers, but as they learn *kana* characters, they learn to rely predominantly on moraic segmentation procedure. Moreover, awareness of the simple consonant-vowel combination of moras is less phonologically complex than awareness of syllables. Thus, the complexity level of syllable awareness which Japanese L1 speakers achieve might be lower than that of English L1 speakers.

Figure 2.3: The model of developmental progression of phonological awareness by English speakers

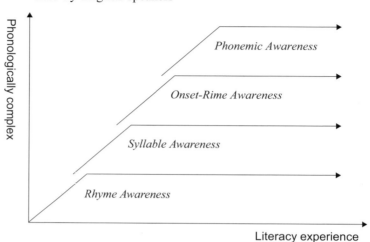

1. Each level of phonological awareness develops in a quasi-parallel manner.
2. In order to read in English, multiple levels of phonological awareness are needed such as syllable awareness and phonemic awareness.

At the same time, by becoming familiar with alphabetic symbols and words of foreign origin in their daily lives, children may develop the ability to manipulate smaller phonological units methodically on demand (i.e., *implicit* phonemic awareness). However, this ability will not go beyond the *implicit* level spontaneously because children are not required to use it *consciously* in learning to read in Japanese, and it is difficult to predict to what extent they would enhance it. Moreover, as the phonological category of intrasyllabic units such as onset-rime, which is characteristic to English phonology, cannot be found in Japanese, the facilitation of the development of phonemic awareness by such intrasyllabic awareness may not be recognisable.

Then, in *Roma-ji* learning in Grade 3, children learn to know that most Japanese sounds can be represented by combining a vowel letter and a consonant letter of the alphabet, and their awareness of moras, and possibly phonemes, strengthens.

Finally, when children are exposed to English speech in FLA in Grade 5, because they are not accustomed to consonant clusters and words ending with a consonant, they might recognise or pronounce English word sounds inserting a vowel sound between or after consonant sounds. If children begin to learn early English reading without explicit understanding of the phonological differences between Japanese and English and not realising that *Roma-ji* is not English script, they are likely to add a vowel after consonants also in reading aloud English words.

On the other hand, mora awareness which Japanese children develop in Japanese literacy acquisition seems to overlap syllable awareness to a large extent. Syllable awareness is important in learning to read commonly in both Japanese and English. However, since English is a phonologically inconsistent language, it also requires awareness of smaller phonological units such as phonemes to be read. Unfortunately, the transfer of phonological awareness is unlikely to occur between Japanese and English where English as L2 has a more complex phonological structure than Japanese as L1. Therefore, phonological awareness in Japanese may not facilitate the development of awareness at the phoneme and onset-rime levels which are uniquely related to learning to read in English. Thus, in order to have phonological awareness needed to acquire early English literacy, Japanese children have to develop *purposefully* additional units of awareness such as phonemic and onset-rime awareness, by making their *might-have* (i.e., implicit level of) phonemic awareness *explicit* to the extent they can use it consciously in analysing English phonological structure.

2.6.3. The importance of teaching phonological awareness to Japanese elementary school children

Some researchers (Cunningham, Perry, Stanovich, & Share, 2002; Share, 1995; Snowling, 2000) have argued that phonological awareness might not necessarily have an effect on the outcome of learning to read and it might decrease as children become more skilled in reading and more able to apply alternative strategies such as reading by analogy. Indeed, phonological awareness is not the only factor that predicts reading development because the processes of learning to read and of reading *per se* are complexly multifaceted and causally determined by various causal factors. However, phonological awareness seems to at least boost the process of learning to read. Especially in the context of EFL learning in Japan, as long as it seems unlikely that phonological awareness in Japanese spontaneously facilitates the development of phonological awareness in English because of the different phonological units of importance, children should be 'explicitly taught' *rudimentary* awareness of specific phonological units which is a prerequisite for learning to read in English in order to make sure that they have readiness for it.

Here, with regard to the *explicit instruction* of phonological awareness to Japanese children, the necessity of considering the explicit-implicit dichotomy in language learning research was acknowledged. The terms *instruction* and *learning* may not be used interchangeably (Schmidt, 1990), and the term *explicit* or *implicit instruction* here refers to the intentionally-organised instructional practices to elicit *explicit* or *implicit learning* respectively on the learners' side, following the definition proposed by Dörnyei (2009). Explicit learning is "input processing with the conscious intention to find out whether the input information contains regularities and, if so, to work out the concepts and rules with which these regularities can be captured" (Hulstijn, 2005, p. 131), while implicit learning "takes place without either intentionality or awareness" (Ellis, 2009, p. 7) and requires massive amount of input (Dekeyser & Larson-Hall, 2005). Moreover, in relation to the age effects on L2 acquisition, it is argued that younger children acquire their L1 in an implicit natural manner whereas older L2 learners may rely on or benefit from explicit learning due to the limited amount of input and the use of cognitive system different from what was necessary for L1 acquisition (Dekeyser & Juffs, 2005). The advantage of young learners in implicit learning has been claimed in relation to the critical period hypothesis: It has been assumed that the ability of learning implicitly comes to be lost and a shift to explicit learning is observed in the post-critical period of language learning (Dekeyser, 2000; Dekeyser & Larson-Hall, 2005), and therefore that "the instructional approach should be different depending on age" (DeKeyser, 2003, p. 335). On the other hand, some researchers who are sceptical about such mutually exclusive conceptualisation of explicit and implicit learning before and after the critical period claim the necessity of combining both instructional approaches, i.e., providing learners with explicit explanation of the concepts and rules once they have been extensively exposed to a large amount of L2 input which could trigger implicit learning (Dörnyei, 2009; Norris & Ortega, 2000; Singleton & Muñoz, 2011; Singleton & Ryan 2004).

On the basis of this understanding about explicit and implicit learning, it should be noted why this research emphasises the explicit approach to the instruction of phonological awareness. Phonological awareness is a facet of metalinguistic awareness, making it possible to demonstrate the skills such as segmenting, blending, deleting, and substitution at various phonological levels. Therefore, considering that the development of metalinguistic awareness is encouraged in explicit teaching (Ellis, 2009), it might be argued that phonological awareness instruction should necessarily have some aspect of this. However, in fact, the distinguishing feature of explicit and implicit phonological awareness instruction generally lies not in its metalinguistic properties, but in whether letter-sound correspondence is introduced and then the phonological awareness skills are directly connected to early word reading (Adams, Foorman, Lundberg, & Beeler, 1998; Cunningham, 1990; Snow, Burns, & Griffin, 1998). In other words, in both 'explicit' and 'implicit' instruction of phonological awareness, children first learn these skills by intensively experiencing them through the focused 'oral' activities, rather in a decontextualised manner. Then, in the explicit instruction of phonological awareness, the newly acquired skills are directly applied to demonstrating how to read words on the basis of the knowledge about letter-sound correspondence, while the implicit instruction will make no further association between these skills and word reading. Thus, the instruction of phonological awareness that the current research aims to propose needs to adopt the explicit instructional approach as it attempts to incorporate the introduction of letters and early reading.

In the theory of reading as an interactive and culturally constructed process, two types of strategies are thought to play important roles. First, 'inside-out' strategies are based on the reader's knowledge and cultural expectations and provide the scaffolding as a means of instructional, emotional, and cognitive support. On the other hand, the 'outside-in' strategies provide the reader with new information, new cultural experiences, and new aspects of language through various activities such as reading stories from the target culture (Gregory, 1996). Bus and van IJzendoorn (1999) suggest that, especially for the development of early reading, both 'outside-in' factors such as emergent literacy and 'inside-out' factors such as phonological awareness stimulated by the appropriate instruction should have an essential role in shaping its process. The perspective of *emergent literacy* presumes that literacy-related abilities acquired during the preschool period are the most legitimate and important in the continuum of literacy development. The view originates from the idea of distinguishing reading from pre-reading, and in the *reading readiness* approach phonological awareness is thought to be one of the pre-reading skills needed to benefit from the formal reading instruction (Whitehurst & Lonigan, 1998; Lonigan, Burgess, & Anthony, 2000). In this sense, phonological awareness instruction might serve as a preventive intervention in the pre-reading stage so that children would not fail to have the readiness for formal instruction (Lundberg, Frost, & Peterson, 1988).

Moreover, there are some empirical findings claiming that in the case of English as a language of deep orthography, learning to read words written in an alphabetic script does not guarantee that children would spontaneously induce the alphabetic principle which is reflected in its phonological structure, especially at the phoneme level (Byrne, 1998). Two explanations were given to this claim based on a series of studies summarised in Byrne (1996) that preliterate children do not hypothesise any level of phonological representation when they are first exposed to alphabet symbols, and that even for children who have realised that letters reflect the phonological structure of a language it is difficult to detect phonemes because they have characteristics not shared by other larger phonological units such as syllables. The former was supported by the finding that children failed to detect the target phoneme *s* and syllable *er* in the written word pairs which shared the same position in the phonological structure such as *bug-bus* and *corn-corner*, whereas they could readily detect the targets in the word pairs distinguished by the comparative morphemes such as *hats-books* and *small-smaller*, showing that they might focus on meaning aspects of distinctive letters. Therefore, if English is a language that poses difficulty in deducing alphabetic principles, teaching those principles explicitly to children should facilitate their recognition of them, and the instruction of phonological awareness must be the first necessary step.

2.7. The instruction of phonological awareness

Many L1 studies have investigated the effects of the phonological awareness instruction on the acquisition of phonological awareness and other reading-related outcomes (e.g., word reading, spelling, and reading comprehension). However, the phonological awareness programs used in those studies differ widely in terms of content, duration, and characteristics of students. With the increasing interest in the ingredients of effective programs for teaching children to read, the meta-analyses of studies that examined the effects of phonological awareness instruction were carried out by Bus and van IJzendoorn (1999) and National Reading Panel (2000) which is reported in Ehri, Nunes, Willows, and Shuster (2001). Whereas these meta-analyses were mainly based on the studies in the English-speaking context, their findings should give essential information which needs to be considered in the phonological awareness instruction for Japanese children.

The study reported in Ehri et al. (2001) was a replication and extension of that of Bus and van IJzendoorn (1999). The common statistical method of meta-analysis was primarily effect size, which indicated whether and by how much performance of the instruction group exceeded that of the control group. The sample in the study of Bus and van IJzendoorn (1999) included 36 studies which tested effects of training programs on phonological awareness and 34 studies which tested effects on reading with some overlap, and Ehri et al. analysed a set of 52 studies that met their criteria and it contributed 96 cases comparing the outcomes of instruction and control groups.

Generally, with regard to outcome measures which investigated the effects of phonological awareness instruction, the results of both studies commonly showed that phonological awareness instruction was remarkably effective in helping children acquire phonological awareness and in facilitating its transfer to reading (word-level decoding ability). Moreover, the studies agreed on the following: (1) The effects of phonological awareness instruction were limited to literacy outcomes as shown in the low effect size of phonological awareness instruction on math posttests, (2) Phonological awareness instruction is more effective than alternative forms of instruction used in the control group or no instruction in teaching phonological awareness and in facilitating transfer of phonological awareness skills to reading, (3) Phonological awareness instruction taught phonological awareness very effectively and had long-term effects so that children retained the acquired skill after instruction, and (4) Phonological awareness instruction yielded statistically higher effects for the acquisition of segmentation and deletion skills than for blending skills.

2.7.1. Features of the effective phonological awareness instruction

Below, the major findings on the effective instruction of phonological awareness are summarised. As Ehri et al. (2001) points out, effect sizes analysed in their studies might not represent the whole database. However, even though their findings may be tentative and suggestive and should not be considered to be definitive, they are certainly insightful in making future instructional plans including the phonological awareness intervention in this study.

Target students

The meta-analyses found that pre-schoolers and kindergarteners gained the most phonological awareness although the number of comparisons was small, and the effect of phonological awareness outcomes in kindergarteners was statistically larger than the effect in first graders and in second-to-six graders. The explanation was given to this result that pre-schoolers and kindergarteners had just started out with the least phonological awareness and had more to learn than older children did. In addition, phonological awareness instruction transferred to reading to a similar extent among kindergarteners, first graders, and second-to-six graders. Although the effect size for pre-schoolers was statistically much larger, it was again assumed to be due to the small number of comparisons and the outcome tested with simplified word recognition tests. Furthermore, it was found that at-risk readers gained as much phonological awareness as normal developing readers and more than disabled readers, and especially they showed statistically larger transfer effects on reading.

As for the difference in children's L1, phonological awareness instruction exerted a statistically larger impact on phonological awareness acquisition as well as transfer to reading by English-speaking students than by the non-English-speaking students. One possible reason for the larger effect sizes in English was presumed to be that the English writing system is not as transparent in representing phonemes as it is in the majority of the other languages. Based on these results, Ehri et al. (2001) argued that explicit phonological awareness instruction may clearly teach children the phonological units at the higher phoneme level and how they are linked to graphemes in English.

Skills taught

Focusing instruction on one or two skills was demonstrated to be more effective for teaching phonological awareness than focusing on multiple skills simultaneously. Similarly, transfer of the learnt skill(s) to reading was statistically greater when the instructional focus was on one or two phonological awareness skills than when multiple skills were taught. Moreover, the advantage of instruction persisted in the follow-up test, with statistically larger effects on reading especially when two skills, not one, were focused. Further analysis revealed that, out of the various combinations of skills for phoneme manipulation, the instruction of segmenting and blending might play a central role in learning to read words (Lewkowicz, 1980). In fact, teaching the skills to segment and blend statistically benefited reading more than the multiple-skills approach did.

Letter use

Phonological awareness instruction with letters created statistically greater effect sizes on reading, which were almost twice as large as the effect size of phonological awareness instruction without letters, and the same statistically significant pattern was yielded at the follow-up test as well. It was claimed that the instruction of phonological awareness might make a stronger contribution to reading performance when the instruction involves teaching children to manipulate phonemes with letters than when the instruction is limited to speech, although disabled readers did not benefit either type of instruction in any case.

The unit of Instructional delivery

In fact, the point is that the findings of two studies were not fully consistent. Whereas Bus and van IJzendoorn (1999) found larger effects for individualised instruction than for small groups in teaching phonological awareness but not in promoting transfer to reading, Ehri et al. (2001) demonstrated that small groups were more effective than tutoring for both teaching phonological awareness and reading outcome. Phonological awareness was taught most effectively in small groups where the effect size was very large, over twice the size of effects for tutoring and for classrooms. Ehri et al. (2001) interpreted that small groups were more effective because they might enhance children's attention, or social motivation to achieve, or the chances of observational learning, and attributed the failure in replicating the results of Bus and van IJzendoorn (1999) to the small number of studies that used group as a statistical unit of analysis.

The length of the instruction

Bus and van IJzendoorn (1999) reported that the amount of time spent for the instruction might be weakly related to the effect sizes for reading, but not for phonological awareness. Similarly, Ehri et al. (2001) demonstrated that effect sizes for phonological awareness outcome were statistically larger for the two middle time periods lasting from 5 to 9.3 hours and from 10 to 18 hours, and the periods that were either shorter or longer than this were statistically less effective for teaching phonological awareness. Effect sizes for reading were also larger for shorter time periods than for longer time periods. Thus, it was assumed that phonological awareness instruction might not need to be lengthy to exert its strongest effect on the acquisition of phonological awareness and reading.

2.7.2. The implications for the phonological awareness instruction for Japanese children

Based on the findings of the above meta-analyses and what has been discussed so far in this chapter, the following practical suggestions for the instruction of rudimentary phonological awareness for Japanese children can be drawn.

(1) The instruction may have more effect on the acquisition if it teaches phonological awareness combining letter practice, and a purely phonetic training might be less effective. Letters are expected not only to improve children's acquisition of phonological awareness in that they provide concrete, lasting symbols for sounds which are harder to grasp, but also to give additional support for linking phonological processes to reading (Bus & van IJzendoorn, 1999). Moreover, it was indicated that well organised phonological awareness instruction might benefit children regardless of with or without the training of articulatory awareness (Wise, Ring, & Olson, 1999).

(2) The instruction may be more effective if it focuses on segmenting and a blending skills. It was argued that a blending skill is needed to transform graphemes into recognisable words in word decoding, while phoneme segmentation skill is necessary for reading words from memory by sight, and that both may be required to read words by analogy (Ehri et al., 2001). In addition, it was demonstrated that one trained skill of phonological awareness is unlikely to transfer spontaneously to another untrained skill (Slocum, O'Connor, & Jenkins, 1993) and that the instruction of a blending skill alone might be of relatively little value unless children have developed the basic skill of segmentation (Fox & Routh, 1976).

(3) The instruction does not necessarily have to be long, but needs to be intensive (Byrne & Fielding-Barnsley, 1993, 1995; Byrne, Fielding-Barnsley, & Ashley, 2000). For this purpose, it might be possible to suggest that the phonological awareness instruction should include words in dense phonological neighbourhoods (i.e., having many similar-sounding words) rather than words from sparse lexical neighbourhoods (i.e., having few similar-sounding words) because children are expected to show more accurate performance on phonological awareness tasks including such words. A statistical analysis has shown that in English those are words that share rime portions (De Cara & Goswami, 2003).

(4) Concerning the unit of delivery, small group instruction may work better. Recently in Japanese elementary schools, different from other subject classes where a homeroom teacher teaches alone, more adults such as voluntary local people and university students with a certain level of English ability are participating in English classes to support the teaching. Under these circumstances, it might be possible to make the most of small-group activities.

(5) Considering the potential development of phonological awareness at

both larger and smaller units through literacy experience in Japanese, the focus of the instruction might not necessarily have to be comprehensive. Rather, the emphasis should be placed on the phonological elements that are found in English sound system but not in Japanese system and that are different between English and Japanese. The former category of elements may involve the phonemic sounds which are not included in Japanese sounds such as /r/ and /v/, the alphabets which are not used in the *Roma-ji* writing system (i.e., *c, f, j, l, q, v,* and *x*), consonant clusters, and onset-rime distinction. Focusing on rimes rather than on vowels alone is thought to be particularly important in helping children learn to decode words (Adams, 1990). Moreover, the awareness of both consonant clusters and onset-rime distinction seems to be important to prevent the mora-based segmentation of sounds in words and 'vowel epenthesis.'

(6) Children need to be encouraged to apply phonological awareness skills learnt to reading and spelling so that they can maintain longer effect of instruction. It has been demonstrated that whereas the phonological awareness instruction does effectively teach component skills, more elaborated instruction which emphasises their application is also necessary for not only utilising these component skills (Cunninghan, 1990; Qi & O'Connor, 2000) but also promoting broader transfer of skills (O'Sullivan & Pressley, 1984). Cunningham (1990, p. 434) compared the phonological awareness instruction based on a "skill and drill approach" where the procedural knowledge of phoneme segmentation and blending was taught and the instruction based on a "metalevel approach" that explicitly emphasised the application and utility of phonemic awareness to word reading. The result supported the facilitative role of phonological awareness in reading development at the beginning stages. Moreover, it revealed that the "metalevel" instruction was more effective for the transfer to reading ability than the "skill and drill" instruction. Thus, phonemic awareness gained through the instruction might be able to be supplemented by further instruction in how to apply the knowledge. In the case of the intervention reported in the following chapters, these advanced activities are simple word reading and picture book reading.

(7) The conceptualisation of phonological awareness as *a unitary construct* suggests that the instructional tasks should be appropriate for children in terms of the levels of both linguistic complexity and cognitive maturity. In other words, as children's phonological awareness develops,

both the tasks that can best evaluate their concurrent skills and abilities for phonological awareness and the linguistic levels of phonological awareness they can prove to have may vary. It is necessary, therefore, to select tasks which can assess most effectively not only the level of phonological awareness that a child has just acquired, but also the level that is currently in the course of development. By taking account of these developmental variances of phonological awareness, better results and outcomes should be undoubtedly obtained.

(8) According to the *quasi-parallel* progression model which assumes the overlap among developmental stages of phonological awareness, "children learn and refine variety of phonological sensitivity [awareness] skills simultaneously" (Anthony et al., 2003, p. 482). Thus, the phonological awareness instruction may not necessarily have to be mastery-oriented because mastery at one stage is not a prerequisite to the next.

2.8. The factors affecting the item difficulty in the phonological awareness assessment

A variety of tasks have been used for assessing phonological awareness, such as *adding* sounds to words, *deleting* sounds from words, *blending* sounds together to make words, *segmenting* words into smaller sound units, and *substituting* one sound for another in a word (Morais, 1991; Muter et al., 1998; Torgesen & Mathes, 2000; Torgesen, Wagner, & Rashotte, 1997). These tasks are used not only for measuring phonological awareness but also for its instruction. However, in earlier studies, there seems "little standardization within individual phonological awareness tasks" (McBride-Chang, 1995. p. 179).

As indicated in Section 2.7.2, for the objectives of the present study, it is important to consider the factors that affect the item difficulty in the assessment and instruction of phonological awareness. These may be categorised into the following three perspectives: (1) levels of phonological awareness tapped, (2) linguistic complexity of target phonological units, and (3) differences in the tasks used (Anthony et al., 2002, 2003; Pufpaff, 2009; Lewkowicz & Low, 1979; Vandervelden & Siegel, 1995). Below, the effects of each factor will be discussed based on the findings from previous studies.

2.8.1. The target levels of phonological awareness

As discussed in Section 2.2.3, the skills necessary for segmenting larger phonological units such as syllables have been demonstrated to be more accessible and acquired earlier, and therefore easier, than the skills of segmenting more sophisticated level of phonological units such as phonemes (Leong & Haines, 1978, Treiman & Baron, 1981).

As for the studies that empirically investigated the influence of phonological awareness levels on the task difficulty, Liberman et al. (1974) is one of the earliest that demonstrated that the task of segmenting words at the syllable level is easier than at the phoneme level. Moreover, the study of Treiman and Zukowski (1991) is important in the sense that it underpinned the existence of the onset-rime awareness between syllable awareness and phonemic awareness. It found that the onset-rime condition was easier than the phoneme condition and more difficult than the syllable condition, regardless of whether the shared phoneme is part of an onset (e.g., <u>s</u>teak-<u>sp</u>onge) or part of a rime (e.g., sm<u>oke</u>-t<u>ack</u>) in the phoneme condition.

Fox and Routh (1975) demonstrated not only that segmenting words into syllables was generally easier for children than segmenting syllables into phonemes, but also that the ability for phoneme segmentation increased between the average ages of three and six and reached the ceiling between the ages of six and seven. The similar result was found in Goldstein (1976) that the segmentation and deletion tasks at the phoneme level were more difficult for four-year-old children to perform accurately than those at the syllable level. Moreover, children's performance in the tasks which require them to recognise intrasyllabic units of spoken words was relatively better than in the tasks of separating phonemes (Bowey & Francis, 1991; Kirtley, Bryant, Maclean, & Bradley, 1989). Considering these results from a developmental perspective, Treiman and Zukowski (1996) proposed the *linguistic status* hypothesis which "maintains that syllables always have an advantage over intrasyllabic units, which in turn always have an advantage over individual phonemes" (p. 194).

2.8.2. Task differences

Many studies have attempted to describe the order of the difficulty in phonological awareness tasks. Vendervelden and Siegel (1995) demonstrated that the tasks requiring multiple cognitive operations such as manipulation were more difficult, and especially 'multiple operations and production' was found to be the most cognitively demanding. Chafouleas and Martens (2002) found that segmentation was more difficult for first-graders than phoneme blending and deletion.

Yopp (1988) administered 10 phonological awareness tasks to 54 kindergarteners with an average age of 5;10 and found that the tasks which requires the skill for rhyme detection was easiest followed by the tasks tapping the skills for phoneme blending, isolation, counting, segmentation, and deletion. Later, Schatschneider et al. (1999) administered a battery of seven phonological awareness tasks of 105 items to 945 English-speaking kindergarteners. It was revealed, slightly different from Yopp's, that tasks for phoneme segmentation, phoneme blending, and phoneme deletion were more difficult than tasks for onset-rime blending, phoneme matching, and phoneme categorisation. These contradicting results, however, seem to be caused by the less strict experimental design and data analysis. Then, Stahl and Murray (1994) revealed that phoneme isolation was significantly easier than blending, and deletion was easier than segmentation. However, they claimed that the linguistic complexity of the target stimuli might have more influence on the difficulty in the phonological awareness assessment.

Moreover, it needs to be noted that, in addition to these factors, the difference of cognitive operations required in a task such as *recognition* or *perception* might also affect its difficulty. For example, recognition tasks (e.g., to detect whether *duck* and *dog* begin with the same sound) seems to be easier than production tasks (e.g., to say the beginning sound of *dot*) (Yopp, 1988). Then, tasks assessing *analytic* skills such as segmenting and deleting are assumed to be more difficult than those assessing *synthetic* skills such as blending and adding (Perfetti, Beck, Bell, & Hughes, 1987). This implies that the characteristics of each task and the quantity of tasks used in the assessment might also influence the results. For example, the task asking children to detect a word which does not rhyme with other three words might require them to hold all the four words in memory while judging, and therefore confounds their ability for short-term memory with their rhyme detection skill (Wagner & Torgesen, 1987).

2.8.3. The linguistic complexity of target phonological units

2.8.3.1. The number of phonemes in the target stimuli

The factor of the number of phonemes in the stimuli might affect the difficulty of the phonological awareness tasks; that is, the more phonemes a target stimulus has, the more easily it may be detected by children (Gipstein, Brady, & Fowler, 2000). Walley, Smith and Jusczyk (1986) demonstrated that kindergarteners' performance in the non-word classification task became better as the number of phonemes increased from one to three. However, regarding such *unit size* effect, Treiman and Zukowski (1996) pointed out that in earlier studies the linguistic *levels* of phonological units might have been confounded with their *sizes*, as the number of phonemes shared in the syllable condition was larger than that in the onset-rime condition, which was in turn larger than that in the phoneme condition. Therefore, they attempted to disentangle *linguistic status* and *unit size* by designing tasks in which phonological units shared the same number of phonemes, and found that children judged the similarity of words which shared complete syllables more easily than those which shared the same number of phonemes but these phonemes did not constitute whole syllables, supporting the *linguistic status* hypothesis on the whole.

On the other hand, the effect of the number of consonants within a consonant cluster on the task difficulty is widely recognised (Stahl & Murray, 1994). Treiman and Weatherston (1992) demonstrated that, when the initial consonant was in the consonant cluster and a part of a larger linguistic unit (i.e., an onset), it was harder for children to pronounce the consonant separately than if the consonant is an onset on its own. More specifically, McBride-Chang (1995) revealed that deleting a consonant from a word without a consonant cluster was significantly easier than deleting the same stimulus from a cluster of two or three consonants, but no significant difference in the difficulty of phoneme deletion was found between clusters of two and three consonants. Later, Bouwmeester, van Rijen, and Sijtsma (2011) reported not only the similar result in a Dutch context that a consonant cluster rendered the task of segmenting words more difficult, but also that a cluster of three consonants was significantly more difficult to segment than a cluster of two consonants.

2.8.3.2. The position of target phonemes

Regarding the influence of the position of target phonemes in a word, Marsh and Mineo (1977) demonstrated that tasks which require children to focus on the syllable-final consonants to be harder than those which require them to focus on the syllable-initial consonants. Similarly, Stanovich, Cunningham, and Cramer (1984) administered ten phonological awareness tasks to 49 kindergarten children. It was found that, while three tasks which tapped rhyme awareness were at ceiling, other seven phonemic awareness tasks with the target phoneme in different positions (e.g., segmentation, detection, blending, or deletion of the initial or the final phoneme) seemed to vary in terms of their cognitive demand. Generally, tasks in which the critical sound contrast was at the beginning of the word were easier than those in which the critical sound was at the end of the word.

More specifically, with regard to phoneme identification, Helfer and

Huntley (1991) claimed that there were no position differences in consonant identifiability in many conditions but, when such differences did occur, initial consonants were favoured over the final consonant. Moreover, Redford and Diehl (1999) demonstrated that, although final consonants were more identifiable when preceding a vowel, they were still less identifiable than initial consonants. They explained the advantage of initial consonants in terms of their greater acoustic distinctiveness. Schreuder and van Bon (1989) also found that consonant clusters in the coda are more difficult to segment than vowel-consonant combinations.

McBride-Chang (1995) demonstrated that phonemes in the middle position were significantly more difficult to identify than those in the initial or final positions, but no significant difference between the initial and final position was yielded. In contrast, it was also found that, in phoneme deletion, all three position factors were significantly different: Phonemes in the middle position (i.e., part of an initial or final consonant cluster) were the most difficult to delete as in Lewkowicz (1980), and final phoneme deletion was much easier than initial phoneme deletion. The advantage of final phonemes was attributed not only to the recency effect stronger than the primacy effect that initial phonemes had, but also to the perceptual similarity of the task to familiar rules of English grammar such as making a plural word singular or a past tense word present tense (e.g., *hellts / helt*, or *ginkt / gink* in non-word targets).

The difficulty of the medial consonant was also demonstrated in the task of segmenting (Lewkowicz & Low, 1979). In their study, although there was no significant difference in the difficulty for children to segment between CV words (e.g., *toe, tie,* and *sew*) and VC words (e.g., *out, ice,* and *ask*), kindergarteners trained on the segmentation of CV words did significantly better on the task of segmenting CVC words (e.g., *suit, coat,* and *sock*) than those trained on VC words.

2.8.3.3. The types of target phonemes

The aforementioned study of Redford and Diehl (1999) also found that types of consonants influenced the results: For example, consonants /k/ and /ʃ/ were not statistically more identifiable in initial position than in preconsonantal final position, while consonants /t/, /k/, and /ʃ/ were as identifiable in prevocalic final position as in the initial position.

Similarly, there are some earlier studies that carried out the systematic investigation of the effect of phoneme types on the task difficulty. In the tasks of identification, stop consonants are significantly more difficult to identify than fricative consonants (Marsh & Mineo, 1977; McBride-Chang, 1995; Treiman & Baron, 1981). Moreover, In the task of segmentation, liquid were easiest for children to segment, followed by nasals, and obstruents were the most difficult to segment (Stahl & Murray, 1994), while McBride-Chang (1995) yielded no significant difference in children's performance between on fricatives and on plosives. Stahl and Murray (1994) argued that certain consonant clusters such as /st/ and /pl/ might be difficult for children to segment, but nasal blends (like /nk/, /nd/ and /mp/) and liquid blends (/ld/) in rimes seemed easier to segment.

Specifically with regard to the vowel-consonant combination in a target word, considering the sonority of consonants, Treiman (1984) hypothesised that liquids (e.g., /l/ or /r/) tend to adhere more closely to the vowel than nasals (e.g., /m/ or /n/), which in turn adhere more closely to the vowel than obstruents (i.e., plosives such as /p/ or /k/ and fricatives such as /s/ or /g/). Later, the results of Geudens, Sandra, and van den Broeck (2004) showed that plosives and fricatives are easier to separate from a vowel than liquids and nasals, but they pointed out that this pattern was characteristic in particular for VC combinations and not as clear-cut for CV combinations. Recently, partly supporting Treiman (1984), Bouwmeester et al. (2011) demonstrated that, as in English, Dutch vowel-liquid combinations are the most difficult to segment followed by vowel-plosive or vowel-fricative combinations, but not so different from vowel-nasal combinations.

2.8.4. Summary

The task difficulty of phonological awareness could be affected by various factors. Generally, in English L1 studies, the tasks tapping larger phonological units are assumed to be easier than those tapping smaller units. In terms of the task differences, it seems that segmentation is the most difficult task followed by deletion and blending, and identification (isolation) is the easiest. However, the difficulty of individual tasks might be further affected by whether they need multiple skills (manipulation) or by the position of target phonemes within stimuli or their types. In C_1VC_2 words, for example, manipulation of the final consonant (C_2) may be more difficult than the initial consonant (C_1). Moreover, manipulating consonants in clusters may be more demanding for children than manipulating single consonants not comprising clusters. These will be considered in deciding not only the target phonological skills or sound categories for the intervention but also the order of introducing them to the participating children in the methodological chapter.

2.9. Chapter summary

This chapter first provided a detailed discussion about the facilitative role of phonological awareness in English L1 development. Considering the differences in phonology and orthography between Japanese and English, it was assumed that Japanese children need to develop multiple levels of phonological awareness to learn to read in English. Indeed, English has more complex phonological characteristics than Japanese, which exposes little possibility of phonological awareness transfer, and therefore the significance of its explicit instruction to Japanese children was claimed. In addition, due to the orthographically transparent L1 and the influence of *Roma-ji* learning, it might not be assumed that Japanese children spontaneously develop smaller linguistic units of phonological awareness necessary for learning to read in English. Based on these arguments, a hypothesis of Japanese elementary school children's phonological awareness development in English was proposed. Finally, the features of effective phonological awareness instruction and the factors that affect the task difficulty was summarised based on the findings from earlier research in order to establish the framework for the interventional instruction in a Japanese elementary school carried out later in this study.

Chapter 3

Methodology

This chapter provides a detailed account of the research methodology employed for this study to investigate the research questions outlined in Chapter 1, along with the specific research approaches and methods. First, the main component of the research design, i.e., exploratory intervention, is presented with the justification of choosing this. Then, a thorough description of additional adopted research methods as well as tools and procedures for data collection and analysis follow. Based on the hypothesis of the developmental progression of phonological awareness by Japanese children learning English (Section 2.6.2.2) and the roles that phonological awareness plays in learning to read in English (Sections 2.3 and 2.5), a careful deliberation about the empirical matters of research on early English reading instruction in the Japanese EFL context will also be provided, considering the ethical issues related to this study and the author's role as the instructor in the implementation of the intervention. Below, the term "instructor" is used interchangeably with "author," especially in the description of the interventional sessions and discussion based on them.

3.1. Research Design

The aim of the intervention was to make a resolute attempt to investigate the feasibility of introducing early English reading in normal classrooms through the provision of phonological awareness instruction. Due to the fact that very few previous training studies and empirical findings could be found on learning to read in English in an EFL context like Japan, this interventional instruction was exploratory in nature, and necessarily adopted a more qualitative approach which had been regarded as an effective way of looking into such "new, uncharted areas" (Dörnyei, 2007, p. 39). Furthermore, considering the scope and depth of research questions to be answered, the necessity of supplementing the phenomenological view of the reality in the author's subjective perception in the qualitative approach with the objective perspective of reality in the quantitative approach was also recognised. They are indeed "complementary parts of the systematic, empirical search for knowledge" (Silverman & Marvasti, 2008, p. 57). Therefore, also in the microstructure of the intervention design, the qualitative data collected during the period of instruction was complemented by quantitative data which consisted of the test results of children's phonological awareness and early English reading ability as well as the questionnaire information about their attitudes toward the interventional sessions. In contrast, these quantitative details were further triangulated with the qualitative data of semi-structured informal interviews with children.

Thus, overall in this research, each of the methods employed was considered as "a 'composite,' with considerable possibility for internal validation" (McDonough & McDonough, 1997, p. 95) and located with its distinct significance in the hierarchical structure of the research design. The whole protocol of both questionnaires and the intervention will be described in detail below to assure the reliability of this research.

3.2. The intervention

3.2.1. The context

The intervention took place in M Elementary School during Terms 2 and 3 (from September to March) of the academic year preceding the official introduction of FLA. The school is located in a city which has been growing as a commuter town next to a regional central city in the middle area of Japan. The total number of pupils is around 700 annually, and there are usually three or four classes of less than 35 pupils in each of the six grades. This elementary school had been designated for research on education for international understanding between the academic years of 2003 and 2005, and was one of the schools which had established their own in-house curriculum of ECA before the official announcement of the introduction of English teaching in elementary schools in 2008. When the intervention was conducted, ECA was held once a week in all grades but Grade 1 beginning in Term 2, and voluntary local residents (i.e., mothers of pupils) and university students with interests and English ability played the role of teachers. Most homeroom teachers joined the sessions and took a role of assisting voluntary teachers with the instruction, whereas some took part in planning lessons and teaching more actively. Thus, English classes were normally taught by one main voluntary teacher, one or more assistant voluntary teachers, and the homeroom teacher. The general content of sessions such as key words and expressions words in particular communicative situations as well as possible activities and games, was provided by the in-house curriculum of this elementary school. However, the actual way of instruction was left to the main voluntary teachers.

Considering that this intervention was an attempt to teach phonological awareness and early English reading in the normal classroom practice of elementary school English teaching, M Elementary School was an ideal school because its curriculum for English instruction had represented what English teaching should be like according to the *Course of Study for Elementary Schools*. That is, children in this school can become familiar with English and encourage positive attitudes toward communication through ECA in the PIS from Grade 1 to Grade 4, and then move on to FLA in Grade 5. This very feature of the practice of English teaching was an advantage in establishing the external validity of the intervention which related to the *generalisability* of the findings beyond the immediate case of the site in the present study. Because of its exploratory characteristics, this intervention needed to investigate English classes typically following the Japanese national curriculum "within their *real-life* context" (Yin, 2009, p. 83). Moreover, in the sense that M Elementary School had decided to use *Eigo Note 1* as a teaching material for children in Grade 5, this intervention was carried out in the real FLA classroom, which was the most desirable situation for investigating the proposed research questions. The site of the intervention was Class 5-2, one of the four classes in Grade 5. The number of children participating was 31, consisting of 15 boys and 16 girls.

3.2.2. Methods of data collection and the role of the researcher

During the sessions, it was hardly possible for the instructor to jot down every detail and think about the session on site. Therefore, in addition to the field notes written promptly after each session, other tools were used for data collection in order to establish the construct validity of the intervention design: (1) the instructor's research journal, (2) the diary of the assistant student teacher (AST), (3) video and audio recording of the sessions, (4) informal interviews with children held after session and during breaks, and

(5) semi-structured interviews with the teachers who had observed or participated in the sessions.

One of the considerations that needed to be discussed was reliability of the data collection in the intervention. During the process of instruction, the instructor as well as the HRT and the AST were actively involved in activities as facilitators. In this sense, it seems difficult to assure that the perspectives reflected in the research journal and diary kept by these *participants* or in the interviews would give an *objective* description of their observations of the English classes. Objectivity in qualitative research might be, as Corbin and Strauss (2008) speculate, "a myth" (p. 32). Therefore, instead of tackling the question of how to establish objectivity head-on, it will be considered from the different perspective of sensitivity which is a contrasting concept with objectivity and means "having insight, being tuned in to, being able to pick up on relevant issues, events, and happenings in data" (p. 32). As Dey (1993) argues that "there is a difference between an open mind and an empty head. To analyze data researchers draw upon accumulated knowledge. They don't dispense with it. The issue is not whether to use existing knowledge, but how" (p. 63), and professional experience could be a solution to it (Corbin & Strauss, 2008). Therefore, throughout the intervention, the teachers participating and the instructor were encouraged to be mindful of the necessity to always compare professional knowledge and experience with what was happening before their eyes, and to observe the reality of the data without being distracted by their own perceptions of it.

3.2.3. The content and methods for the instruction

3.2.3.1. Target skills for phonological awareness, sound categories, and spelling rules

Based on the knowledge about the development of phonological awareness (Adams, 1990; Anthony & Francis, 2005), its instruction (Bus & van IJzendoorn, 1999; Ehri et al., 2001), and the factors affecting its assessment (Stahl & Murray, 1994; McBride-Chang, 1995) obtained through the literature review in Chapter 2, the four phonological awareness skills to be taught during the intervention were set as follows:

Skill	Examples of tasks
Blending	What is the word which is made up of the sounds /p/, /e/, and /t/? [*pet*] (phoneme level)
	What is the word which is made up of the sounds /m/ and /ɑp/? [*map*] (onset-rime level)
Segmenting	What are the sounds in the word *bag*? [/b/, /ɑ/, and /g/]
Deleting	What is the word if you delete the initial sound of *cat*? [*at*]
Substitution	What is the word if you change the initial sound of *hen* to /t/? [*ten*]

The activities and tasks in which these skills are focused on either at the onset-rime level or at the phoneme level were prepared following the ideas and tips for the instruction in the phonological awareness programmes which are commercially available; e.g., *Road to the code* (Blachman, Ball, Black, & Tangel, 2000), *Road to reading* (Blackman & Tangel, 2008), and *Intervention for reading success* (Haager, Dimino, & Windmueller, 2007), or which can be downloaded from the website of the reading research institute; e.g., Florida Center for Reading Research (http://www.fcrr.org/curriculum/SCAindex.shtm).

Deciding on the target sound categories and spelling rules to be dealt with in these activities and tasks was full of challenges, because, first of all, how much and in what ways the children participating had been exposed to English words before the intervention was not clear. In the previous grade, they were in different classes and experienced different instruction with different teachers. Moreover, there were some children who were taking or used to take English lessons outside school. Since the aim of this intervention was to evaluate the feasibility of instructing phonological awareness and early reading skills in the normal curricular context of FLA, it seemed most reasonable to follow its potential curriculum. In fact, the curriculum was embodied in *Eigo Note 1* (for the structure and its content, see Appendix 3.1), which was published by MEXT in 2009 so that elementary schools all around Japan could achieve the objectives of FLA in Grade 5 by using it as a common material. Thus, it was settled that sounds and spelling rules which could be taught referring to the words in this textbook should be targeted in the interventional instruction. In other words, it was envisaged that, by mastering target sounds and spelling rules, the children would be able to read words of *Eigo Note 1* which were officially expected to be presented aurally.

However, there was another practical problem to be faced. According to *The Guidebook for Teacher Training of 'Foreign Language Activities'* (MEXT, 2009), the number of target words in *Eigo Note 1* is 211, and even after adding five words representing fruit names needed to be taught for activities in a certain lesson, it was 216. Moreover, in addition to this small number of words which are expected to be taught in Grade 5, these words were not selected nor organised considering their phonological complexity (i.e., sounds and spelling rules) as Kan (2010) explained that the words included in *Eigo Note 1* and *2* were those which had been used by many designated schools for research for the past 10 years. In other words, they are a mixture of words which children would come across in various situations. Therefore, the number of words which could be used to introduce each of potential target sound categories (e.g., diphthongs, or double vowel-letters pronounced as long vowels) and spelling rules (e.g., word-final *e* or consonant doubling) differ considerably from one another. For example, whereas the number of appearances of a long vowel *ee* is 13 out of 216 words, those with diphthongs such as *aw*, *ow*, and *ou* are 2, 2, and 3 respectively. It seems natural that words are not graded according to their phonological characteristics so that children would gradually develop basic word reading skills because word reading skills are not expected to be taught in elementary school. Additionally, the following factors were considered in selecting the target content for the instruction:

- What Japanese EFL children need to be explicitly taught in order to learn to read in English in terms of the phonological differences between English and Japanese
- The number of words in each lesson of *Eigo Note 1* which could be used as examples for a particular sound category or a spelling rule
- The total number of sessions for the intervention
- The complexity of targets and cognitive demand for children

Thus, the following seven sound categories and spelling rules were selected as the instructional targets.

Sound categories
1. short vowels
2. basic consonants
3. digraphs (*sh*, *th*, *ch*, *ck*, *wh*)
4. long vowels (*ee*, *oo*)
Spelling rules
5. V-e rule
6. consonant doubling (*bb, cc, dd, ff, ll, pp, rr, mm, ss, tt*)
7. consonant clusters (*bl, br, cr, dr, fr, gl, gr, sk, sl, sp, st, str, sw, tw*)

These were not only frequently found in words of *Eigo Note 1* but also widely taught in published phonological awareness programmes. Especially, consonant doubling was included as a target not because of its role as a marker of a preceding short vowel, yet because it was necessary to teach the Japanese children participating that English consonant doubling does not make a geminate sound as in *Roma-ji*. If a sound category or a spelling rule applies to many letter combinations, those which can be found in words of *Eigo Note 1* were selected as targets and are presented in the parentheses above.

These target content was used not only for making the plans for interventional sessions, but also as the standards for selecting words used in the instruction of target phonological awareness skills as well as other tasks and activities. On the other hand, the necessity of flexibly adjusting these targets according to the actual knowledge of English the children had at the beginning of the intervention had been realised.

3.2.3.2. Session plans

In making plans for a series of sessions, two approaches to the implementation of the phonological awareness instruction at the classroom level suggested by Gillon (2004) were considered. One was *the informal approach* in which phonological awareness activities are integrated into not only language class content but also content for other curricular subjects including simple classroom routines. The other was *the structured approach* in which a structured phonological awareness programme is implemented for a defined length of time.

It was assumed that the present intervention should be primarily based on *the informal approach* as the suggested phonological awareness instruction needed to be able to be administered in the normal classroom practice of FLA. However, there were indeed some content areas which had to be taught intensively in a structured manner such as the difference between letter names and letter sounds. Thus, the main approach taken was one integrating both *informal* and *structured* approaches. It was also necessary to utilise children's knowledge of *Roma-ji*, once they had understood that *Roma-ji* is one of Japanese writing systems, not English. Table 3.1 summarises characteristics of target sounds and spelling rules for the interventional instruction which were taught referring to the difference from and the similarity to those of Japanese writing system and *Roma-ji*.

Table 3.1: The summary of target sound categories and spelling rules for the instruction and the assessment

	Categories & Rules	Targets (letter sounds or spellings) *	Purposes for instruction
Sounds	short vowels	a, e, i, o, u	1. To make children acquire basic knowledge of English vowel sounds 2. To teach children differences and similarities of vowel sounds between English and Japanese (1) /e/, /i/, and /o/ are similar as *e* for え, *i* for い, and *o* for お respectively (2) /æ/ is pronounced by saying *a* for あ with mouth stretched horizontally (3) /ʌ/ is pronounced by saying *a* for あ with mouth stretched vertically
	consonants	b, c, d, f, g, h, j, k, l, m, n, p, q, r, s, t, v, w, x, y, z	1. To make children acquire basic knowledge of English consonant sounds 2. To teach children differences and similarities of consonant sounds between English and Japanese (1) Consonant sounds applicable from *Roma-ji* are /b/, /d/, /g/, /h/, /k/, /m/, /n/, /p/, /s/, /t/ (2) The sounds /ti/ and /tu/ are remarkably different from *ti* for ち and *tu* for つ respectively (3) The sound pairs which are not discriminated in Japanese are /b/ and /v/, /r/ and /l/, and /f/ and /h/
	digraphs	sh, th, ch, ck, wh	1. To make children have an understanding of basic digraphs. 2. To teach children that there are consonant combination which are pronounced as individual phonemes
	double vowel-letters	ee, oo	1. To make children understand that *ee* is pronounced as long vowels and *oo* has both long and short sounds
Spelling rules	Split-grapheme rule (V-*e* rule)	a-e, e-e, i-e, o-e, u-e	1. To make children understand that the final *e* "has a marking function, indicating the value of preceding consonant or the previous vowel as long" (Carney, 1994, p. 308) 2. To make children aware that in Japanese (and *Roma-ji*) there is no silent letter
	consonant doubling	bb, cc, dd, ff, ll, pp, rr, mm, ss, tt	1. To make children understand that the function of consonant doubling is different between English and *Roma-ji* (1) In Japanese (and *Roma-ji*), doubling consonants makes the geminate (Q) of っ (2) In English, double consonant letters "do not normally follow long vowels" (Carney, 1994, p. 115)
	consonant clusters	bl, br, cr, dr, fr, gl, gr, sk, sl, sp, st, str, sw, tw	1. To make children understand that in English it is allowed that two or more adjacent consonants are blended together keeping each individual sound, with no intervening vowel 2. To make children aware that in Japanese, consonant blends are not found, and that Japanese learners of English tend to insert a vowel after the initial consonant of blends (most frequently the sound /u/)
Others	Intrasyllabic structure (onset-rime)	e.g., C / VC	1. To make children aware of onset-rime units 2. To help children understand that the speech segmentation procedure is different between English and Japanese (In Japanese, the intrasyllabic structure of words is not recognisable, and spoken words tend to be segmented based on the phonological unit of mora.)

* : Target letter sounds and spellings were selected from those included in words of *Eigo Note 1*

Furthermore, basic concepts of planning the course of sessions were as follows:

1. After having experienced several oral activities of phonological awareness, short vowels and basic consonant sounds will be introduced with their corresponding letters at a stretch.
   — Special care was taken with regard to the fact that some of the alphabet are not used in *Roma-ji*. That is, in introducing short vowel and consonant sounds in this intervention, the children were first presented with short vowel sounds in the words with the CVC structure, and all consonant letters contained in these words were ones which children had already got familiar with in *Roma-ji* learning. Then, sounds of the same set of consonant letters were introduced before the rest including the seven consonant letters which cannot be found in *Roma-ji* writing system.

2. Once basic sounds for corresponding vowel and consonant letters were taught, various activities and tasks to enhance the children's phonological awareness will be *integrated* with the normal classroom activities (i.e., curricular content based on several activities in each of nine lessons in *Eigo Note 1*) in every session. When the intensive instruction for other categories of sounds is necessary, 20~25 minutes of a 45-minute session is allowed for it.

3. Words with which the children are familiar in their daily lives will be used as target words in each session, in addition to the words included in *Eigo Note 1*. (e.g., loan words such as *bus*, *tape*, and *tube*)

4. Key phrases (or expressions) in each session will be introduced with their written forms, raising the children's awareness about constituent letter sounds.

In this way, the plans for 22 sessions and a stock of activities which could be used according to the children's progression or as supplementary materials were prepared in advance of the intervention.

3.2.4. The assessment and questionnaires before and after the intervention

Both before and after the period of the intervention, several abilities of the children in relation to phonological awareness and early English reading ability were tested. In addition, information was collected on their attitudes toward English learning. That is, at the beginning of the intervention, a questionnaire followed by informal interviews was administered to explore the children's attitudes toward English learning including letters and literacy skills, English learning experience outside school, and confidence in *Roma-ji* reading and writing. Then, at the end of the intervention, another questionnaire was used, in which some items were slightly adjusted so that they could elicit changes in the children's attitudes during the period of the intervention as well as their general reaction to the instruction. The purposes of this initial and final assessment and questionnaires were as follows:

1) To evaluate the children's development of skills which were targeted in the instruction
2) To clarify the influence of the interventional content and the intervention itself on their attitudes to English learning in general and interest in English literacy skills.

Table 3.2: The list of tools for the assessment and information gathering before and after the intervention

		Before the intervention	After the intervention
Tests	Written	Letter name knowledge	
		phonological awareness tests	Sound categorisation
			Initial phoneme recognition
			Phoneme recognition & location
			Sound manipulation
	Oral	Word reading [real words and nonwords]	
	(Written)	(Word spelling [real words and nonwords])	
Questionnaire and a follow-up interview with children		> Attitude toward English learning > English learning experience outside school > Confidence in *Roma-ji* > Exposure to English in daily life	> Attitude toward English learning > Reactions to the intervention
Interview with the homeroom teacher and assistant teachers (OR Questionnaire and a follow-up interview)		> Attitude toward elementary school English teaching and introduction of literacy skills > Children's exposure to English in other school activities and subjects > The way *Roma-ji* was taught	> Attitude toward elementary school English teaching and introduction of literacy skills > Reactions to the intervention

Table 3.2 is the comprehensive list of the content of the initial and final assessment as well as other information gathering (i.e., questionnaires and interviews) before and after the intervention (see Appendix 3.2 for the detailed summary). In addition, the children were given a short *reflection sheet* about five minutes after each session in order to elicit their reaction

to it. The sheet included common five-scale questions such as 'How much did you enjoy today's session?' and 'How much effort did you make in today's session? Give the mark,' as well as several open-ended questions about the most enjoyable or difficult activities and what they learnt in the session. Other questions were all five-scale items and asked the children to judge how much they understood or came to be able to perform individual instructional content in the session.

3.2.4.1. Tests for the initial and final assessment of phonological awareness

In both the initial and final assessment, the children's skills for phonological awareness and literacy skills were measured with the same battery of tests. These were a letter name knowledge test, four kinds of phonological awareness tests (sound categorisation, initial phoneme recognition, phoneme recognition and location, and phoneme manipulation), a real word and non-word reading test. In fact, a real word and non-word *spelling* test was also administered both before and after the intervention just in case that the oral part of the assessment (i.e., sound manipulation and word reading tests) could not be administered individually due to unexpected events, because the strong relationship between spelling and word reading ability in early stages of literacy development has been claimed (Caravolas & Bruck, 1993; Foorman & Francis, 1994; Gentry, 2000; Lesaux, Rupp, & Siegel, 2007; Sirois, Boisclair, & Giasson, 2008; Martins & Silva, 2006; Read, 1971; Richgels, 1995; Stage & Wagner, 1992). However, as the oral part was successfully given to the children on the individual basis in both the initial and final assessment, the results of spelling tests were not included in the analysis.

Among four phonological awareness tests, the sound categorisation test was adapted from Kirtley, Bryant, MacLean, and Bradley (1989), and the rest of three tests were developed by Vandervelden and Siegel (1995) and adapted by Jongejan, Verhoeven, and Siegel (2007). The advantage of using these tests was that they had been administered to English-speaking children in a wide range of ages (i.e., 5;6 to 7;3 years old in Kirtley et al. (1989) and 6;7 to 9;10 years old in Jongejan et al. (2007)), including relatively older children similar to the participants in this intervention.

Below, the details of the six tests used in the assessment will be summarised.

The letter name knowledge test

This test asked the children to listen to a letter name spoken aloud by the instructor and find the corresponding letter out of five options. All option letters were in lower-case, and there were 20 items. This test was used because it was necessary to evaluate how much knowledge of letter names and their corresponding shapes children had acquired through *Roma-ji* learning and daily exposure to them at the beginning of the intervention. In fact, 19 out of 26 letters (i.e., except seven consonant letters such as *c, f, j, l, q, v,* and *x*) are used in *Roma-ji* writing system, and components of *Roma-ji* spellings are commonly taught by referring to alphabetical symbols with their names (e.g., The teachers says, "A *kana* character か is spelt by combining the letters *k* and *a*."). Therefore, depending on the children's knowledge of letter names, the content of the course and the amount of time used for the revision of letter names as well as the instruction of unfamiliar letters had to be adjusted.

Moreover, only in the final assessment, a test on the correct sound of letters (i.e., a letter sound knowledge test) was administered using the same set of items as in which the sound of each target letter was presented instead of the name of the letter.

The sound categorisation test

This test had 40 items of three C_1VC_2 words, following four practice items. The original set of this test developed in Kirtley et al. (1989) had 64 items, which were further subcategorised into two tasks of 32 items: (1) an opening sound task which asks the children to identify the odd word based on the difference in the sound part of C_1V and (2) an end sound task which requires discriminating the odd word based on the difference in the sound part of VC_2. There were four conditions, each of which differed in terms of the sound(s) shared between two words and the nature of the odd word. Those conditions are summarised in Table 3.3. Precisely speaking, because all test items consisted of monosyllabic C_1VC_2 words, Condition 1, 2, and 4 in the opening sound task assessed the children's *phonemic* awareness in the word-initial position (i.e., onset), while Condition 2, 3, and 4 in the end sound task measured their *intrasyllabic* rime awareness.

Moreover, Condition 3 in the opening sound task asked the children to categorise C_1VC_2 words on the basis of the difference in the vowel sound (V) following the initial consonant (C_1 = onset) which were common in all three words. Similarly, in Condition 1 in the end sound test, the children had to recognise the difference in the final consonant sound (C_2) which was one constituent of the word's rime (VC_2) as the other constituent (V) was different from one another among all three words. Thus, these two conditions also assessed the children's phonological awareness at the phoneme level.

Table 3.3: The summary of four conditions in the sound categorisation test [adapted from Kirtley et al. (1989), p. 234]

Type of oddity tasks	Form of categorisation [shared sound(s) in two words]		Nature of the odd word		Examples	
	Opening sound	End sound	Opening sound	End sound	Opening sound	End sound
Condition 1	C_1	C_2	different C_1	different C_2	deck, cap, cough	leek, sock, *hid*
Condition 2	$C_1 V$	VC_2	different C_1 and V	different V and C_2	lap, lad, *pet*	*hop*, bead, seed
Condition 3	$C_1 V$	VC_2	different V same C_1	different V same C_2	can, *cot*, cap	tip, lip, *top*
Condition 4	$C_1 V$	VC_2	different C_1 same V	different C_2 same V	*pet*, deck, den	hop, *rock*, mop

C_1 = the initial consonant
C_2 = the final consonant
V = vowel sound

Correct answers *in italics*

With regard to the number of the items used in the present study, not all items of the original study were adapted considering the amount of time necessary for administering the whole set of seven tests as well as the cognitive demand for children. Generally, for the purpose of equating tests, it is assumed that "no fewer than 20 items or 25% of the total test, whichever is larger" (Downing & Haladyna, 2006, p. 458; Kolen & Brennan, 2004), needs to be included in both tests so that these items (i.e., anchor items) would reflect the content and difficulty level of either test. Therefore, in this study, 20 items of both opening sound and end sound oddity tasks were adapted, making the maximum score 40. When administered, the children were first told that they would hear three words, two of which sounded like each other but the other one did not, and then instructed to identify the odd word. Items for opening sound discrimination and those for end sound discrimination were mixed together, and the total 40 items were divided into two subtests of 20 items. One of the subtests was administered at the beginning of the series of phonological awareness tests and the other at the end so that children would not get bored with or tired from the repetition of the same task.

The initial phoneme recognition test

In this test, the children were aurally presented with a target sound, and were then asked to decide if that particular sound was in the initial position of the word they heard (e.g., /t/: *pen*, *tape*, *top*, *duck*). Two of four words in each test item had the initial sound that was targeted, and there were 10 test items and three abbreviated practice items. In order to increase the discrimination level of the test, different from the scoring method in Jongejan et al. (2007), one point was given when each of words with or without the target sound was correctly identified, making the maximum score 40. This test and the next 'phoneme recognition and location test' measured awareness of smaller phonological units (i.e., phonemic awareness) as some of the items in the above sound categorisation test did. However, the disadvantage of the categorisation test is that its results may be confounded with participants' ability for short-term memory because it requires children to hold the sound of all four target words in memory while judging the odd one (Wagner & Torgesen, 1987; see Section 2.8.2). In this sense, the test of initial phoneme recognition could assess the children's phonemic awareness with the simplest (i.e., less cognitively demanding) task. Then, the test of phoneme recognition and location could measure the same awareness with a more demanding task, because the task requiring multiple cognitive operations is more difficult (Vendervelden & Siegel, 1995; see also Section 2.8.2). The use of different tasks for assessing a particular level of phonological awareness was necessary because it was expected that the high percentage of correct responses (i.e., ceiling effect) would be achieved for some tasks by the children who are relatively older in the present study. This helped obtain more detailed information about the level of phonological awareness which children had before the intervention.

The phoneme recognition and location test

This test asked the children to listen for a target sound which had been aurally presented to them and then decide if that particular sound was in the first part of the word they heard, the last part, or not in the word (e.g., /s/: *neck*, *sun*, *class*, *grass*, *sick*, *pen*). When all words containing the target sound in a test item were identified, the item was considered correct. There were four abbreviated practice items and nine test items, and each test item comprised six words. The maximum score on this test was 54.

The phoneme manipulation test

This test aimed at assessing the children's higher phonological awareness skills than the ones measured in other tests, since phonological awareness was expected to develop through the intervention. This oral test was administered individually, and all responses of the children were audio-recorded. As the discussion about the relative complexity of phonological awareness tasks in Section 2.8.2 suggests, deleting phonemes is considered more difficult for children than phoneme identification and location, and in turn manipulating (e.g., substituting) phonemes requires more sophisticated phonological processing than deletion. This test was adopted from Jongejan et al. (2007) and assessed the children's ability of either removing a consonant sound from the presented words or changing a consonant sound in the words. There were three subtasks which were different in the position of the target consonant sound in the presented word (i.e., initial, final, or one phoneme which is in the middle of the words and comprises consonant clusters), and each subtask contained six items. In three of the items, the children were asked to remove a sound in the target position of the word, and in the other three items they had to change a sound in the target position to another presented sound. For example, in the subtest of clusters, they were instructed to remove /l/ from *slip*, and change /l/ in *slip* to /n/. The test consisted of two practice items and 18 test items with the maximum score 18.

Table 3.4: Target words for the word reading test in the initial and final assessments

	three-letter words (CVC)	words with a final *e*	words with a digraph	words with a long vowel	others
Real words from *Eigo Note 1* (*n*=17)	*yes* *six*	*name* *five* *cute* *home*	*black* *jellyfish* *this* *thank* *sandwich* *what*	*green* *cool*	*book* [to compare with *cool*] *octopus* [for the sound /u/] *study* [for sounds /u/ & /di/]
Original non-words (*n*=19)	*yag* *sed* *wib* *cof* *puz* [to compare with words with a final e] *hul* [for sounds /h/ & /l/] *qun* (*quen*) [for the sound /q/]	*yage* *sede* *wibe* *cofe* *puze*	*chax* *tock* *shem* *rith* *whov*	*jeen* *koot*	

The real word and non-word reading test

This test was administered individually in order to measure the exact level of the children's achievement of this skill. Target words (Table 3.4) had phonological characteristics relating to one or more sound categories and rules that were going to be taught to the children in the subsequent interventional instruction. A set of real word targets was selected from *Eigo Note 1* originally for this study. Although the children might not know some of them at the time of the initial assessment, it was assumed that they would have become familiar with all of them by the time of the final assessment because they were presented to children several times through tasks and activities in the intervention.

Out of 17 real words, two were three-letter CVC words, four were words with a final *e*, six with a digraph (i.e. *ch*, *ck*, *sh*, *th* for /θ/ and /ʒ/, *wh*), two with a long vowel (i.e., *ee* or *oo*), and three with some other phonological characteristics (e.g., *oo* for a short /u/ sound). On the other hand, a set of 19 monosyllabic non-word targets were also originally made for this study. There were seven non-words which had the three-letter CVC structure, five V-*e* non-words which were made by adding a silent *e* to the final position of five CVC target non-words, five non-words with a digraph in either initial or final position, and two non-words with a long vowel sound (i.e., *jeen. koot*). In these sets of target words, consonant letters were included at least once in either initial or final position if it was permissible in terms of orthographic constraints (see Section 3.3.4.3 below). Moreover, five short vowel sounds appeared at the similar rate in the middle position, so that a rough idea of children's understanding of each of letter sounds would be obtained.

3.2.4.2. Mini assessment

During the intervention, following the completion of each target content area, the children's ability to use the newly learnt skill or knowledge was assessed with a written test. Five tests were administered to assess their ability for (1) identification of a vowel in the middle of a CVC word, (2) identification of a word-final consonant, (3) identification of the initial and final consonants in a CVC word, (4) recognition and identification of a substituted phoneme, and (5) phoneme substitution and identification. Each test was administered as a form of a worksheet activity, without telling the children that it was a test to assess their understanding of the skill learnt in the previous session.

Originally, there was no plan to carry out mini assessment, and the worksheet activities intended to familiarise the children with written activities using the skills learnt. However, when the children were given the first worksheet activity, most of them appeared to get serious and worked on it as if they were taking a real test. Therefore, it was decided to use the rest of worksheet activities as mini assessment in order to check the children's understanding of the target content in the process of the intervention.

3.2.4.3. The letter combination in non-word targets

In making non-word targets for reading and spelling tests, there was a problem of how much possible influence of *orthographic regularity* in English writing system should be taken into account in order to maintain the *authenticity* of non-words as targets used in phonological awareness tests *in English*. The concept of orthographic regularity concerns "language users' awareness of permissible positions of letters in words when these seem to be determined purely on a visual basis" (Rixon, 2007, p. 11). The knowledge of orthographic regularity is assumed to begin to emerge from an early age among L1 English-speaking children (Treiman & Bourassa, 2000). For example, Treiman (1993; cited in Treiman & Bourassa, 2000) investigated the confounding effect of pronounceablity in testing children's knowledge of orthographic constraints. Kindergarteners, first-graders, and second-graders were asked to judge which of two words looked more like a real word. Each of the 16 target pairs included a non-word which conformed to the regular spelling pattern but the other non-word did not (e.g., *ckun / nuck, beff / ffeb, bei / bey, chym / chim, gri / gry,* and *dau / daw*), whereas both were pronounceable. The result showed that all three age groups of children chose the conforming target significantly more than 50% of trials above chance level.

The orthographic constraints in English seem complex and wide in scope and may be different between British and American usage (Cook, 1997), as Carney (1994) summarised 226 text-to-spelling correspondence rules which were further followed by detailed information about their limitations, relative importance and efficacy. Moreover, they are thought to be one of the most difficult aspects in English spelling that may cause problems for many English learners (Cook, 1999). With regard to words with a simple phonological structure such as CVC, there are several constraints which affect the appearance of a particular letter in each position of a word as well as the sound which a sound make in a particular position. For example, the letter *x* is pronounced as /z/ in the initial position but /ks/ in the final position, the letter *h* is not pronounced after a vowel, the letter *q* in the initial position is always followed by the letter *u* and make a consonant sound /k/, and the letter *k* for the sound /k/ only appears in the final position and the cluster *ck* is used in the final position (Carney, 1994). These explicit characteristics of consonants were considered in the process of *inventing* 19 target

CVC non-words for the present study.

In fact, Japanese elementary school children's exposure to written English words was so limited that it could hardly be envisaged that they would recognise unnaturalness of the target word structure due to the lack in the knowledge of orthographic regularity. Rather, it was expected that children would rely on what they had been explicitly taught during the intervention when they were asked to read aloud English words in the final assessment. However, the advantage of administering a non-word reading test was to evaluate to what extent the children would read unfamiliar English words mechanically based on their phonological awareness and knowledge of letter sounds acquired through the interventional instruction.

3.2.5. Ethical issues related to the intervention

In obtaining the consent for the intervention, the author visited M Elementary School and explained to the principal its purposes as well as detailed session plans. A few days later, a response from the principal came saying that they would accept the intervention with acknowledgement by the assistant principal and the teacher in charge of academic affairs. Then, cautious discussions were held before the target grade was decided on Grade 5.

What the author felt ethically most responsible for was the fact that the intervention itself and the content of exploratory instruction should not have a negative effect on the children's attitudes toward English learning and place extra burden on them even though the instruction included the content which was not usually expected to be taught in elementary school English education. In order to adjust its methodology and content, the author asked opinions about each session of every teacher who was involved in or observed the session. Moreover, since the participants were elementary school children in Grade 5, every effort was made to build a rapport with them and to get to know and understand them by means of paying frequent visits to the class even on the days when there were no English sessions and including fun activities especially in earlier sessions of the intervention. In addition, the author tried not only to explain the purpose and process of the intervention very clearly to them but also to convince them that they were allowed to ask questions and tell their difficulty and anxiety to any teacher in the school. By doing so, it was assumed that problems which had not been recognised would be illuminated and then could be solved appropriately.

Finally, any recorded data and information were kept securely so that the confidentiality to the children and teachers partaking in the intervention would be assured, and special codes for their names were used at the stage of transcribing recordings and interviews as well as describing the results in this book whenever necessary.

3.2.6. Data analysis procedures

All of the children's responses in the initial, final, and mini assessment were put on a database of IBM SPSS Statistics 19 in order to analyse their development in individual target instructional content. On the other hand, the qualitative data such as the instructor's field notes and diaries and the transcription of video-recording and interviews were categorised according to the content so that both qualitative and quantitative data could be complemented in discussing the results of the intervention from various angles.

3.3. Chapter summary

This chapter introduced the methodology for this study. In order to answer the set of research questions addressed, an exploratory intervention was carried out. The session plans for the intervention were originally constructed for the aims of this study. In this process and later discussion, the data obtained from the survey on teachers' beliefs and principles related to the instruction of letters and early English reading in elementary school (Ikeda, 2013, 2014) provided insightful information throughout the process of the intervention.

Chapter 4

The Results

In this chapter, an overview of the interventional sessions will first provided in Section 4.1, describing a typical pattern of a session for introducing new instructional content. Then, from Section 4.2 below, the results will be given, presenting the detailed description on how each of target instructional content (i.e., phonological awareness skills, sound categories, and spelling rules) was introduced as well as the children's reactions. This qualitative data is then followed by a discussion of the quantitative assessment data which serves to substantiate these results. The data for this chapter was obtained from different sources such as the research journal (RJ) kept by the instructor, the AST's diary of classroom observations, informal interviews with the children and the HRT, various tasks for assessment (i.e., initial, final, and mini), and reflection sheets completed by the children. Furthermore, in order to describe the sessions, the session videos were made full use of so that the children's reactions as well as classroom interaction could be depicted more accurately than would have been possible relying solely on the RJ.

4.1. Actual sessions

The total number of sessions was 22, slightly fewer than had been expected at the beginning because two sessions were cancelled due to a school event and an influenza epidemic. Apart from these teaching sessions, one session was used for conducting the written part of the initial assessment test and another for that of the final assessment. The oral part of these assessments was administered individually using periods of class activities and the break time such as between classes or after lunch.

Table 4.1: Participating children in the intervention (sorted by the total score in the final assessment)

ID		Group	Initial Written (Max. 154)	Oral Sound Manipulation (Max. 18)	Oral Word Reading (Max. 34)	Initial Total (Max. 206)	Written (Max. 154)	Initial Oral Sound Manipulation (Max. 18)	Oral Word Reading (Max. 34)	Final Total (Max. 206)	Letter Sound (Max. 20)
P10	Boy	A	141	10	11	162	141	19	28	188	20
P31	Girl	A	124	16	31	171	135	18	32	185	—
P27	Girl	A	130	8	21	159	137	19	28	184	20
P6	Girl	A	137	7	21	165	143	15	22	180	18
P1	Girl	A	129	5	17	151	144	12	18	174	—
P13	Boy	C	122	6	6	134	138	13	14	165	20
P14	Boy	A	93	6	13	112	139	13	9	161	20
P7	Girl	B	122	8	5	135	137	12	12	161	20
P15	Boy	A	121	4	5	130	130	12	14	156	20
P12	Boy	C	119	4	0	123	134	11	10	155	18
P8	Boy	B	128	10	16	154	125	13	16	154	18
P20	Girl	C	101	7	1	109	130	11	12	153	20
P25	Boy	C	116	5	0	121	137	7	7	151	16
P18	Girl	C	93	1	2	96	132	6	12	150	19
P2	Girl	A	100	2	4	106	126	10	11	147	18
P3	Boy	C	113	12	9	134	120	13	13	146	17
P26	Boy	C	99	3	0	102	128	10	4	142	20
P21	Boy	A	111	7	10	128	116	9	15	140	20
P19	Girl	B	113	6	0	119	117	10	11	138	18
P29	Boy	A	116	4	3	123	124	7	4	135	15
P11	Boy	B	104	5	2	111	129	—	—	—	16
P24	Girl	C	95	6	0	101	121	6	1	128	16
P9	Girl	C	87	4	1	92	112	4	2	118	12
P22	Boy	C	97	5	1	103	108	8	2	118	13
P30	Boy	C	94	1	7	102	99	8	11	118	17
P32	Girl	C	92	4	0	96	109	4	5	118	—
P16	Boy	C	86	2	0	88	74	2	0	76	8

The total number of children included in the analysis was 27 (12 boys and 15 girls with the average age of 11;6 years). The children were divided into three groups according to their English learning experience outside school revealed in the initial questionnaire: Group A comprises of 10 children who were learning English outside school at the time of the intervention, Group B includes four children who used to learn English outside school but quit, and Group C are 13 children who had never learnt English outside school.

Table 4.1 above illustrates the children together with the group they belong to, their IDs in the following accounts of sessions, and their test scores in the initial and final assessments. Group A and C included one boy (P29 and P3 respectively) whose mother is from the Philippines, and other groups had no remarkable characteristics of children's family background. Moreover, unfortunately, because one boy (P11) in Group B was absent in the oral test of the final assessment, the total number of children in its analysis was 26. Below, a comparative analysis in terms of these three groups will be reported wherever necessary, remembering that the test scores should be cautiously discussed due to the uneven numbers of children among groups, especially the significantly small number of Group B.

In each session, the HRT of Class 5-2 played roles of encouraging the children and calling a child's name when he or she volunteered to answer the questions from the instructor, and the AST helped the instructor by putting up picture cards on the blackboard, playing CDs, and demonstrating the activities. The AST was also asked to take note of the children's behaviour as well as their spontaneous speech in class. Sessions were usually held in the second period on Thursdays from 9:45 to 10:30 a.m., but sometimes the length of a session was five minutes shorter due to the school events, which caused much difficulty in reorganising instructional activities.

Different sessions followed different patterns according to their aims. For example, there were sessions in which most time was spent on communicative activities from *Eigo Note 1* (Sessions 7 and 21) or activities for seasonal events such as Halloween (Session 6) and Christmas (Sessions 13). A typical flow of a session focusing on introducing and practising new content was the following, and 11 out of the total 22 sessions followed this (see Appendix 4.1 for the timetable for the introduction and activities of the target content and Appendix 4.2 for full description of the activities and target words):

1. Initial greeting
2. Revision of content that has been already learnt
3. Introduction of a new content
4. Activity (or activities) for consolidation of the new content
5. Filling in a reflection sheet
6. Final greeting

The stages 1, 5, and 6 in this flow were common in all 22 sessions, but the reflection sheet was not administered only in Session 22 for lack of time remaining.

Table 4.2: Summary of the assessment tasks

	Date	Test type	Tasks	Target skill / knowledge	Section
Initial Assessment	9 September	Written	Letter name knowledge	Letter name knowledge	4.2
		Written	Sound categorisation	Segmenting	4.3.1.2
		Written	Initial phoneme recognition	Segmenting	4.3.1.2
		Written	Phoneme recognition & location	Segmenting	4.3.1.2
	10–16 September	Oral	Sound manipulation	Deleting Substitution	4.3.3.2 4.3.4.2
		Oral	Word reading test [real words and nonwords]	Word reading (Blending) Split-grapheme rule Digraphs Double vowel-letters (long vowels)	4.5.1.2 4.5.2.2 4.5.3.2 4.5.4.2
Mini Assessment	Session 12 9 December	Written	Middle vowel identification	Segmenting	4.3.1.2
	Session 13 16 December	Written	Final phoneme identification	Segmenting	4.3.1.2
	Session 13 16 December	Written	Initial and final phoneme identification	Segmenting	4.3.1.2
	Session 16 20 January	Written	Recognition and identification of a substituted phoneme	Substitution	4.3.4.2
	Session 17 24 January	Written	Phoneme substitution and identification	Substitution	4.3.4.2
Final Assessment	24 February	Written	Letter name knowledge	Letter name knowledge	4.2
		Written	Sound categorisation	Segmenting	4.3.1.2
		Written	Initial phoneme recognition	Segmenting	4.3.1.2
		Written	Phoneme recognition & location	Segmenting	4.3.1.2
	14–24 February	Oral	Sound manipulation	Deleting Substitution	4.3.3.2 4.3.4.2
		Oral	Word reading test [real words and nonwords]	Word reading (Blending) Split-grapheme rule Digraphs Double vowel-letters (long vowels)	4.5.1.2 4.5.2.2 4.5.3.2 4.5.4.2
	10 March	Written	Letter sound knowledge	Letter sound knowledge	4.4.2

Seven sessions did not introduce new content but engaged in revising and consolidating target content which had already been introduced through focused activities. Revision activities were intentionally included in all sessions after Session 2, based on the principle that the best way to help all children master new skills was to make them exposed to them repeatedly, as was the case in other curricular subjects. This overlaps with the characteristics of the effective phonological awareness instruction, as discussed in Section 2.7.2; that is, it does not need to be lengthy, but should be intensively administered for a moderate period of time.

Below, the children's attainment of the elements for early reading development over the intervention will be given, considering first the qualitative observational data and then the pattern of improvement revealed through the quantitative assessment data. The sources of quantitative data (i.e., assessment tasks) are summarised in Table 4.2, with the information about in which section of the current chapter the results of each task will be reported.

4.2. Lower-case letter-name knowledge

Letter-name knowledge was not actually a target instructional content, but it was necessary to make sure that the children had this knowledge to receive the introduction of letter sounds. At the beginning of the intervention, three sessions (Sessions 1, 2, and 3) were used for the purpose of familiarising them with the shapes and names of lower-case letters. The children were expected to have high level of lower-case letter knowledge, because they had been exposed to lower-case letters through *Roma-ji* learning in Grade 4. However, in the initial assessment, "many of the children seemed to be less comfortable with lower-case letters than with upper-case letters" [the instructor's field notes], and the results showed that the ability of the children in Group B and C to recognise lower-case letters by their names was not as high as in Group A. In fact, it turned out that most of the children had already learnt names of *upper-case* letters through *the ABC song* in English. Nevertheless, there was a gap in the *lower-case* knowledge between Group A and C, and it was assumed that the lack of familiarity with lower-case letters could cause the children in Group C more difficulty in learning not only letter-sound correspondence but also any other activity for the intervention because they were to be introduced to lower-case letters. Thus, with the help of the HRT, some of morning class activities were additionally used for revising lower-case letters by having the children randomly recite them.

As a result, the correct response rate of all children significantly increased from the initial (76.85%) to the final assessment (93.15%). Interestingly, although many of them expressed their unfamiliarity with lower-case letters as well as a preference for upper-case letters during the initial assessment, their performance was moderate in this test in which all options were lower-case letters. Figure 4.1 illustrates the correct response rates for all 20 target letters in the letter-name recognition tests in the initial and final assessments together with the letter-sound recognition test in the final assessment. It was found that the rates increased for all letters except letter *v* and, specifically, 10 letters yielded 100% of correct responses and eight letters obtained more than 90% in the final assessment. With regard to the low correct response rate for letter *v*, a further analysis revealed that the large percentage of incorrect responses (11.11% in the initial and 37.04% in the final assessment) was related to the option of the letter *b*. Thus, it seems that the confusion of *v* and *b* was the biggest cause for this. Nevertheless, according to Appendix 4.3, which summarises the statistical significance for the individual test items, letters whose correct responses significantly increased from the initial to the final assessment were *b*, *d*, *g*, *h*, *l*, *n*, and *q*. These included four letters whose shapes might be confusing and difficult for children to distinguish from one another (i.e., *b*, *d*, *g*, and *q*).

Figure 4.1: The results of the initial and final letter-name recognition tests and the final letter-sound recognition test of all children

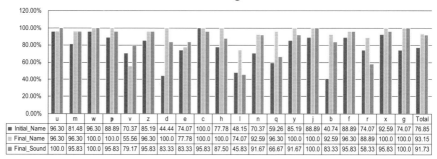

Finally, when the correct response rates were analysed by group, a common tendency was found that, irrespective of the timing of the assessment, the total correct response rate of Group A was the highest, followed by Group B, and the lowest was Group C. Considering that 13 children out of 14 in Group A and B had been exposed to lower-case letters through reading activities outside school as demonstrated in the initial questionnaire, this seems reasonable. On the other hand, a significant increase in the total score was yielded only in Group B and C and, therefore, the development of letter-name knowledge in Group C seems to have raised the standard for the correct response rate as a whole in this test. As for individual letters, whereas the correct response rates increased for all letters between the initial and final assessments in Group A and B, the rate decreased for letters *u* and *v* in Group C, which appears to have contributed to the low rate for letter *v* of 'all children' just mentioned above. In summary, the results show that the Japanese fifth-graders generally could enhance letter name knowledge as they were intensively presented with them both visually and orally through various tasks during the intervention.

4.3. Phonological awareness skills

In this section, the data regarding each of four phonological awareness skills will be given. These skills were basically introduced first without presenting letters to the children and then, after introducing sound-letter correspondence, attempts were made to consolidate them with the aid of letters.

4.3.1. Segmenting and phoneme identification

4.3.1.1. Qualitative observational data

Segmenting was the first phonological awareness skill introduced in the present intervention. An important tool for instruction was Elkonin cards, a kind of picture cards with boxes (Figure 4.2).

Figure 4.2: Sample Elkonin cards

Each box in a card represents a phoneme in a target three-letter CVC word expressed by a picture. For example, an Elkonin card with a picture of *dog* has three boxes under the picture, each of which represents /d/, /o/, and /g/ respectively. First, in Session 4, the children were asked to recite the minimum necessary 20 words represented by pictures on Elkonin cards for later introduction of the correspondence between short vowel sounds and letters repeatedly. There were several words with which the children seemed to be unfamiliar (e.g., *tap*, *log*, *vet*, *web*, and *zip*) (for the full list of words introduced, see Appendix 4.2) but, "after reciting the set of words several times, they came to recite them in a loud voice" [RJ4 (i.e., RJ on Session 4)].

First, the instructor demonstrated how to segment a CVC word (e.g., *dog*) by saying it extending each constituent sound (e.g., /ddddd/, /ooooo/, and /ggggg/) while pointing to a corresponding box. Contrary to her concern that the children might find this task embarrassing or childish, most appeared to be enjoying listening to her demonstration, and some spontaneously began imitating the sounds she made before being asked to do so. The instructor then demonstrated how to make each sound explicitly, overacting the movement of the mouth and the tongue so that the children could see them clearly, and some boys said, "Funny face!", looking at her exaggerated pronunciation. However, the children were generally good at imitating, which was not only recorded in the AST's field notes on Session 4 but also referred to by the HRT after class [RJ4]. Their pronunciation of individual phoneme sounds was mostly acceptable. However, it was also true that there were some difficult sounds for them to pronounce clearly; that is, children showed a sign of vowel epenthesis:

> When some children's pronunciation of /bbbbb/ sounded like /bububububu/ and I told them not to add /u/ after /b/, repeating /b/ and /bu/ several times, they did not seem to understand what I was saying. In other words, they did not appear to have realised that /u/ was added after their /b/. Then, I explained the difference between a consonant sound and a consonant sound followed by a vowel sound /u/ using another example phoneme /p/, and it worked! Because /p/ is a voiceless plosive, its difference from /pu/ was obvious. Thus, I thought it is important to use appropriate letters or sounds as examples according to what is being introduced. Also, I decided to say each of segmented phonemes just once, making it very short, because the repetition of each phoneme might be likely to cause the children to add a vowel sound after it. They seemed to find this easier than extending a phoneme. [RJ4]

Another difficulty for the children was to pronounce unvoiced sounds, although most could overcome it before long. When presented with the way of placing their fingers on the throat in order to feel the difference between the voiceless plosives (e.g., /p/, /t/, and /k/) or fricatives (e.g., /s/ and /f/) and their corresponding voiced plosives (e.g., /b/, /d/, and /g/) or fricatives (e.g., /z/ and /v/), they enjoyed this very much and a boy (P13) said, "This is fun! When I put my fingers here, the sound changes!" His remark may mean that he learnt how to correct pronunciation of these sounds by himself.

Around when having segmented a half of the target words, it was noticed that some children (mostly those in Group A) were getting bored. Actually, by then, many children came to be able to segment a CVC word by themselves: They made a sound for a box on the card before the instructor's demonstration. Whereas they were 'saying' segmented phonemes, they looked as if they were losing interests in the task, presumably because of its monotony. Then, a boy (P29) shouted, "How much longer are we going to do this?", the instructor wondered later in the day:

> They might have developed some ability of segmenting phonemes (i.e., the very beginning level of phonemic awareness) naturally in their developmental process. Although (1) the initial and final sounds they made frequently sounded like a combination of a consonant sound and an inserted vowel sound (e.g., /fʊ/ in *fan* or /to/ in *hot*), and (2) a middle vowel, especially when it was /ɑ/ or /ʊ/, was not differentiated from each other, most children were able to say 'one sound' in each box on the card I was pointing to. [RJ4]

Therefore, the instructor quickly finished segmenting the rest of cards, encouraging the children, and went on to the second segmenting task: All 20 Elkonin cards were put on the blackboard and the children were asked to say a sound in the box to which the instructor was randomly pointing. They seemed to like this task very much. Their faces lit up, and they shouted the sound in a very loud voice. However, here again, the same problem mentioned just above was encountered:

> Because the children got very excited and wanted to be the first to say a sound, almost all consonant sounds made by them were combined with a following vowel sound, and vowel sounds /ɑ/ and /ʊ/ in the middle position both sounded like a Japanese vowel /ɑ/. It is impossible to pronounce some consonants such as voiceless plosives loudly. I guess they hadn't realised this. But I didn't want to stop them from doing so, because they were especially enjoying this task and at least able to segment a CVC word into three sounds (but not phonemes). [RJ4]

The instructor did not explicitly tell the children that their pronunciation was *wrong*, but demonstrated the correct phoneme sound after they shouted the answer. In the informal interview with the HRT after this session, she said:

> I was surprised to hear the children make the correct sounds of English. They can pronounce English correctly when they are explicitly taught how to do so, can't they? But some sounds they made when you pointed to boxes one by one were *very Japanese*! (laugh)

In relation to this "very Japanese" characteristics in the children's segmentation skill, the following question was recorded:

> Most of the children seemed to be aware that a CVC word consists of three sounds because they were able to say <u>three sounds</u> [moras] (e.g., /jɑ/, /ɑ/, and /mʊ/) when I pointed to boxes representing three constituent phonemes of a word (e.g., *jam*). It's different from a Japanese way of segmentation in which a corresponding English loan word *jamu* is divided into <u>two sounds</u> /jɑ/ and /mʊ/. But, unless they come to pronounce phonemes correctly without vowel epenthesis, isn't it safe to say that they have developed the ability of segmenting? [RJ4]

A more advanced task of segmentation and categorisation was used in Session 15. In this task, the children had to segment two words, recognise which sound was common between them, and select the correct position of the sound in words (initial, middle, or final). This was administered in a form of a pair worksheet activity in which the children identified the position of a common sound by putting a double-picture card on one of the three boxes representing the initial, middle or final sound. Before going on to a new target pair, the instructor demonstrated the pronunciation of words and the children repeated after her several times. Target words (e.g., *juice / jar*, *hive / kite*, and *drum / game*) did not always have a structure of CVC and the number of phonemes in them varied. Even though the structure of a target word was sometimes more complex than CVC, a common sound was either in the initial or final position. Whereas the children sometimes appeared to be answering by guessing, their answers were mostly correct. However, some children said, "It's easier to find *different* sounds than *common* sounds!" or "The same sounds between these two words ... difficult!" Considering that this task asked children to segment words into the smallest sounds because a common sound was just one phoneme, it might be more demanding than a task to find a different sound in which all sounds except for one were the same. Thus, this task was found to be useful in making the children focus on recognising a smallest sound by segmentation, and many children seemed to have developed their segmenting skill sufficiently to tackle it by then.

4.3.1.2. Quantitative assessment data

Table 4.3 on the next page summarises the descriptive statistics of children's scores in all the tests of both the initial and final assessment, and Table 4.4 shows the results of *t*-test for the test scores in which a significant difference was found between the initial and final assessment.

Table 4.3: The descriptive statistics of the results of the initial and final assessment

				N	Minimum	Maximum	Mean	SD
Total	(208 items)	Initial	All Children	27	88	171	123.22	24.23
			Group A	10	106	171	140.70	23.62
			Group B	4	111	154	129.75	19.00
			Group C	13	88	134	107.77	15.37
		Final	All Children	27	76	188	147.04	25.32
			Group A	10	135	188	165.00	19.84
			Group B	4	129	161	145.50	14.62
			Group C	13	76	165	133.69	24.05
Written	Letter Name (20 items)	Initial	All Children	27	6	20	15.37	3.79
			Group A	10	16	20	18.80	1.48
			Group B	4	14	19	16.00	2.45
			Group C	13	6	17	12.54	3.07
		Final	All Children	27	15	20	18.63	1.52
			Group A	10	19	20	19.60	.52
			Group B	4	18	20	19.00	.82
			Group C	13	15	20	17.77	1.74
	Sound Categorisation (40 items)	Initial	All Children	27	18	33	24.74	4.34
			Group A	10	21	33	26.60	4.09
			Group B	4	21	30	25.50	3.87
			Group C	13	18	30	23.08	4.29
		Final	All Children	27	10	35	25.78	7.13
			Group A	10	12	35	28.70	6.96
			Group B	4	12	28	22.25	7.32
			Group C	13	10	35	24.62	6.91
	Initial Phoneme Recognition (40 items)	Initial	All Children	27	22	38	29.67	4.91
			Group A	10	22	38	31.10	4.75
			Group B	4	22	38	30.75	6.70
			Group C	13	22	36	28.23	4.46
		Final	All Children	27	19	40	34.37	4.84
			Group A	10	29	39	35.70	3.02
			Group B	4	36	40	38.00	1.63
			Group C	13	19	39	32.23	5.70
	Phoneme Recognition & Location (54 items)	Initial	All Children	27	21	53	40.70	7.42
			Group A	10	21	53	43.70	9.52
			Group B	4	40	52	44.50	5.45
			Group C	13	31	43	37.23	4.28
		Final	All Children	27	26	54	46.59	6.72
			Group A	10	44	54	49.50	3.69
			Group B	4	46	49	47.75	1.26
			Group C	13	26	54	44.00	8.51
Oral	Sound Manipulation (18 items)	Initial	All Children	27	1	16	5.85	3.36
			Group A	10	2	16	6.90	3.93
			Group B	4	5	10	7.25	2.22
			Group C	13	1	12	4.62	2.90
		Final	All Children	27	0	19	10.07	4.79
			Group A	10	7	19	13.40	4.25
			Group B	4	0	13	8.75	5.97
			Group C	13	2	13	7.92	3.52
	Word Reading (36 items)	Initial	All Children	27	0	31	6.89	8.20
			Group A	10	3	31	13.60	8.96
			Group B	4	0	16	5.75	7.14
			Group C	13	0	9	2.08	3.12
		Final	All Children	27	0	32	11.59	8.56
			Group A	10	4	32	18.10	9.21
			Group B	4	0	16	9.75	6.85
			Group C	13	0	14	7.15	5.06

108 *Introducing Phonological Awareness and Early Literacy Instruction*

Table 4.4: The results of *t*-test for the initial and final assessment

		t	df	p
All Children	Total	8.63	26	**
	Letter Name	5.51	26	**
	Initial Phoneme Recognition	5.25	26	**
	Phoneme Recognition & Location	3.92	26	**
	Sound Manipulation	6.03	26	**
	Word Reading	5.09	26	**
Group A	Total	6.18	9	**
	Initial Phoneme Recognition	3.42	9	**
	Sound Manipulation	6.63	9	**
	Word Reading	2.42	9	**
Group B	Letter Name	3.29	3	**
Group C	Total	5.67	12	**
	Letter Name	6.28	12	**
	Initial Phoneme Recognition	3.04	12	**
	Phoneme Recognition & Location	3.28	12	**
	Sound Manipulation	3.96	12	**
	Word Reading	4.79	12	**

* $p < .05$ ** $p < .01$

Initial phoneme recognition (initial and final assessment)

The initial phoneme recognition test aimed to assess the children's phonemic awareness with the simplest task, which asked them to judge whether or not the initial sound in a word was the same as the target. In order to answer correctly in this test, the children had to be able to segment the initial phoneme sound in order to compare it with a target.

Figure 4.3: The results of the initial phoneme recognition test of all children

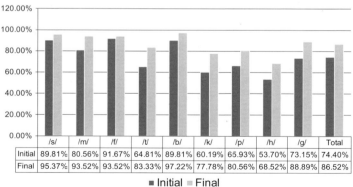

According to Tables 4.3 and 4.4, the mean scores of all children, Group

A, and Group C in the final assessment was significantly higher than those in the initial assessment. Figure 4.3 illustrating the correct response rates of all children in terms of individual target phonemes shows that all percentage figures increased from the initial to the final assessment and, specifically, a statistically significant increase was yielded in the phonemes /m/, /t/, /k/, /p/, and /g/ (Appendix 4.3). Among them, however, phonemes /t/, /k/, and /p/ were the ones whose correct response rates were still lower than 85% in the final assessment together with /h/. All these phonemes are voiceless sounds which are also found in Japanese phonology. The difficulty that the children had in segmenting and recognising voiceless sounds in the word-initial position might be supported by the instructor's observation during the intervention that many of them had trouble with blending C_1 with VC_2 in a C_1VC_2 word (see Section 4.3.2 below).

Phoneme recognition & location (initial and final assessment)

A task of recognising and locating a target phoneme is more demanding than a simple recognition task but less demanding than a categorisation task. That is, the estimated difficulty of a phoneme recognition and location test lies between a sound categorisation test and an initial phoneme recognition test. In this test, the children had to segment initial and final phonemes in a word and see which of them was the same sound as the target.

Figure 4.4: The results of the phoneme recognition and location test of all children

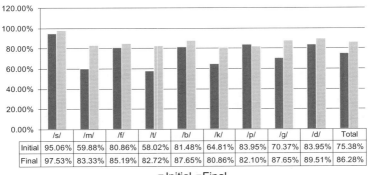

The mean scores of all children and Group C significantly increased between the initial and the final assessment (Tables 4.3 and 4.4). Figure 4.4 illustrating the correct response rates of all children for individual target

110 *Introducing Phonological Awareness and Early Literacy Instruction*

phonemes shows that, for all items except /p/, the percentages in the final assessment were higher than those in the initial assessment. The decrease in the correct response rate for /p/ seems to be due to a drop of the rate in Group B.

In particular, the increase in the rates for phonemes /m/, /t/, /k/, and /g/ are statistically significant (Appendix 4.3). Considering that phonemes /m/, /t/, and /k/ were the ones whose correct response rates at the beginning were quite low (lower than 65%), the children might compensate for the lack of ability for segmenting and recognising these phonemes rapidly through the instruction. Phonemes /t/, /k/, and /g/ were also the ones whose correct response rates were similarly low at the beginning in the above initial phoneme recognition test but significantly increased in the end, although the final rates of /t/ and /k/ were still slightly lower than other phonemes.

Middle vowel identification (mini assessment)

In this worksheet task, the children had to segment an orally presented CVC word, identify its middle sound, and decide which of the two vowel letters as options represented the sound. The average correct response rate was 87.69% and, among five short vowels in English, /o/ seems to have been the easiest for the children to associate with its letter (Table 4.5).

Table 4.5: The results of a middle vowel identification test (N = 26)

Question No.	1	2	3	4	5	6	7	8	9	10
Target word	*hat*	*run*	*jam*	*bed*	*six*	*hot*	*sit*	*mop*	*big*	*ten*
Correct option	a	u	a	e	i	o	i	o	i	e
Wrong option	u	a	e	i	o	a	e	u	e	i
N of correct responses	20	20	19	25	25	26	23	25	22	23
N of wrong responses	6	6	6	1	1	0	2	0	4	2
N of blanks	0	0	1	0	0	0	1	1	0	1
Correct response rate	76.92%	76.92%	73.08%	96.15%	96.15%	100.00%	88.46%	96.15%	84.62%	88.46%

Here, it needs to be remembered that the children generally appeared to find an English sound for a certain letter difficult to learn if it is distinctly different from a Japanese sound for the letter. As mentioned above, when the sound /ʌ/ for the letter *u* was introduced in Session 5, many children got confused because it was markedly different from a Japanese sound /u/ for *u*. Moreover, they had difficulty in differentiating /ʌ/ from /æ/ for the letter *a*, and /æ/ from /e/ for the letter *e*, in both listening and pronouncing. Such difficulty seems to have manifested itself in the results of this test: The items which asked the children to choose the letters *a* and *u* for *hat* and *run* respectively obtained the second lowest correct response rates (76.92%), and the item in which the children had to answer the letter *a* for the middle sound in *jam* yielded the lowest correct response rate (73.08%). In the former cases, of course, it might be possible that the children chose the letter *a* for the middle sound of *hat* only because the wrong option *u* is pronounced /ʊ/ in Japanese and clearly different from a segmented middle sound. However, considering that a moderate number of the children (76.92%) could answer the letter *u*, not the letter *a*, for the middle sound of *run* correctly, the possibility seems to be small. Another cause of wrong responses (15.38%) was a choice of the letter *e* for the middle sound of *big*, which seems to have elicited from the similarity between the middle sound /i/ and the name of the letter *e*.

Final phoneme identification (mini assessment)

This task asked the children to segment the final sound of orally presented words, and identify and write a letter for it. The average correct response rate was 92.62%, slightly higher than that in the middle sound identification test, whereas there were some words which yielded lower rates (less than 90%) such as *pen*, *gum*, and *kid* (Table 4.6). Especially, the letters *m* and *n* tended to be confused with each other, but the letter *m* was also misunderstood as *b* or *z* by one child each. Other examples of errors were answering the letter *d* for /t/ in *hat*, *p* for /s/ in *bus*, *b* for /g/ in *pig*, and *b* or *g* for /d/ in *kid*. It seems that the confusion of these letters might be caused by their resemblance to one another either in sound or in shape.

Table 4.6: The results of a final phoneme identification test (N = 26)

Question No.	1	2	3	4	5	6	7	8
Target word	*hat*	*bus*	*pen*	*gum*	*quiz*	*pig*	*cap*	*kid*
N of correct responses	25	25	22	22	25	24	24	22
N of wrong responses	1	1	4	4	1	2	2	4
Correct response rate	96.15%	96.15%	84.62%	84.62%	96.15%	92.31%	92.31%	84.62%

Initial and final phoneme identification (mini assessment)

In this task, the children had to segment an orally presented word, identify both its initial and final sounds, and write down letters for them. The average correct response rates are 79.23% for the initial sounds and 82.30% for the final sounds. Although final phoneme identification was a common task with the previous test, the correct response rate was lower in this test. A possible explanation for this might be that the present task was more cognitively demanding for the children because they had to retain two phoneme sounds (i.e., the initial and final phonemes) in their memory in order to identify their letters.

Also as in the previous test, the sound /b/ seemed to be easy for the children to connect with its letter, regardless of its position in a word (initial or final) (Table 4.7). On the other hand, the children seemed to have difficulty in identifying the letter *d* for the sound /d/ in *bed*. Two children confused it with letter *g* and three with letter *t*. The letter *f* for the sound /f/ in *fox* was misunderstood with the letters *b*, *p*, *q*, *h* and *k*. Therefore, the results from this test also show that there were some children who could not differentiate letters which share a similar shape or sound even at the end of the intervention.

Table 4.7: The results of an initial and final phoneme identification test (N = 26)

Question No.	1		2		3		4		5	
Word	*mat*		*tub*		*fox*		*bed*		*big*	
Taeget place	initial	final	initial	final	initial	final	initial	final	initial	final
Correct answer	m	t	t	b	f	x	b	d	b	g
N of correct responses	22	24	21	20	18	22	21	17	21	24
N of wrong responses	4	2	5	6	8	4	5	9	5	2
Correct response rate	84.62%	92.31%	80.77%	76.92%	69.23%	84.62%	80.77%	65.38%	80.77%	92.31%

With regard to the cases of two sounds which were tested in both the initial and final positions (/t/ and /b/), the number of children who answered the letter *b* for /b/ in the initial position (21) was not so different from that in the final position (20). However, the number of children who correctly answered letter *t* for the final /t/ (24) was slightly larger than that for the initial /t/ (21). These findings may suggest that a phoneme in the word-initial position is more difficult for Japanese children to identify. A similar tendency, as opposed to the pattern of task difficulty for L1 English-speakers discussed in Section 2.8.2, was also revealed in the results from other tests such as the oral substitution test which will be reported in Section 4.3.4.2 below.

Sound categorisation (initial and final assessment)

In this task, in order to detect an odd word out of three words, the children had to categorise target C_1VC_2 words by segmenting them after C_1 (an onset) or before C_2 (a coda). As seen in Table 4.3, the mean score of all eight conditions increased from the initial to the final assessment, although the difference was not statistically significant (Table 4.4). Indeed, under a half of all the conditions, the correct response rates of all children decreased in the final assessment (i.e., Opening Sound 1 and 2, and End Sound 1 and 2). With a closer look of Figure 4.5 presenting the correct response rates by condition, however, it seems that the children's performance was influenced by these conditions: That is, the mean scores were rather preferable under the following conditions: End Sound 2 (e.g., *hop* / *bead* / *seed*), 3 (e.g., *tip* / *lip* / *top*), and 4 (e.g., *hop* / *rock* / *mop*) (more than 70% of correct response rates in the final assessment and more than 60% in the initial assessment), and Opening Sound 1 (e.g., *deck* / *cap* / *cough*) and 2 (e.g., *lap* / *lad* / *pet*) (more than 60% in both assessment).

Figure 4.5: The correct response rates of the sound categorisation test of all children

[O: *Opening Sound* Condition   E: *End Sound* Condition]

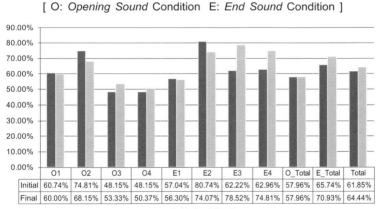

With regard to the End Sound oddity tasks, according to the developmental process of phonological awareness summarised in Section 2.2.3, it is reasonable that End Sound 2, 3, and 4, in which the children had to categorise words based on their rime sound (i.e., a large unit), were easier than End Sound 1 (e.g., *leak* / *sock* / *hid*) which required the children to recognise an odd word based on the final phoneme sound only (i.e., a small unit). Among the former three conditions, moreover, the mean score was statistically significant only in End Sound 3 where the children only had to pay attention to a middle vowel sound (V) as a part of a rime (VC$_2$) in order to detect an odd word because all word-final consonants (C$_2$) were the same. Thus, it could be argued that, at the end of the intervention, the children's phonological awareness was generally high enough to identify a word

114 *Introducing Phonological Awareness and Early Literacy Instruction*

with an odd rime, but not sufficiently sophisticated so that they could detect an odd word by the difference in a single phoneme.

On the other hand, Opening Sound 1 (e.g., <u>deck</u> / cap / cough), 2 (e.g., lap / lad / <u>pet</u>), and 4 (e.g., <u>pet</u> / deck / den) assessed the children's onset awareness (i.e., the awareness of the word-initial consonant). Based on the discussion in Section 2.6, it was assumed that Japanese children would be likely to find an odd word by segmenting target words after the initial consonant and vowel combination (C_1V) because the phonological unit of L1 Japanese is a mora (CV). Therefore, it seems reasonable that Condition 2 was easiest for the children because, in this condition, the common words share not only an initial consonant sound but also a vowel sound (C_1V), while the odd word did not share any sound with common words. However, the assumption does not seem to have applied to Condition 3 (e.g., can / <u>cot</u> / cap) and 4, where common words share the same combination of C_1V but the odd word also had either the same initial consonant or vowel as common words respectively. A possible explanation is as follows: As mentioned in Section 2.4.2, Japanese children learn *kana* characters using a *kana* matrix (Figure 2.1). In this matrix, *kana* characters which share the same initial consonant are located in the same column (e.g., か/ka/, き/i/, く/ku/, け/ke/, and こ/ko/) and characters which share the same vowel are in the same row (e.g., あ/a/, か/ka/, さ/sa/, た/ta/, な/na/, は/ha/, ま/ma/, や/ya/, ら/ra/, わ/wa/). Since children usually learn *kana* characters by reciting the matrix by column or by row and come to consider characters in the same column or row as a group, it is assumed that Condition 3 (i.e., all C_1V combinations are in the same column) and Condition 4 (i.e., all C_1V in the same row) were more difficult for the children to categorise. On the other hand, the correct response rate of Condition 1 which could assess purely the awareness of an onset without the influence of a vowel adhering to it (i.e., all different vowels) remained the same and moderate between the initial and final assessment.

To summarise, the results of the sound categorisation test show that, although the increase in the mean score of all conditions was not significant from the initial to the final assessment, the intervention could promote the children's development of rime awareness which is a lower-level phonological awareness and usually develops earlier than a higher-level phonemic awareness, but it was not sufficient to make them fully develop the awareness of onset as a word-initial single consonant (i.e., phonemic awareness). However, it needs to be considered that a categorisation task used in this test was more complex and demanding than the tasks of recognition and location of a single phoneme used in other tests for the assessment, as discussed in Section 2.8.2.

4.3.2. Blending

Blending was the skill which was demonstrated first without letters by using Elkonin cards, and then practised and assessed with letters through the integrated tasks such as substitution or word reading. Thus, in this section, only the observational data is presented when it was introduced and the children's improvement in this skill is discussed together with the test results of these advanced skills.

Blending at the phoneme level

Following the instruction of a segmenting skill, a new task of blending was introduced with the same tool of Elkonin cards in Session 4. After giving the instruction of "Now, let's do math. Add the sounds you hear to make a word you know," the instructor segmented a CVC word (e.g., /t/, /ɑ/, and /p/ in *tap*) showing only boxes but not a picture in an Elkonin card. The children shouted the word when they could blend the phonemes. As in the case of segmenting, many children performed well in a confident manner. However, there were two episodes in relation to the difficulty of this blending task for the children:

1) It seemed that relatively many children (including P9, P13, P20, P22, and P30 in Group C) could not blend constituent phonemes of particular words such as *tap*, *pin*, *hot*, and *fan*. I don't know *why*, but they pronounce the initial consonant and the middle vowel separately. They were trying to blend these two phonemes, but ended up in producing two separate sounds pronounced very quickly in an awkward way. On the other hand, they easily blended the middle vowel and the final consonant. So, their blending of these CVC words sounded as if they were segmenting a word at the onset-rime distinction; for example, "/t/, /ɑp/." [RJ4]

2) Some cannot blend /n/ or /m/ in the final position with a preceding vowel. When trying to blend /ɑ/ and /n/, for example, they make two sounds of /ɑ/ and /N/ [a Japanese nasal coda consonant]. However, when I asked them to repeat after my *fan* or *jam*, they could do it correctly. [RJ4]

At this time of the intervention, the instructor was not convinced that these instances indicate important characteristics of the children's blending skill,

116 *Introducing Phonological Awareness and Early Literacy Instruction*

which would be revealed later again through onset-rime activities or the sprit-grapheme (V-*e*) rule introduction.

Blending at the onset-rime level

Tasks of blending an onset and a rime (e.g., /m/, /ɑt/) were aimed at developing not only children's blending skill but also onset-rime awareness. This was demonstrated first by sliding the author's finger on one box for an onset and two boxes for a rime separately on the Elkonin card. Then, with the aid of letters, two main tasks were used: Onset-rime slides in Session 8 and speed reading in Session 11.

Figure 4.6: Sample onset-rime slide

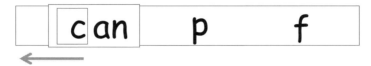

An onset-rime slide (Figure 4.6) is a tool consisting of two sheets combined. A rime part of words (e.g., *en*) is printed on a cover sheet. By sliding the inner sheet on which five onset letters (e.g., *e, h, m, p,* and *d*) are written sideways, these letters appear one by one in a square window on the cover sheet. After reciting a rime part several times, the children were asked to blend an onset in the window and a rime on the cover sheet, checking what the resulting word means with a picture card presented by the instructor. Due to the small size of the slides, the children were told to come forward and gather around the instructor, which helped the observation of their reactions and behaviours closely during the task. The manifestation of the children's difficulty in blending particular pairs of an onset and a rime, just as mentioned in Section 4.3.1 above, was also recorded:

> When asked to blend C_1 and V (e.g., /p/ and /e/ in *pet*) in a C_1VC_2 word, many children had trouble in making a sound part /pe/ and their pronunciation sounded like two separate sounds pronounced quickly (e.g., /p/, /e/). In such a case, their pronunciation of a voiceless plosives /p/ was very clear and correct, and they appeared to be wondering how they could pronounce the 'two independent' sounds smoothly. [RJ8]

Moreover, the video data of Session 8 recorded the following struggle of two boys clearly:

> P26: /p/ /en/. /p/ ... /en/, uh ..., /pu/ /en/, no, not that, /p/ ... /p/ ... I can't

combine them!
P13: /f/ /æn/, /f/, /æ/, ... They won't stick together!

In fact, there were quite a few children who could segment an orally presented word *pet* into three phonemes (i.e., /p/, /e/, /t/) correctly or at least into three sounds with vowel epenthesis (i.e., /pu/, /e/, /to/), but could not blend a particular onset with rimes (e.g., /p/ with /et/) when these were presented separately (i.e., visually in different colours or orally with a break between them). In contrast, it was observed in Session 8 that, when the children were visually presented with three-letter C_1VC_2 words, many could read them easily. Considering the fact that the children had learnt how to read *Roma-ji* (i.e., One C+V combination stands for one *kana* letter.), they might read those C_1VC_2 words in a *Roma-ji* way, segmenting them after the middle vowel (i.e., C_1V+C_2). If so, it may be assumed that they have an ability of blending C_1 and V. Then, the instructor wondered why they could not blend C_1 and VC_2 when they were presented separately.

A clue for answering this question was obtained from the observation of the children in a speed reading task in Session 11. They were presented with a set of words which shared a rime and were arranged from top to bottom on the screen (e.g., *mat, sat, pat, hat, cat, bat, fat,* and *rat* lining up in a column). Onsets are written in red and rimes in blue. The children had to read these words as quickly as possible. Because there were many options of onsets in this task, an analytical description was possible:

> I hadn't expected that this task would be that difficult for the children. No, not this task itself, but some onsets were difficult for them to blend with a rime. They can read rimes—all rimes, I can say—very well. But there were words with a particular onset they cannot read. These onsets are, based on my observation, voiceless consonants, but not all of them. Voiceless fricatives such as /s/ and /f/ were O.K., but voiceless plosives such as /p/, /t/, f/, and /k/ seemed to be troublesome. [RJ11]

Thus, it seems that the children had difficulty in blending an onset and a rime when the articulation to make the onset sound does not smoothly link to that which makes the following vowel sound. Moreover, from the observation that some children were keeping their fingers on their throat when trying to blend an onset of a voiceless plosive and a rime (e.g., /t/ and /op/), their attempt to prevent a lack of vibration (i.e., voicelessness) for an initial consonant before a middle vowel might cause difficulty because the voiceless part before the vowel could hardly be felt once they were blended.

4.3.3. Deleting

4.3.3.1. Qualitative observational data

As discussed in Section 2.8.4, *deleting* is considered to be the most difficult for native speakers of English among skills that require single processing (cf. *substitution* which requires multiple processing of identifying, segmenting, and then blending). Also considering the effect of the phoneme position on the task difficulty (see Section 2.8.3.2), deletion of the word-initial phoneme was first introduced and later deletion of the word-final phoneme was demonstrated in Session 13.

The instructor introduced seven words with an initial consonant cluster (*clip, clock, ski, snail, stop, train,* and *swing*) showing the children seven picture cards they represented. Because all of the words but *snail* and *swing* are widely used in Japanese as English loan words, the children soon came to recognise and recite them in a loud voice. Actually, this was the children's first encounter with consonant clusters but, because the ability of pronouncing consonant clusters correctly was not so much required for recognising phoneme deletion, the instructor gave them only a short explanation that there was no vowel sound between initial two sounds (e.g., /kl/ not /kʊl/ in *clip*). Consonant clusters were formally introduced in Session 17, which will be reported in Section 4.5.6 below.

After putting up picture cards of the words with an initial consonant cluster together on the left side of the blackboard, the instructor took out another seven picture cards (*lip, lock, key, nail, top, rain,* and *wing*), pronounced them, and asked the children to repeat after her. In fact, these were the words that could be made by deleting an initial phoneme of the seven words that had already been introduced. Most of the children learnt to say a word for a picture card gradually presumably because most of these target words are also used in their daily lives as English loan words. The instructor put up the picture cards together on the right side of the blackboard, making two groups of seven cards. Then, asked "Why do you think I made two groups of cards here?", the children showed a perplexed expression on their face. As there was a long silence for more than 15 seconds, the instructor decided to give them a clue and drew a line between the groups. A girl said, "Oh!", and shouted:

> P27: There are no initial <u>words</u>!
> T: Initial ...?
> P27: ... initial <u>things</u> ...
> P13: Initial <u>sounds</u>!

P29 (and some others): Oh yes! No initial sounds!
P10: There are initial sounds in this (pointing to the left group of words with an initial consonant cluster) and no initial sounds in that (pointing to the right group of words).

When the instructor explained that words in the right group could be made by deleting an initial sound of the words in the left group, a commotion arose in the classroom. Some children shouted, "Wow!", "Interesting!", "I didn't know that!", or "Well, that's a surprise!" one after another. She then took the group of the picture cards on the right side off and, pointing to the remaining cards one by one, said to the children, "What word is left when you subtract an initial sound from this?":

> The children, almost all of them, were very good at answering the resulting words. Even though some still pronounced the original words with vowel epenthesis like [kʊlip] for *clip*, they correctly answered /lip/ when asked to delete an initial sound. Because I sometimes made the children focus on a target 'phoneme' by saying, for example, "Subtract the sound /k/ from this (word)!", the children should have understood a target sound to delete was /k/, not /kʊ/. So, the children who said /kʊlip/ might not have recognised that their /k/ sounds like /kʊ/ and think that they are pronouncing /k/ correctly. On the other hand, the final /p/ was not a problem. In order to make children notice the difference between /p/ and /pʊ/, I only had to put my fingers on my throat. The children soon remembered that /p/ should not be /pʊ/ and check that by imitating me. [RJ13]

After having the children recite the words used for initial phoneme deletion, the instructor went on to the task of final phoneme deletion. As it was expected that the children might be able to delete the final phoneme by themselves based on their responses to the initial phoneme deletion task, after having introduced the target words, the instructor decided to ask them to do so without her demonstration. The children were presented with a picture card of a *tent*, encouraged to say the word, and then asked if they could subtract the final, not the initial, sound from the word. Whereas a few children stopped at /te/, many children shouted /ten/ in a loud voice. Considering that there were some children who needed additional time to think before answering, the instructor told them not to shout until she said O.K. and continued the task with the remaining seven pairs of words (i.e., *date / day*, *note / no*, and *seat / sea*). Apart from the pairs of *rose / row* and *train / tray*, most of the children could say the right word after deleting a final phoneme even though the four target pairs included a diphthong, which was not included as a target instructional content for the present intervention, in the middle position. Thus, in this case, the cause of difficulty seemed to be *not* the complexity of target words, i.e., inclusion of an unfamiliar diphthong, *but* that the children could not recognise the meaning of the resulting words. In fact, many of the children did not know the word *row* and could not notice that the English word tray (/tre̱i/) is the same as the loan word トレー (/tore̱ː/) in Japanese because of the difference in the vowel sound.

Thus, most children seemed to be enjoying the task of deleting an initial or a final phoneme from a word. The HRT said to the instructor after class;

> The children got excited about your demonstration (of initial phoneme deletion), didn't they? They were so interested that they listened to you and recited the words very seriously. It seemed that their curiosity got stimulated today.

Moreover, the AST recorded the following observation of the children in her diary entry for Session 13:

> In the '*clip-lip*' activity, as in the session where the Magic-*e* rule was introduced, the children looked very excited and impressed to know how to make a word from another. I was also glad to see children say, "Wow!" and "Fantastic!" Judging from their loud voices in reciting words, it seemed that the children were fully motivated, and even the children who seem to have an awareness of difficulty in learning English such as P16 and P22 appeared to be happy today, probably because the content was very clear to them. I think the way of explaining today's content—the addition and subtraction of a sound—attracted the children's attention effectively. They were not reciting words somehow today, but they were saying words with confidence as well as fully understanding the content.

In this session, the instructor fully realised that both a quiz-like way of presenting instructional content and the meaningfulness of the task (i.e., a familiar word changes into another familiar word through a simple processing) worked well in introducing phoneme deletion. It should be noted that the task in this session was rather *passive*, in that the children looked for a word made by deleting a phoneme from an original word only after they had practiced reciting both words. A more-demanding *productive* task of phoneme deletion was incorporated in that of substitution which was introduced later in Session 17, to be reported in the next section.

4.3.3.2. Quantitative assessment data

Oral sound manipulation (initial and final assessment)

Table 4.8: Paired Samples *t*-tests of children's performance on the oral sound manipulation test in the initial and final assessments (N = 26)

	M	(%)	SD	df	t	p
Total				25	6.23	.000
Initial assessment	5.85	32.48	3.43			
Final assessment	9.27	51.50	3.85			
Deletion						
Total				25	6.02	.000
Initial assessment	3.23	35.90	1.93			
Final assessment	5.19	57.69	2.17			
Initial consonant (IC)				25	4.87	.000
Initial assessment	.58	19.23	1.03			
Final assessment	1.65	55.13	1.13			
Final consonant (FC)				25	2.07	.049
Initial assessment	2.00	66.67	.98			
Final assessment	2.46	82.05	.71			
Initial consonant cluster (ICC)				25	3.14	.004
Initial assessment	.19	9.62	.49			
Final assessment	.54	26.92	.76			
Final consonant cluster (FCC)						
Initial assessment	.46	46.15	.51			
Final assessment	.54	53.85	.51			
Substitution						
Total				25	4.06	.000
Initial assessment	2.62	29.06	1.65			
Final assessment	4.08	45.30	2.10			
Initial consonant (IC)				25	5.14	.000
Initial assessment	.92	23.08	.94			
Final assessment	2.04	50.96	.96			
Final consonant (FC)						
Initial assessment	1.27	63.46	.83			
Final assessment	1.38	69.23	.64			
Initial consonant cluster (ICC)						
Initial assessment	.31	15.38	.47			
Final assessment	.42	21.15	.64			
Final consonant cluster (FCC)						
Initial assessment	.12	11.54	.33			
Final assessment	.23	23.08	.43			

122 *Introducing Phonological Awareness and Early Literacy Instruction*

In this task, the children had to delete a target consonant sound from an orally-presented word. Targets can be categorised according to their position in a word: an initial consonant (IC), a final consonant (FC), an initial consonant cluster (ICC), and a final consonant cluster (FCC). As shown in Table 4.8 which summarises descriptive statistics and *t*-test results of the oral sound manipulation test (both deletion and substitution parts), it was found that in the deletion task the total mean score as well as scores by target position increased in the final assessment and, in particular, the increase was statistically significant in the total, IC, FC, and ICC. Thus, the children's performance in deleting a word from a word was generally better in the final assessment (Figure 4.7).

Figure 4.7: The results of oral sound manipulation tests

	IC_D_ fill / ill	IC_D_ cup / up	IC_D_ bat / at	IC_S_f ill / till	IC_S_f ill / bill	IC_S_ cup / pup	IC_S_ bat / sat	FC_D_ goat / go	FC_D_ make / mei	FC_D_ seal / sea	FC_S_ cup / cut	FC_S_ bite / bike	ICC_D _slip / sip	ICC_D _stick / sick	ICC_S _slip / snip	ICC_S _stick / slick	FCC_ C_nest / net	FCC_ S_ crest / crept	V_S_p et / pat	V_S_ mop / mip
Initial	14.81	22.22	18.52	22.22	48.15	11.11	7.41%	55.56	81.48	66.67	62.96	66.67	3.70%	14.81	18.52	14.81	44.44	11.11		
Final	65.38	38.46	61.54	46.15	84.62	42.31	30.77	92.31	84.62	69.23	65.38	73.08	19.23	34.62	15.38	26.92	53.85	23.08	61.54	57.69

■ Initial ■ Final

Moreover, from a comparison of the correct response rates (Table 4.9) instead of mean scores because the item number for each target consonant position (IC, FC, ICC, or FCC) varied, it can be deduced that the children's performance was affected by the position of a target in a word: That is, there seems to be a tendency that deleting a phoneme within a consonant cluster is more difficult than deleting an individual consonant and, in turn, deleting a consonant in the word-initial position is more difficult than deleting a consonant in the word-final position. The disadvantage of a phoneme within a consonant cluster has been demonstrated in various L1 research with English-speaking children (Section 2.8.3.2), and it can be claimed that the present investigation replicated it with Japanese-speaking EFL-learning children. A general discussion on the results of an oral sound manipulation test will be undertaken together with the findings from the substitution part in Section 4.3.4.2 below.

Table 4.9: The average rates of correct responses of each test item of all children

		Correct response rate (All Children)	
		Initial	Final
Test items	IC_D	18.52%	55.13%
	IC_S	22.22%	50.96%
	FC_D	67.90%	82.05%
	FC_S	64.81%	69.23%
	ICC_D	9.26%	26.92%
	ICC_S	16.67%	21.15%
	FCC_D	44.44%	53.85%
	FCC_S	11.11%	23.08%
Manipulation task	Deletion	35.03%	54.49%
	Substitution	28.70%	41.11%
Position of a target phoneme	Word-initial	16.67%	38.54%
	Word-final	47.07%	57.05%

IC = Initial Consonant
FC = Final Consonant
ICC = Initial Consonant Cluster
FCC = Final Consonant Cluster
D = Deletion
S = Substitution

4.3.4. Substitution

4.3.4.1. Qualitative observational data

As mentioned in Section 2.8.4, the skill of substituting a phoneme in a word requires multiple operations such as identifying a target sound in a word, segmenting it in order to replace it with a new phoneme, and blending the new phoneme with the rest sounds of the word. It is considered to be the most difficult of all the four phonological awareness skills and, therefore, was the last skill introduced during the intervention.

First, in Session 15, the children were asked to recognise what sound (initial, medial, or final) was different between two words. The instructor put up three picture cards as headers, each of which represented a head, a body, or a tail of an animal respectively, on the blackboard. Showing two pairs of two-picture cards (i.e., *rug / bug* and *rain / rake*), she pronounced the words and had the children repeat after her. Then the children were asked, "What sound is different—initial, medial, or final—between *rug* and *bug*?" Most of them answered, "Initial!" right away, but a few kept silent and looked puzzled. Therefore, the instructor segmented target words slowly in an exaggerated way such as "/r/, /u/, /g/" and "/b/, /u/, /g/" and, making sure that the children who could not answer at first nodded and could say the answer together with other children, put up the card under the header of the animal's head.

Then, the children were told to come to the front in turn and complete the same task individually with a two-picture card handed to them by the instructor. Target words were CVC, CCVC, CVCC, or CVC*e* words and different for each child (e.g., *lap / cap, map / mop, sing / sink, pig / pin*, and *sleep / sleeve*). Because most of the target words were new to the children, it was decided to make them recite a pair of target words which a child in the next turn was to work with so that lack of familiarity with the words would not adversely affect the task. Most of the Group A children could answer the position of a substituted sound without the instructor's help, but she had to segment target words for many children in Group B and C. The AST described the children's reactions to the task in her diary entry for Session 15:

> Because the children had to perform the task individually in front of other children, they were very nervous but the boys especially looked very excited. Some who were not in the current turn repeated target words many times just like they were making certain of a different sound between them. But, to my surprise, all of the children could finally answer the position of different sounds, with some help from the instructor. There were, of course, some (P30, P26, P24, etc.) who took longer to think of the answer, but they could do it by themselves in the end. Their happy faces after giving the right answer made me happy too.

Moreover, with regard to the difficulty in recognising the position of substituted sounds, the instructor recorded as follows:

> My intuition tells me that recognition of phoneme substitution was the easiest when a target phoneme was in the final position, then by a narrow margin when it was in the initial position. The most difficult seemed to be when the target phoneme was in the medial position. [RJ15]

That is, C_2 following a C_1V combination in a C_1VC_2 word might be segmented automatically and it is easier for the children to compare with its counterpart in the other word. Moreover, it is assumed that an initial phoneme might be easier than a medial vowel for Japanese-speaking children to segment because it is important for them to recognise which column the CV belongs to in the *kana* matrix (see Figure 2.1), whereas a medial vowel is likely to be incorporated in a CV combination and difficult to separate.

It should also be mentioned that the children generally did not seem to worry too much about unfamiliar vowel sounds in words (i.e., diphthongs or long vowels which were not the target instructional content). For instance, they seemed to accept a diphthong as a single sound rather than trying to segment it into two short vowels. Only one girl (P31), who spent her early school years in an international school where English is spoken and moved to the target school at the beginning of Grade 5, said to the instructor during the task, "There are four sounds and I don't know which is the middle one," showing her card of '*lake /cake.*' The AST recorded her own feeling then in her diary entry for Session 15:

> When P31 said there were four sounds, I thought I had never thought of such a thing. This is probably because I was taught that /ei/ is a diphthong and counted as one sound deductively in junior-high school—or was it in high school?

This was surprisingly the same as what the instructor thought, and she added the following:

> When I didn't segment a target word as a clue for the children, some boys, mostly who are learning English [Group A], began mumbling segmented sounds and naturally other children imitated them to identify the position of where substitution occurred. Even in such cases, the children didn't segment a word with a diphthong in the middle position, e.g., *house*, as /h/, /ɑ/, /u/, and /s/. They seemed to say "/h/, /ɑu/, /s/" quite casually. Does this mean most children have not yet developed phonemic awareness as sophisticated as P31 showed?
> Indeed, with regard to this, I was particularly surprised to hear a boy (P29) spontaneously segment a target word *gate* as "/g/, /e/, /i/, /t/" when revising the split-grapheme (V-*e*) rule in Session 18. Was that because in this case the children were presented with spellings? In other words, the number of letters in the word *gate* may have induced the children to segment it into four sounds. [RJ15]

Later in Session 16, the same task was administered as a pair worksheet activity for revision. As with other worksheet activities, most of the children liked it and showed more concentration on the task. They discussed with their partner how to segment a pair of target words and thought about their difference. After familiarising with the task of recognising phoneme substitution in this way, the instructor decided to give them its production task in Session 17. The children were presented with a target word (e.g., *mop*) and a target initial phoneme in it (e.g., /m/) and asked to substitute a new phoneme (e.g., /t/) for it, say the resulting word (e.g., /top/), and then choose a right picture of it in their worksheet. Some children kept silent while thinking, whereas many others tried segmenting a word (e.g., "/m/, /o/, /p/, /m/, /o/, /p/ ....") and, when the target phoneme was identified, replaced it with a new phoneme and blended all sounds (e.g., /m/, /o/, /p/, ... /t/ ... /t/, /o/, /p/, /to/, /p/ ... /top/"). Such explicit behaviour was not observed at the time of the oral sound manipulation test in the initial assessment, in which the children appeared to be trying to think and come up with an answer. Thus, it may be claimed that many of the children came to be able to apply what they had learnt in the intervention (i.e., how to segment and blend sounds) to a new task. Especially, there were two children in Group A (P10 and P14) who wrote down constituent letters in a blank space, marked a letter for the target phoneme with a ×, then wrote a letter for the new phoneme on it, and finally read the resulting word looking at its spelling.

Finally, a tendency in relation to the children's blending was noticeable through this substitution task. That is, in attempting to blend sounds after replacing a target phoneme, regardless of the position of a target phoneme for substitution (initial or final), their resulting word frequently sounded like CV+C (e.g., "/to/, /p/"). Indeed, this was the tendency that was also observed among the children in a simple blending task (Section 5.8.2) but, because they were encouraged to say blended sounds in one breath in that task, most of them could say a word without pausing after CV. In the substitution task, on the contrary, the children were absorbed in trying to recognise what the resulting word represented, not in pronouncing the word correctly, and therefore, they might have read a word with a pause after CV unintentionally as they do in Japanese.

4.3.4.2. Quantitative assessment data

Oral sound manipulation (initial and final assessment)

Here, it needs to be remembered that, because all the targets in the sound manipulation test were phonemes in this study, the abilities assessed were deletion and substitution skills at the phoneme level. The substitution part in this test assessed the following complex skills; identifying a phoneme sound that is the same as a target in a word, replacing it with a new sound, and blending all constituent sounds. As shown in Table 4.8 above, mean scores in the total sound manipulation items and by consonant position all increased in the final assessment, whereas a significant difference was found only in the total and IC (initial consonant substitution). Moreover, Table 4.9 shows that, as in the case of the deletion part in Section 4.3.3.2 above, a phoneme within a consonant cluster seems to be more difficult for the children to substitute than an individual phoneme. Whereas the advantage of a consonant in the word-final position over the word-final consonant was also yielded in this substitution task, the difference was not so distinct compared with that in a deletion task, presumably because the children's performance was generally better on a deletion task than a substitution task.

In the process of analysing the items which yielded low correct response rates in the oral sound manipulation test, a very interesting feature was found in the children's incorrect responses (for the descriptive statistics of the children's responses in this test, see Appendix 4.4). This was frequently recognised in the target words with consonant cluster. For example, when asked to delete a phoneme /l/ from a word *slip*, 11 children out of 26 pronounced a word whose middle vowel had been changed into /ʊ/ such as /sʊp/, /sʊːp/, or /sʊːpʊ/. Similarly, when asked to substitute a phoneme /l/ for /t/ in a word *stick*, 13 children pronounced a word with a middle vowel /i/ changed into /ʊ/ such as /s(ʊ)lʊː/ or /s(ʊ)luk/. In order to interpret these tendencies, it needs to be remembered that one of the most common epenthetic vowels inserted after a consonant when vowel epenthesis happens in Japanese speakers' speech in English tends to be /ʊ/ (Section 2.4.2.2). In the above cases, it can be assumed that, while children were trying to delete or substitute a target phoneme while retaining the other constituent sounds of a word, a vowel sound (specifically /ʊ/) was added after individual consonants and, consequently, the original vowel sound might drop off. Most children did not seem to have noticed that they had changed a vowel sound as well.

Recognition and identification of a substituted phoneme (mini assessment)

This worksheet task administered as a part of mini assessment included two stages: First, the children had to recognise which sound (initial, medial, or final) was different between two orally-presented words (16 target word pairs). Second, they were encouraged to identify and write down the two substituted letters if they could. Thus, this task assessed the children's ability to recognise and identify substituted phonemes in a word pair.

Table 4.10 illustrating the results of this test shows that, as in the above oral substitution task (i.e., production task), the children's performance in recognising substituted phonemes were affected by their position in CVC words. The rate of successful recognition of substituted phonemes in the word-initial, medial, or word-final position was 85.19%, 66.67%, and 89.63% respectively. Moreover, it seems that, as demonstrated in the deletion task (Section 4.3.3.2), substitution of *initial* phonemes was slightly more difficult for the children to recognise than that of *final* phonemes. On the other hand, the low correct response rate for word-medial phonemes might be partly explained by the inclusion of unfamiliar diphthongs and long vowels as targets. However, when the rate for substitution only in medial short vowels was calculated, it became 68.52% and not so much different from the rate including the diphthongs and long vowels. Thus, it could be assumed that the children were generally tolerant toward the complexity of middle vowel sounds in C_1VC_2 words (i.e., diphthongs or long vowels). In fact, a girl (P31) who pointed out that there were four sounds in *lake* and *cake* in Session 15 (Section 4.3.4.1) checked her understanding during this task, saying to the instructor, "So, /ei/ in *rake* and *cake* is one sound, isn't it?"

Moreover, the findings from this test might suggest an idea that recognising substitution in a middle vowel sound was the most difficult of all three constituent sounds (i.e., C_1, V, and C_2) for Japanese children to recognise, as demonstrated with English-speaking children in McBride-Chang (1995). However, careful consideration is needed on this point because almost all the children who failed in recognising substitution in a *middle* position in a word chose an option of *initial* instead, suggesting as a possibility that they regarded a CV combination in a CVC word as an initial sound as they do in Japanese.

On the other hand, quite naturally, no children could identify (i.e., spell correctly) a diphthong or a long vowel as substituted middle vowels, except four Group A children who wrote down the letter *a* accurately for a middle vowel in *ball*. Then, concerning target sounds whose correspondence to letters were introduced during the intervention, the results indicate that only about half of the children who succeeded in recognising the position of substitution could identify letters for substituted sounds correctly, and the correct response rates significantly varied according to the target word pairs. Generally, the children could identify more original phonemes than new phonemes after substitution, irrespective of their position in a word, which might be explained by the primacy effect on their memory of substituted sounds.

Table 4.10: The results of a recognition and identification of a substituted phoneme test (N = 27)

Question No.	1		2		3		4		5		6	
Target pair of words	hat	ham	rake	cake	bell	ball	gate	game	book	hook	boat	coat
Place of substitution	Final		Initial		Medial		Final		Initial		Initial	
N of option: Initial	0		20		10		0		24		12	
N of option: Medial	1		4		15		2		2		3	
N of option: Final	26		0		1		24		0		1	
N of blanks	0		3		1		1		1		1	
Correct response rate	96.30%		74.07%		55.56%		88.89%		88.89%		77.78%	
Substituted phoneme	t	m	r	c	e	a	t	m	b	h	b	c
N of correct responses	17	18	7	4	9	4	12	11	14	5	11	6
Correct response rate	62.96%	66.67%	25.93%	14.81%	33.33%	14.81%	44.44%	40.74%	51.85%	18.52%	40.74%	22.22%

Question No.	7		8		9		10		11		12	
Target pair of words	seed	seal	feet	meat	map	mop	nose	toes	mug	bug	cat	can
Place of substitution	Final		Initial		Medial		Initial		Initial		Final	
N of option: Initial	0		22		7		24		27		1	
N of option: Medial	2		3		19		0		0		3	
N of option: Final	23		0		1		3		0		23	
N of blanks	1		2		0		0		0		0	
Correct response rate	85.19%		81.48%		70.37%		88.89%		100.00%		85.19%	
Substituted phoneme	d	l	f	m	a	o	n	t	m	b	t	n
N of correct responses	11	7	9	11	12	14	10	11	10	8	14	11
Correct response rate	40.74%	25.93%	33.33%	40.74%	44.44%	51.85%	37.04%	40.74%	37.04%	29.63%	51.85%	40.74%

Question No.	13		14		15		16	
Target pair of words	moon	man	kite	coat	dice	dime	dog	dig
Place of substitution	Medial		Medial		Final		Medial	
N of option: Initial	8		5		0		9	
N of option: Medial	18		20		1		18	
N of option: Final	0		2		25		0	
N of blanks	1		0		1		1	
Correct response rate	66.67%		74.07%		92.59%		66.67%	
Substituted phoneme	oo	a	ai	oa	ce	m	o	i
N of correct responses	0	8	0	0	0	12	13	12
Correct response rate	0.00%	29.63%	0.00%	0.00%	0.00%	44.44%	48.15%	44.44%

Phoneme substitution and identification (mini assessment)

In this task, after listening to a target word and instruction of what sound in it should be changed into what sound (e.g., "Change /b/ into /h/ in a word *bat*."), the children were asked to choose one of two pictures which represents the resulting word. Some of the target word-medial vowels were diphthongs, and there were 10 items in total. Different from the previous recognition task, this was a manipulation task in which the children had to substitute a sound in a word by themselves.

Table 4.11 shows that the correct response rates were generally high in most of the items. From an examination of two items which yielded the lowest correct response rates, causes of wrong answers seem to be as follows: (1) confusion of sounds /r/ and /l/ as in a wrong choice of a picture of *lock* after substituting /r/ for /s/ in *sock* (44.44%), or (2) confusion of sounds /e/ and /æ/ as in a wrong choice of a picture of *pen* after substituting /æ/ for /i/ in *pin* (22.22%). With regard to an effect of a target position in a word, the correct response rates were 81.49%, 93.33%, and 100.00% for substitution of the initial, medial, and final sound respectively, whereas there was only one item of substitution in the word-final phoneme. The finding that an initial phoneme was more difficult for the children to substitute than a final phoneme also seems to be consistent with a common tendency found in their performance in Sections 4.3.3.2 and 4.3.4.2.

Table 4.11: The results of a phoneme substitution and identification test (N = 27)

Question No.	1	2	3	4	5	6	7	8	9	10
Target word	*fan*	*sock*	*mop*	*can*	*pin*	*bike*	*bat*	*cane*	*phone*	*sax*
Substitution	/f/→/k/	/s/→/r/	/m/→/t/	/n/→/p/	/i/→/a/	[ai]→[ei]	/b/→/h/	[ei]→[or]	[ou]→[i]	/a/→/i/
Place of substitution	Initial	Initial	Initial	Final	Medial	Medial	Initial	Medial	Medial	Medial
Option 1	can	rock	top	cap	pen	book	hat	corn	fin	six
Option 2	pan	lock	hop	cat	pan	bake	mat	can	fan	socks
Correct answer	1	1	1	1	2	2	1	1	1	1
N of correct responses	23	15	26	27	21	27	24	25	26	27
N of wrong responses	3	12	1	0	6	0	3	2	1	0
N of blanks	1	0	0	0	0	0	0	0	0	0
Correct response rate	85.19%	55.56%	96.30%	100.00%	77.78%	100.00%	88.89%	92.59%	96.30%	100.00%

4.4. Letter sounds — Short vowels and basic consonants

4.4.1. Qualitative observational data

The correspondence of letter sounds to their letters were introduced in Session 5 and 6. Specifically, in Session 5, five vowel letters were presented first and then 11 consonant letters which are used in *Roma-ji* (i.e., *b, d, g, h, k, m, n, p, d, t, z*) were connected with their sounds. The rest of 10 consonant letter sounds were introduced in Session 6. However, as the instructor had not expected that the children would learn all letter-sound correspondences within these two sessions, the revision activities were included thereafter throughout the intervention, using not only session periods but also time for morning class activities organised by the HRT.

After revising segmenting and blending skills with Elkonin cards, the instructor put cards of *big*, *pin*, *zip*, and *lip* on the blackboard and asked the children to recite these words. She segmented their constituent phonemes like "/b/, /i/, /g/," and "/p/, /i/, /n/," pointing to their corresponding boxes in the cards, and the children repeated after her. Then tapping the middle box in all cards, she asked them to say the sound. When the children realised that all middle sounds were /i/, the instructor said, "This /i/ sound is represented with this letter *i*," showing a lower-case letter card of *i*. She further explained that all English letters have names and sounds, and that names of letters are not identical to their sounds as in Japanese. However, most of them showed a confused expression on their faces, and words from a boy (P10) in Group A may represent how children were feeling then:

> There are names and sounds in English …? I didn't know this. Interesting! Then, "/eɪ/, /biː/, /siː/ …" in *the ABC song* are names? Well, then, what are sounds? [RJ5]

The instructor tried to convince the children that *letter name* is what they use when they are referring to a particular letter, while *letter sound* is used when they pronounce a particular letter or a word of which it is a constituent, but it seemed to be a little difficult for them to understand.

Another source of confusion seemed to be the correspondence of a vowel sound /ʌ/ to the letter *u*, as had been predicted from its clear difference from Japanese /ʊ/ sound for this letter. When the instructor explained that /ʌ/ is written with the letter *u*, about five or six children said one after another, "But that's Japanese あ (/ɑ/)!", showing their knowledge that the letter *u* is pronounced differently in *Roma-ji*. However, presumably because this was a relatively marked difference between Japanese and English, some children soon came to be able to pronounce the letter *u* correctly in a focused task, but others struggled in saying the sound of /ʌ/ correctly still at the end of the intervention (e.g., P24 "/ʊ/, not /ʊ/, but /ʊʌ/, /ʊʌ/, … /ʌ/.").

Moreover, an interesting feature was recognised in the children's responses when they were asked say a sound in a particular position in a CVC word:

> When I was introducing consonant letter-sound correspondence, I put up Elkonin cards that shared the same consonant in the initial position on the blackboard and said to children, "What do you think is the common

sound in the initial box?" Then, most of the children who volunteered to answer shouted the name, not the sound, of a letter for the initial box. Why? [RJ5]

This was observed many times at the initial and middle stages of the intervention. For instance, in Letter-sound *Karuta* activity (Session 5) in which the children had to find a letter card whose sound the instructor pronounced as well as in the 'word *Karuta*' activity (Session 14) in which they were asked to find a letter card which represented an initial sound of a word the instructor pronounced, there were some children who were looking for a card mumbling its name. They were mostly Group C, who learnt sound-letter correspondence for the first time in this session. As it was unrealistic that the children came to directly connect all phoneme sounds to corresponding letters within this first learning opportunity, it might be assumed that it was easier for them to refer to a letter by its name once they could summon up its visual image based on its sound.

As mentioned above, letter sounds were constantly revised for the rest of the intervention. For revision, the instructor visually presented letter cards one by one to the children, and orally gave a cue of "Name" or "Sound" randomly to answer. Sometimes she pointed to the letter cards on the blackboard, and asked the children to say their names or make their sounds as quickly as possible. Also in the earlier sessions, a commercially available phonic video song specifically designed for the consolidation of letter-sound correspondence was used in order to make the revision of these links enjoyable for the children (e.g., They sing "/ɑ/, /ɑ/, *ant*!" looking at the lower-case letter *a* that blinks on the screen twice followed by a picture of an ant.). The instructor came to realise what an amazing power audio-visual materials are in their ability to attract the children's attention and leave a strong impression in their memory and mind. They riveted their eyes on the screen of the electronic interactive board and, against her worry that they might find the song and video a little childish and not show any interest, their faces brightened up repeating the song. In fact, when the song was first introduced in Session 8, they asked the instructor to play the song many more times.

Some of the children reflected on their experience of revision activities in an informal interview with the AST (A) and the instructor (I) while having school lunch together after Session 15 [RJ15]:

I: Well, you learnt letter names and sounds, and as in the session this morning, you did an activity in which I asked you to say a name or a sound of a letter, didn't you? Do you think this was difficult or easy?

P27: I can say the names of letters correctly, but when it comes to their sounds, I still get confused.

P20: A little difficult ... but I came to be able to do it well. I want to do it more.

P7: Because you say "Name!" and "Sound!" in English, I learnt these English words. I'm happy.

P24: Some of letter shapes were very confusing ... for example, *p* ... and *q* ... and *b* ... *d*? Sometimes you said "Name!" to a letter whose sound I know ... I get panicked ... difficult.

A: Did you enjoy the review song? ... "/ɑ/, /ɑ/, *ant*." Can you sing it well?

P14: Perfect! Too easy!

P11: I liked that because it was enjoyable!

A: That's good! Then, can you say a name or a sound correctly when T shows you a letter card?

P30: Yes, of course. ... But T sometimes plays a trick on us by saying "Name!" while asking us to say sounds ... that's difficult! I get confused and can't say which is a sound and which is a name.

P26: (singing) /ks/, /ks/, *x*! I've remembered this song because we sang it many times this morning. I think I've learnt almost all sounds, but sometimes ... I feel a lack of confidence. I think I need a bit more time. ... I'm almost there.

Table 4.12: Children's responses to the revision activity of letter sounds in the reflection sheets

[1 (I don't understand it at all – 2 – 3 (Neither) – 4 – 5 (I understand it very much)]

Session		N	Minimum	Maximum	Mean	SD
5	Introduction	27	1	5	3.74	1.06
7	Revision	27	1	5	4.26	1.10
8	Revision	26	1	5	4.19	1.13
14	Revision	27	2	5	4.33	0.88
15	Revision	26	2	5	4.23	0.86
16	Revision	27	2	5	4.22	0.80
17	Revision	27	2	5	4.30	0.87
18	Revision	27	2	5	4.30	0.82
19	Revision	25	3	5	4.52	0.65
20	Revision	25	2	5	4.52	0.77
21	Revision	27	3	5	4.44	0.80

According to Table 4.12 which shows the children's responses to the question in the reflection sheet about "how much they have come to understand letter sounds," they might find letter-sound correspondence a little difficult in Session 5 where they were first introduced. In later sessions, the lowest response of 1 cannot be seen and mean responses slightly increased, but the differences were not significant.

Indeed, the HRT's cooperation was indispensable for the children's development of letter-sound knowledge. She conducted revision activities using 10 to 15 minutes in morning class activities three or four times a week, and made the following comment regarding their progress:

> Almost all children now can say letter sounds correctly. This is great! I think, if they keep receiving the instruction of letter sounds as they do now next year [in Grade 6], this knowledge will certainly help them learn English in junior-high school. But ... probably, they will forget most of what they learnt this year once they stop revising them. But, it's interesting ... children came to sing that song changing some of the words ... like "/ɑ/, /ɑ/, *ari* [a Japanese word meaning an *ant* in English], /b/, /b/, *buta* [a Japanese word meaning a pig in English]." [RJ15]

Her words reminded the instructor of the importance of considering English learning environments in Japan: In an EFL situation like in Japan, the amount of natural English input is so limited that it is difficult to retain knowledge and skills without revising them constantly. This was a kind of sad reality, but the latter half of her comment was really encouraging. The children seemed to have developed ability for categorising Japanese words according to their initial phonemes, not moras.

4.4.2. Quantitative assessment data

The children's ability to recognise letter-sound correspondence, which was assessed with the same items as in a letter-name knowledge test only in the final assessment, was generally high: 91.73% on average among all children, and almost as high as their letter name knowledge (Figure 4.1 above). The letters which yielded the correct response rate lower than 80% were *r*, *l*, *q*, and *v*, and these are either letters which are not used in *Roma-ji* (*q* and *v*) or letters which had been assumed to be difficult for Japanese learners to distinguish from each other (*r* and *l*) because the letter *r* is used in *Roma-ji* but its pronunciation is closer to English /l/, not /r/. Indeed, the correct response rates for the recognition of letters *r* and *l* by their sounds were the worst two of all 20 targets (58.33% for *r* and 45.83% for *l*) in 'all children.' A detailed analysis revealed that letters *r* and *l* were confusing for many of the children, because 33.33% of children who could not recognise letter *r* answered with the wrong option of letter *l* and 54.17% of children who failed in recognising the letter *l* by choosing the letter *r*.

Considering the fact that an isolated consonant sound cannot exist alone in Japanese spoken language (Section 2.4.2.2), it is unlikely that the children were exposed to individual consonant sounds in their daily lives and, therefore, it could be argued that it was mostly through the intervention that they developed the letter-sound knowledge. In fact, there was only one boy (P10) in Group A who told the instructor at the time of the oral test in the initial assessment that he had experienced activities to pronounce letter sounds such as /ɑ/, /b/, and /k/, but he "seemed to know only four or five letter sounds such as the ones early in the alphabet order (i.e., sounds for letters *a*, *b*, *c*, *d*, and *e* at the most) and did not differ from other children so much in terms of letter-sound knowledge" [RJ6]. To summarise, the results suggest that the children generally could develop letter sound knowledge up to the same level of their letter-name knowledge through a focused instruction for a certain amount of time; in other words, it may be claimed that Grade 5 is a grade where not only English letter sounds but also their difference from letter names could be introduced as a part of English teaching.

4.5. Skills and knowledge for early word reading

4.5.1. Word reading

4.5.1.1. Qualitative observational data

Word reading is an applied task in which children have to make full use of their knowledge about letter sounds and spelling rules as well as phonological awareness skills. In the present intervention, materials used for the focused activities on beginning-level word reading were three-letter CVC word cards (Session 8) and simple phonic stories (Sessions 10 and 12).

After having introduced letter-sound correspondence in Session 5, the children were asked to recite sounds or names of letters on the instructor's random cues for revision in the following two sessions. Then, in Session 8, judging from their improvement, it was decided to go on to more demanding CVC word reading in order to make the revision task more meaningful. In this advanced task, different from the task of blending orally-presented sounds to which the children had already been exposed in Session 4 (Section 4.3.2), they had to come up with a sound for each of constituent letters by themselves.

All target words were the same as the ones used in the earlier blending and segmenting activity with Elkonin cards in Session 4. First, the instructor held up a C_1VC_2 word card of *dog* and asked the children to say individual sounds for C_1, V, and C_2 one by one. Without her demonstration, many of the children shouted the sound of the letter she was pointing to. Then, the instructor slid her finger from the left to the right under the word. Some children, mostly in Group A, spontaneously blended three phonemes /d/, /o/, and /g/, and instantly others repeated /dog/ after them. Thus, no explanation was needed and the practice was guided only by the instructor's cues. Additionally, in order to ensure that the children realised the meaning of a word they were reading, they were asked, "Do you know what this means?". Some children, who frequently volunteered to answer the instructor's questions, said, "*Inu* (i.e., dog in Japanese)," "*Doggu* (an English loan word in Japanese meaning a *dog*)," or "*Wan-wan* (i.e., onomatopoeia of a dog's barking in Japanese)." This question unexpectedly worked well and it made the children realise the difference in the pronunciation between an English word and a corresponding loan word in Japanese. Showing a picture of a dog, the instructor further said to them, "In Japanese, *Doggu*, but in English?", and again asked them to say its component phonemes one by one. As P1 shouted "Oh, *dog*! This sounds like English!", the children's pronunciation was correct and full of confidence. In other words, once they have developed some letter-sound knowledge, they might find it easier to blend phonemes presented with letters than orally-presented phonemes, presumably because they did not have to retain the sounds they heard while blending.

At the same time, however, it was assumed that there was a possibility that the children might be reading the words on the basis of their knowledge of *Roma-ji*, segmenting a C_1VC_2 word as $C_1V+C_2(V)$. Especially, it was expected that the children could read aloud words whose vowel letter was *a*, *e*, *i*, or *o* because these vowels have a similar sound to its corresponding vowel sound in Japanese. What the instructor was most concerned about was the vowel letter *u*, whose English sound (/ʌ/) is significantly different from its sound in *Roma-ji* (/ʊ/). However, surprisingly, when a word card of *bus* was presented, many children correctly pronounced it. Then, some boys shouted one after another, "Does this /bʌs/ mean /bɑ-sʊ/ (i.e., a Japanese word バス which means *a bus*)?" or "The word バス is spelt as /bʊ-sʊ/ (i.e., a Japanese word ブス which means *an ugly girl*)!" The instructor became excited to hear them say so, because this might suggest that they read aloud the word *bus* based on their understanding that the sound of the letter *u* is /ʌ/ without realising the meaning of it.

Then, in Session 10, phonic book reading was introduced, which soon became of interest to the children. Target sentences were phonologically simple such as "*A dog is in a pot. A dog is in a bag. A dog is in a box.*" At the start, pointing to every constituent letter of a word, the instructor asked them to say its sound. Regarding the word *is* which could not be read based on the letter-sound knowledge they had learnt so far in the intervention, she pronounced it /iz/ expecting that the children would accept this sound as it is. The following observation was recorded:

> I was concerned if the children might indicate that *is* was not /iz/ but /is/. On the contrary, no child showed a puzzled expression, and obediently repeated after my demonstration. I was a little disappointed, but thought that for some of them it might be easier to learn the pronunciation of the words by imitation, not by blending individual sounds by themselves. This is possible at the present level of learning to read, but the longer words become, the more difficult it would be to learn their pronunciation by heart. What I have to do is to make the children aware of how to *build up* pronunciation of a word by following a sequence of letters. [RJ10]

Moreover, different from single word reading, sentence reading made the variance in the children's reading speed explicit. Nevertheless, due to the advantage of phonologically simple word structure in a phonic book which could be read even in a *Roma-ji* way, the children who could only imitate other children's reading at first gradually began attempting to read by themselves. Another benefit of picture books was that many children enjoyed reading English words more because the illustrations gave them a clue for understanding what they meant.

4.5.1.2. Quantitative assessment data

Word reading (initial and final assessment)

In the oral word reading test, the children were asked to read aloud 17 real words and 19 non-words. In scoring, one point was given to a successful attempt to pronounce a whole target word. For example, /neim/ for a word *name* got one point but no point was given to /neimu/ or /ne:mu/. In fact, many responses failed to gain a point because of inserting a vowel sound after a consonant sound or pronouncing a diphthong (e.g., /ou/) as a long vowel (e.g., /o:/). According to Table 4.4 above, the mean score of 'all children' significantly increased between the initial and final assessments, although the average correct response rates were generally lower than those in other tests (19.14% in the initial and 32.20% in the final assessments). Moreover, by group, the significant increase in the mean score was found in Group A and Group C.

Regarding the differences between real words and non-words, the average correct response rates of real words were 28.32% in the initial and 43.79% in the final assessment, while those of non-words were 10.92% and 21.83% respectively. Considering that real-word targets were frequently presented to the children through various activities over the intervention, it is reasonable that their correct response rates increased and were higher than non-words. However, even in the final assessment, most of the children did not appear to have noticed that there were both real words and non-words mixed in the targets:

> Only two boys surprised me by saying, "Is this a real English word?" or "Is there a word like this in English?," after they had been presented with several non-words. They both said that they had never lived in an English-speaking country but had been learning English at an English conversation school since they were in Grade 1. However, it cannot be assumed that they had developed knowledge of English phonotactics like native speakers with such a limited exposure to English. Considering that target real words used in the intervention were also the ones which are basic and commonly included in various English teaching materials used at private English schools in Japan, they might have been able to identify non-word targets simply because they had never seen or heard them before. [RJ for the final assessment]

Above all, the most remarkable change in the children's performance from the initial to the final assessment was that more children tried to read aloud the target words by making individual constituent sounds in the final assessment, while more children kept silent or gave up soon in the initial assessment (for the descriptive statistics and the phonological description of the children's responses in this test, see Appendix 4.5). It was natural that most children could not read aloud the target words in the initial assessment because they had not learnt how to read in English, and that they could read aloud more words in the final assessment because they were taught early word reading through the intervention. Nevertheless, their attitudes toward reading English words appeared to be different. In other words, many children appeared to be enjoying the reading task, trying to remember the sounds they learnt and blend them. Some of these children's responses were based on the *Roma-ji* way of pronouncing a string of the alphabet and obviously incorrect as English words (e.g., /fibe/ for *five* and /puzu/ for *puz*), but they seemed to have less reluctance to follow individual letters with their eyes in order to read target words.

Table 4.13 shows the correct response rate of all target words in the initial and final word reading tests. With regard to three-letter CVC words, it can be assumed that the children's knowledge acquired through the intervention contributed to the improvement of their performance. As an example, whereas two real-word targets *yes* and *six* seemed to have been fairly familiar to the children and yielded moderate correct response rates even at the beginning (66.67% and 40.74% respectively), the rates showed a considerable increase at the end of the intervention (92.31% and 80.77%). Specifically, in the final assessment, it was obvious that many children pronounced sounds for *y* in a word *yes* and *x* in a word *six* confidently. In fact, these letter-sound correspondences were expected to be difficult for the children to learn because their names and sounds are very different, but a gap between letter name and sound seems to have left such a strong impression on many children that they remembered the sound in a short time, as expressed in a boy's spontaneous speech in class:

> When the sound for letter *y* was introduced, many children looked confused because they could not understand how the sound of the letter *y* whose name is /wai/ could be /j/. P13 said, "Is the sound of *y* is /j/? ... Very different from its name! Where does that /j/ sound come from?." [RJ15]

Moreover, children enjoyed learning a sound for the letter *x* by association:

> The children know that doubling a sound for letter *x* produces a sound similar to an onomatopoeic sound of giggling in Japanese—"*Kusukusu*." In singing a phonic song for revising letter sounds, they were clearly waiting for the letter *x* is coming, and looked very excited to say /ksks/. To my surprise, their pronunciation of /ks/ then had no vowel insertion. [RJ14]

The children's understanding of the sounds for the letters *y* and *x* was also demonstrated in their responses to non-word targets *yag* and *chax*. That is to say, although their correct response rates were 50.00% (13 children) and 26.92% (7 children) respectively in the final assessment, it was found that, when only sound parts of *y* and *x* are concerned, 80.77% (21 children) could make the sound /j/ in *yag* and 53.85% (14 children) could pronounce /ks/ in *chax* correctly.

Table 4.13: The correct response rates of all children in the word reading test categorised by the target word characteristics

	three-letter CVC								
	real words		nonwords						
	yes	six	yag	sed	wib	cof	puz	hul	quen
Initial	66.67%	40.74%	22.22%	14.81%	22.22%	25.93%	14.81%	11.11%	0.00%
Final	92.31%	80.77%	50.00%	38.46%	53.85%	34.62%	26.92%	15.38%	3.85%

	CVCe							
	real words				nonwords			
	name	five	cute	home	yage	sede	wibe	cofe	puze
Initial	7.41%	29.63%	22.22%	3.70%	14.81%	0.00%	3.70%	3.70%	7.41%
Final	53.85%	50.00%	50.00%	26.92%	15.38%	11.54%	19.23%	7.69%	42.31%

	digraph									
	real words					nonwords				
	black	jellyfish	this	thank	sandwich	what	chax	tock	shem	rith	whov
Initial	29.63%	25.93%	18.52%	22.22%	18.52%	25.93%	22.22%	22.22%	7.41%	0.00%	7.41%
Final	42.31%	26.92%	38.46%	19.23%	38.46%	30.77%	26.92%	53.85%	11.54%	0.00%	11.54%

	long vowel			
	real words		nonwords	
	green	cool	jeen	koot
Initial	37.04%	18.52%	7.41%	0.00%
Final	46.15%	19.23%	7.69%	0.00%

	others		
	real words		
	book	octopus	study
Initial	48.15%	40.74%	25.93%
Final	53.85%	57.69%	46.15%

Moreover, it is worth noting that, in attempting to read a target word in the final assessment, many children seemed to focus on the initial letter in it and try to think of a sound for it:

> In this assessment, many children attempted to say the initial sound of target words—only the initial consonant without the following consonant or vowel. This is a great change from the initial assessment in which children—although not so many could read the targets—seemed to be looking for a CV combination in a target word so that they could read it in the *Roma-ji* way; for example, *pu* in a non-word target *puz*. Then, they never

only said an initial consonant sound. Nevertheless this time, there were many children who repeated or extended only an initial sound as a first step (e.g., "/ppppp/" in *puz*). This is exactly what I demonstrated in the sessions, and was glad to see they are beginning to understand an English way of reading a word. [RJ14]

From this perspective, the results of non-word reading are very informative in that the children had not seen non-word targets previously and their responses could be analysed without considering the familiarity effect. Generally, possible causes of the children's failure in reading aloud target words in the final assessment could be summarised as follows: (1) The children had not been fully able to connect the constituent letters of a target word with their sounds properly (e.g., failure in making a correct sound of /ʌ/ in *hul* and *puz* or /kw/ in *quen*), (2) They added a vowel sound after the second consonant (e.g., /-do/ for *sed* and /-zu/ for *puz*), or (3) They pronounced a short vowel like a long vowel (e.g., /ko:f/ for *cof* and /se:do/ or /si:do/ for *sed*).

Then, the correct response rates for the real-word targets categorised as 'others' in Table 4.13 were relatively high in both the initial and the final assessment. In the initial assessment, the children who could read these words appeared to know their meaning or had seen them before. For example, they could recognise the word *book* by sight, not by blending the sounds of '/b/ + /oo/ + /k/.' In contrast, in the final assessment, some children who could not read *octopus* or *study* before could pronounce them correctly and recognise what they mean by producing their constituent sounds individually from the beginning. For example, when presented with the word card of *octopus*, a boy (P8) looked at the individual letters and said, "/o/, /ku/, /to/, /pu/ .... No, not /pu/ but /pʌ/! /okutopʌ/ ... /okutopʌs/!" Many others followed a similar process by saying /pu/ for *-pu-*. Similarly, the word *study* was read correctly if a child could identify its correct pronunciation from an attempt of segmenting the word as '/s(u)/ + /tu/ + /d(u)/.' Some children asked themselves what the sound of the letter *y* was, and then realised *dy* was pronounced /di/.

These findings might show that many children tended to segment a vowel and a following consonant as a unit, just like dividing Japanese speech into moras. Thus, whereas most children appeared to have come to be able to segment simple CVC-letter words into three constituent phonemes over the intervention, they still had difficulty in segmenting words consisting of more letters such as *octopus* correctly even though they were phonologically regular. In other words, it can be argued that, through the instruction, many children began to develop the awareness that English three-letter CVC words can be segmented into individual phonemes, but when it comes to reading longer words, they were likely to return to the habit of segmenting (i.e., pronouncing) a consonant and a following vowel together as they do in their native language.

Below, the children's performance in word reading will be discussed in detail in terms of individual target sound categories and spelling rules.

4.5.2. Split-grapheme rule

4.5.2.1. Qualitative observational data

The split-grapheme rule was introduced in Session 12. Word cards of three-letter CVC words and their corresponding CVC*e* words were prepared. V in a CVC word was in blue, while V and *e* in a CVC*e* word was in red and green respectively. First, pointing to constituent letters of a CVC word of *pin* one by one, the instructor gave the children a cue of "Sound!" and they said a phoneme sound for each letter. Then, she took out a CVC*e* card of *pine* silently and waited until a boy (P29) said, "Teacher! Why is *i* red in this?" She, putting up the card of *pin* again, said, "This word is not the same as the last one. What's the difference?". When some children noticed the letter *e* was added at the end in the card of *pine*, she gave a series of cues, "Sound! Name! Sound! Then, don't read the next!", pointing to the letters *p*, *i*, *n*, and *e*. After repeating this several times, the children were asked to blend the three sounds (i.e., /p/, /aɪ/, /n/).

There were two manifestations of unsuccessful attempts observed among many children in pronouncing a CVC*e* word in this session. First, just as in blending tasks at the phoneme and the onset-rime levels (Section 5.3.2) where the children's difficulty mostly lay in blending C_1 and $V(C_2)$, about two thirds of the children who could not say *pine* correctly had trouble in combining /p/ and /aɪ/. Moreover, they could not blend /aɪ/ with /n/ well. On the other hand, many succeeded in blending three sounds without the final /n/ such as /l/, /aɪ/, and /k/ in *like*. Similarly, an initial /n/ as in *name* was difficult for several children to blend with the following vowel sound, whereas this word had already become a sight word for some Group A children.

Second, there were some children who extended a sound of a vowel in the second position instead of saying its name. For example, four or five children said /tɑːp/ for *tape* and /tiːm/ for *time* in many attempts in Session 12, even after practicing segmentation of their constituent sounds (e.g., /t/, /ei/, /p/, and /t/, /ɑi/, /m/). The following interpretation might be possible with regard to this difficulty: These children were still in the process of learning the differences between letter names and sounds and prone to confuse them. However, because they had intensive practice of letter sounds after these were introduced in Session 5, they might have been more familiar with letter sounds than names. Therefore, when they had to blend three sounds in the order of 'sound, name, and sound' to read a CVC*e* word, a sound of a vowel in the middle position was produced, instead of its name. Consequently, it might be speculated that they remembered that pronunciation of V in CVC*e* words is different from that of CVC words and, as a result, the sound pronounced was inappropriately extended.

Other characteristics in the children's reading of CVC*e* words were the difficulty in pronouncing diphthongs /ei/ and /ou/ as names of vowel letters *a* and *o* correctly: Many children extended the former part of a diphthong (e.g., /e/ in /ei/). Presumably, the biggest cause of this is the conventional way of writing English loan words with *katakana* characters in Japanese. For example, the words *name* and *home* are widely-used loan words in Japan, with the *katakana* spellings of ネーム and ホーム respectively. Here, the prolonged sound mark 'ー' in the middle position indicates a long vowel sound and, therefore, many Japanese learners of English tend to wrongly apply pronunciation of Japanese words ネーム and ホーム to reading English words *name* and *home*. Furthermore, the phonological difference between Japanese and English might also affect this tendency: In Japanese, two consecutive vowels are usually regarded as two independent vowels (i.e., two moras), while in English a diphthong is an independent sound and counted as a phoneme. Thus, it might be difficult for Japanese children to say 'two sounds (i.e., a diphthong)' for a single letter because they are used to a one-to-one correspondence between a sound and a letter in their mother tongue.

Moreover, the children appeared to be confused when they were asked to read CVC*e* words whose V was *u* (i.e., /juː/) such as *cute*, *cube*, or *tube*:

> The children could not blend C and V well in C*u*C*e* words. When I asked them to repeat after my /kjuːt/ showing a word card of *cute*, a boy (P10) said, "Why /k/ and /juː/ makes /kjuː/? When I do it, … /kuju:/." It was all I could do to tell them that /juː/ has a vowel-like sound /j/ at the beginning and ask them to listen to my /juː/ sound to see if they could catch it. [RJ12]

It was assumed that the boy, and probably many others, might not have realised the existence of a semivowel /j/ in /juː/ and wondered why the beginning of the word *cute* sounded like /ki/, not /kʊ/. It is not clear whether the first /ʊ/ in the boy's attempt /kʊjuː/ was vowel epenthesis or induced by the following /juː/. However, when the children learnt to associate *cute* with an English loan word キュート (*kyūto*) in Japanese, their pronunciation of *cute* dramatically improved. A *katakana* character キュ (*kyu*) is a contracted sound beginning with /ki/, and when the children came to read *cute* like a sight word, they seemed to stop trying to blend /k/ and /juː/ and pronounced it in one breath as if they were reading aloud the Japanese word キュート. This tendency of reading an English word referring to pronunciation of a corresponding Japanese word was observed in other words which many children soon came to be able to recognise them by sight (e.g., *fine*, *name*, *cat*, and *dog*).

Later, the HRT showed the instructor a diary entry written by a girl (P19) on the day of Session 12, which may support the effectiveness of *explicitly* teaching children how to read:

> I learnt a rule called 'Magic-*e* rule' in today's English class. *Sensei* [the instructor] said this is a very important rule in order to learn to read English words. It was a little difficult, but I was happy to learn it.

Additionally the instructor informally asked some children, especially those in Group B and C who appeared to be more struggling than those in Group A in class, how they found learning the split-grapheme rule before and after several sessions, and the following are two excerpts [audio-recorded]:

1) *after Session 18*
   P24: Difficult. I don't understand it so much.
   T: What point in the rule do you think you don't understand?
   P24: ... Well ... (11 seconds)
   T: But you were saying a sound or a name correctly on my cues, ... weren't you?
   P24: I can say most of the names and sounds, but ... I cannot say a word.
   T: A word?
   P24: They [three sounds] don't go together.

2) *after Session 20*
   P7: Uhm ... difficult ... a little, but I think it's interesting.
   T: Difficult, but interesting? What do you mean?
   P7: Well, the second sound from the left changes, ... when there is *e* at the end, right? But it is confusing, and I cannot read it [a CVC*e* word]

quickly ... I have to think.

T: Like "This is read by sound, and this is read by name" ..., you have to think how to read each letter?

P7: I can do that. I know the sounds and names. But I'm slow ... it takes time ... I cannot say a word [a CVC*e* word] at once. I want to practice it [the rule] more, because it's interesting.

4.5.2.2. Quantitative assessment data

Word reading (initial and final assessment)

Table 4.13 above shows that the percentage of the children who could correctly read four real-word CVC*e* were generally higher than that of five non-word targets in the final assessment. The rates also increased in all CVC*e* words, regardless of real words or non-words, although many children said that the rule was difficult to understand in class. In the final assessment, some children said that they had noticed the target word had a final-*e*, but that they could not remember how to apply the rule to that word. Thus, it can be argued that the children could learn this rule through instruction but in the current intervention, more practice should have been included so that more children would be able to read the words with a final-*e* following the rule.

One of the reasons for the low rate in the real word *home* (26.92%) was that nine responses (34.62%) were categorised as incorrect because a diphthong /oʊ/ was pronounced as a long vowel /o:/. This tendency to pronounce a diphthong as a long vowel, which had been recognised throughout the intervention (Section 4.5.2.1), was more remarkable in non-word reading. Moreover, the slightly higher rate of correct responses in a word *puze* (/pjuːz/) in the final assessment (42.31%) seems to be partly because its vowel sound was similar to *Roma-ji* pronunciation of *u* (/ʊ/), while this was also a cause of the low rate for a word *puz* (correctly, /pʌz/). However, in the final assessment, as evidenced by the children's correct pronunciation of /pjuː/ for *pu-* in *puze*, they tried blending separate sounds /p/ and /juː/, not pronouncing *pu-* as one sound (like /pʊ/ for *Roma-ji* letter *pu*) as they did in the initial assessment.

Similar to letter-sound correspondenc, this task of reading CVC*e* words according to the split-grapheme rule was revised in the nine sessions after Session 12, using the same set of cards. In each of these sessions, a reflection sheet was administered in which the children had to answer a five-scale question of "How much do you understand Magic-*e* rule?". The results summarised in Table 4.14 indicate that the children's self-evaluation of their understanding of the rule was generally high and became slightly higher as the intervention proceeded, supporting the necessity of practising how to adopt the rule to actual word reading more intensively, as suggested based on the observation data earlier in this section.

Table 4.14: Children's responses about their understanding of the sprit-grapheme rule in the reflection sheets

[1 (I don't understand it at all – 2 – 3 (Neither) – 4 – 5 (I understand it very much)]

Session		N	Minimum	Maximum	Mean	SD
12	Introduction	26	2	5	4.23	.908
13	Revision	25	3	5	4.32	.748
14	Revision	27	2	5	4.26	.859
15	Revision	25	2	5	4.20	.866
16	Revision	27	3	5	4.30	.724
18	Revision	27	3	5	4.41	.797
19	Revision	25	3	5	4.60	.645
20	Revision	25	2	5	4.40	.816
21	Revision	27	3	5	4.48	.753

4.5.3. Digraphs — *ch*, *ck*, *sh*, *th*, and *wh*

4.5.3.1. Qualitative observational data

Five digraphs of *ch* (/tʃ/), *ck* (/k/), *sh* (/ʃ/), *th* (/θ/ and /ð/), and *wh* (/hw/) were included in the instructional content as frequently-used letter pairs which represent a single phoneme sound. The whole Session 20, except some time for routine revision activities of already-learnt content such as letter sounds and the split-grapheme rule, was used for introducing digraphs and then for activities using them.

In fact, the children came across the spelling of *Thursday* in Session 18, when explaining that *th* makes the sound /θ/ and had them practice how to pronounce it with the tip of the tongue touching the bottom of the top incisor teeth lightly. From the instructor's own experience in teaching at a junior-high school, students who are a little older than the children in this study are likely to become embarrassed when they have to do this movement for making the /θ/ sound, because no such movement is necessary for making any sounds in Japanese (i.e., no /θ/ and /ð/ in Japanese) and they feel awkward at the beginning. In contrast, the children in the present intervention "were very good at imitating the instructor's demonstration and the /θ/ sound many of them produced was clear and correct" (The AST's diary entry for Session 18).

In Session 20, the children were first presented randomly with five cards of digraphs and recited them until they came to be able to read the digraphs by themselves. Each digraph was in a different colour that might help the children recognise it visually. Moreover, they were provided with the following clues so that they would come to identify some of the target correspondences between a digraph and its sound:

- The sounds for letters *c* and *k* are both /k/, and when they are combined as *ck*, its sound is also /k/.
- The sound for *sh* is the same sound as what you say when you want someone to be quiet: "/shiː/! (しーっ)." But make it short.
- When you pronounce /θ/ or /ð/, place the tip of the tongue between the top and the bottom incisor teeth just like you are biting it.
- When you see *wh*, say, "What?" and remember the spelling of *what*. It's the initial part of *what*. [The word *what* was one of the most familiar words for the children, as this was included in many phrases (e.g., *What day is today?*, *What time / colour / food / animal?*, or *What do you like / have?*) they had learnt in English classes in the lower grades.]

In addition, in the instructor's attempt to explain the sound of *ch* based on her personal anecdotal episode, many children showed their developing ability for applying English letter-sound knowledge and phonological awareness to word reading, interestingly to reading a Japanese word. In *Roma-ji* instruction for elementary school children, the *Kunrei* system for romanising Japanese is introduced and the instructor's name is written as *Tika* in this system. She had an experience that she became puzzled when told to write her name as *Tika* in a *Roma-ji* class at elementary school because she had learnt at home that her name is *Chika* in English (i.e., in the Hepburn system of *Roma-ji*). Therefore, the instructor wrote *Tika* on the blackboard without saying anything and encouraged the children to read it. Whereas there were three or four children who shouted /chi-kɑ/ correctly as they had learnt in *Roma-ji* learning, many others made the initial sound of /ti/ (i.e., in a way of reading English *ti*) and added the Japanese mora sound /kɑ/ after it. This exchange was recorded as follows:

> Because many children said /ti/ (i.e., an English sound) + /kɑ/ (i.e., Japanese sound), which didn't sound my name, I said to them, "This is *Roma-ji*, not English, and my name. ... You know?" They looked very surprised and confused, saying "Oh, <u>*Tika*</u>!" [underlined for the purpose of marking a Japa-

nese sound for *ti* (i.e., English *chi*)], "That reads *Tika*?", "Is that *Tika*?", or "*Ti* ...*ka*?" Especially P6 said, pointing to *Tika* on the blackboard, "That's *ti* in *ta*, *ti*, *tu*, *te*, *to*! So, that's *Tika*!" (i.e., *ta*, *chi*, *tsu*, *te*, *to* in the Hepburn system used for English spelling) [RJ20]

However, shortly when P27 said, "But, when /t/ is blended with /i/, it makes /ti/ ... doesn't it?", other children who seemed to have been convinced that *Tika* was pronounced in the same way as *Chika* changed their mind and began saying, "That's right! That is what we learnt." and "You said letter *t* is /t/!" Then the instructor told the above anecdote and explained that *Roma-ji* they had learnt was based on a different system from the one used for writing Japanese words in English, and that they had to learn new spellings such as *chi* in her name *Chika* instead of *ti*. The children appeared to find this interesting, and *ch* was the second digraph that many children came to pronounce correctly following *ck* as the first. The HRT said to her after class, "The children could learn the connection between *ch* and its sound more easily than others thanks to your story, which seems to have left a strong impression." [RJ20]

After introducing digraphs in this way, activities using them (digraph roulette, word card reading, write-a-digraph worksheet, and digraph Bingo) were administered. In word card reading that asked the children to read a word based on their letter-sound knowledge, the meaning of the words could be understood by means of the corresponding picture cards and they appeared to enjoy finding a digraph in a series of letters (e.g., *brick*, *ship*, *bath*, *check*, *fish*, and *lock*). Moreover, they also seemed to expect that there was one digraph in a word and, when reading a word with a digraph, they first tried to find a digraph, think of its sound and then sounds for the other single letters, and finally blend all sounds. Because of this, when a word had two digraphs as in *check* and *chick*, it was a little more difficult for some children to recognise both and they needed more time to think. When P13 said, "Oh, there are two! ... That's not fair!", some other children said, "I didn't notice it. *ch* and *ck* ... now I can read it!" The instructor also included a word without a digraph (i.e., *sled*), and the children spent much longer until P10 finally said, "No digraph ..., the teacher?" At around this stage of the intervention, she began wondering about the diversity of the children's reactions in class and how it could be dealt with:

> The children's intellectual curiosity seems to be so intense that they ask for more and more challenging, tough, quiz-like activities such as today's digraph ones. They appear to make efforts at their own pace; for example,

P24 needs more time to learn new content than other children do, as the HRT told me, but she never gives up and is trying to understand the target little by little. I remembered that she and P7 came to me after the session in which onset-rime slides were used. They said that they wanted some slides so that they could revise them later at home. Moreover, they and other five or six children (both boys and girls) stayed in the classroom during break time and practiced reciting words on the slides. Thus, their pace is different from others, and what they might need is individual advice from me as an instructor. [RJ20]

4.5.3.2. Quantitative assessment data

Word reading (initial and final assessment)

According to Table 4.13, the children's ability of reading the words aloud including a digraph remained relatively low in the final assessment, whereas the correct response rates increased in most targets. The most significant cause of this might be that it was difficult to make the children aware of digraphs and understand their pronunciation with a very small number of not only *sessions* but also *words* for practice. That is, the intervention needed to be carried out within the framework of FLA and, therefore, reciting and practicing to read non-words was thought to be meaningless for the children. As a result, real words used to teach digraphs were basically selected from *Eigo Note 1* and were very limited.

Among the target digraphs (*sh*, *th*, *ch*, *ck*, and *wh*), more children could read *ck* even in a non-word target *tock*. In fact, 24 children out of 26 could make the correct sound /k/, or at least /kʊ/ with vowel epenthesis, for *ck* in *tock* in the final assessment. Thus, it might be claimed that the explanation used in Session 20 that digraph *ck* is pronounced in the same way as each of its constituent letters (i.e., *c* and *k*) worked well for the children to remember its sound.

On the other hand, although many children appeared to have mastered a sound for *ch* in revision activities during the intervention, only seven children could read the non-word *chax* correctly. The analysis of wrong responses indicates that seven children made the sound /k/ at the beginning of the word, presumably because they confused *ch* with *ck*.

4.5.4. Double vowel-letters — *ee* and *oo*

4.5.4.1. Qualitative observational data

Double vowel-letters *ee* and *oo* as long vowels were introduced in Session 18 in order to see whether the children could learn to pay attention to vowel combinations. They were selected as targets because both are spelt with a simple repetition of a vowel. Moreover, *ee* frequently appears on word cards based on *Eigo Note 1*, while *oo* as a short vowel consists of sight words for many children such as *good* and *book*.

First, for introducing *ee*, the children were presented with word cards on which *ee* as a long vowel was highlighted in red and asked to recite them after the instructor. Target words for *ee* were words like *green*, *sleepy*, *three*, and *sheep*. Although there were some parts in their spellings which were difficult for the children to read, the instructor did not refer to them and tried to make them focus only on the part of *ee*. Before reading aloud all the target words, a girl (P27) said, "So, you mean ... *ee* makes the sound /i:/?" She continued, "But *e* (i.e., /i:/ as its name) is ... /e/. When *e* is doubled, ... /i:/? Other children were listening to her, and all she had to do was to say, "Yes, P27 is right. When you see *ee* in a word, you read this as /i:/."

On the other hand, in introducing *oo*, the instructor randomly pronounced target words of *book*, *good*, *cool*, and *kangaroo* showing word cards on which *oo* as a long vowel was in red and *oo* as a short vowel in blue. This time, a boy (P13) was quick to say, "Well, red *oo* is /u:/ and blue *oo* is /ʊ/, right?" Most children soon came to be able to read all four target words, but "it was just like children remembered those four words by sight, rather than they read the words following their spellings including *oo*." [RJ18]

Generally, since *Eigo Note 1* was not organised in view of systematic vocabulary instruction, a limited number of possible target words made it difficult to make the children aware of this sound category. In fact, when *oo* was taught as a long vowel, no child pointed out that its pronunciation is different from that of *oo* in *book* and *good*.

4.5.4.2. Quantitative assessment data

Word reading (initial and final assessment)

As shown in Table 4.13, the correct response rates for target words including a long vowel *ee* or *oo* were the lowest of all in the final assessment. As with the case in digraphs, the small number of words for practice and consolidation seems to be the main cause of the children's inability in applying what they were taught to other words. Regarding long vowel *oo*, three children made the sound /ʊ/ and two of them made it long in the final assessment, although their responses were not counted as correct as they added a vowel sound after the final consonant. On the other hand, more than half of children made the sound /o/ or /o:/ for *oo* in the non-word target *koot*. It could be assumed that, looking at the spelling of *koot*, some children remembered the explanation about consonant doubling and pronounced it as a single consonant /o/. However, considering that the similar tendency was found in their responses in the initial assessment, it seems more appropriate to state that they read the target in a *Roma-ji* way: A vowel sound for the *Roma-ji* letter *o* is mostly the same as /o/ in English.

4.5.5. Consonant doubling

Consonant blending was formally introduced in Session 17. The word *formally* is intentionally here because the children had seen words with consonant doubling when they were reciting words for communication activities in *Eigo Note 1* in earlier sessions but these words were not pointed out then. As described in Section 3.3.3.1, the aim of referring to consonant blending in this intervention was simply to teach the children that it does not make a geminate consonant sound (i.e., a short っ /tsu/ sound) in English as it does in *Roma-ji*, and the focused assessment of the children's understanding was carried out on this spelling rule.

In order to attract the children's attention to consonant doubling, they were first presented with a *Roma-ji* word card of *happī* on which consonant doubling was highlighted in green. They were asked what language it was. Many children shouted "English!" but, when the instructor asked them to read the word, about half the children could read it correctly in a *Roma-ji* way with confidence and some others only hesitatingly. Listening to their Japanese pronunciation for the word *happī*, the instructor said to them, "Is that English?" P29 said, "Wow! No, it's not English, but Japanese!" and others seemed to have noticed it, too. Then, holding up a corresponding English word with consonant doubling in red (i.e., *happy*), she asked them to read it. It was expected that at least Group A children could read it correctly, not only because the spelling had been presented to the children many times from the first session (e.g., in reciting "I'm happy!") but because we can see this word in many places and on many things such as stationery in Japan. In other words, it should have become a sight word for some children. When the instructor heard a boy (P10) say, "*Happy!*", she asked, "*Happī* or *happy*?" pronouncing them very slowly. Many children instantly said, "*Happy!*" However, when she asked them what the difference was, she had to wait for a while until a boy (P13) finally said, "... don't say

152 *Introducing Phonological Awareness and Early Literacy Instruction*

っ." Then, she explained that a *Roma-ji* rule for doubling a consonant does not apply to English words and the children's reactions were as follows:

> The children didn't seem to be convinced when I explained the difference in the roles of consonant doubling between Japanese and English. When I said to them, "So, you don't have to bother about making a small /tsu/ sound when you come across consonant doubling. You only have to read it as if it were a single consonant," the children were as if they had no idea what I was saying. I was really upset, but the children came to read target words by themselves after enough practice of reciting them after me. [RJ17]

Looking back to the intervention, it seems apparent that the cause of inefficacy in this instruction might be the fact that the children's awareness, or understanding, of the function of doubling a consonant in *Roma-ji* was still not sufficiently high. However, we cannot be certain here as their *Roma-ji* ability was not considered in this research.

4.5.6. Consonant clusters

As mentioned in Section 4.3.3.1, the children were provided with a short introduction of consonant clusters in Session 13 but more formal focus was placed on it in Session 17. In order to make the children realise the existence of consonant clusters which cannot happen in Japanese, pairs of an English word with an initial consonant cluster and its corresponding *Roma-ji* word which is actually an English loan word in Japanese (e.g., *black* / *burakku*) were used. The purpose of introducing consonant clusters was to prevent the children from inserting an unnecessary vowel sound after a consonant sound, yet some children referred to this as "'a practice to pronounce English words in an English-like way' when they were telling me about their reactions to it after the session or in a reflection sheet" [RJ19].

First, the children were presented with a word card of *burakku* with *bur* in green. After they recited it, the instructor put up a word card of *black* with *bl* in red and had the children read it aloud after her. When she asked them what the difference between these two words was, a boy (P13) said, "English and Japanese!", which made the whole class burst into laughter. Then, a girl (P6) said, "There is no /ʊ/ (i.e., the sound for the Japanese vowel letter *u*)!" She thought "That's good!" and seized the opportunity to explain that, in an English word *black*, the sound /ʊ/ does not come after the initial /b/ and the final /k/. If the girl had said that there was no letter *u*, it would have been more confusing for the children to understand the concept of vowel epenthesis. Regarding the difference between /r/ and /l/, their pronunciation was demonstrated many times so that the children came to realise them by themselves.

Then, the instructor presented children with a set of words including an initial consonant cluster from *Eigo Note 1* (e.g., *sleepy*, *cream*, *black*, *dress*, *green*) and had them listen to both the correct English way (e.g., /str-/ for *strawberry*) and the Japanese way (e.g., /sutoro-/) of pronouncing it. The practice of making sounds for constituent consonant of a cluster separately and then blending them together without inserting /ʊ/ or /o/ was repeated for all target words several times. Regarding the difficulty in pronouncing consonant clusters for the children, the following observation was recorded:

> The children appeared to become confused with whether or not they were pronouncing a consonant cluster well, especially when the first phoneme was a voiced sound such as /g/ in *green* and *grape* or /b/ in *black* and *blue*. In contrast, when the first consonant was a voiceless sound such as /s/ in *sleepy* and *skirt* or /k/ in *cream* or *crafts*, they seemed to be more confident as a result of being able to check their pronunciation by putting their fingers on the throat. However, regardless of whether the first consonant was voiced or voiceless, when the second phoneme was a semivowel /w/ as in *swim* and *sweater*, children seemed to struggle to check whether there was an inserted vowel sound in their pronunciation. [RJ17]

In fact, the instructor was also feeling the difficulty in catching all the children's pronunciation of consonant clusters precisely due to the relatively large class size. Therefore, considering that just an awareness of consonant clusters may help the children come to pronounce them correctly, they were repeatedly revised in the following sessions by reciting the same set of word cards used for introduction. Focused assessment was not administered on consonant clusters. Instead, the children's reading performance in the various tests were analysed when the target words included them.

4.6. The results of children's questionnaires before and after the intervention

The purpose of the initial and final questionnaire to be completed by the children was to elicit the changes in their attitude toward learning English as well as their appreciation of the intervention. The findings from the initial questionnaire for the children were helpful in that they provided the instructor with important information about their English learning background as well as their attitude toward English learning, which enabled various approaches to be tried according to their familiarity with English and the possible difficulty in learning new content. For example, the children's exposure to English varied and 14.81% answered that they see or hear English words outside school 'every day,' but more children said once or twice 'a week' (22.22%), 'a month' (22.22%), or 'a year' (7.41%).

In this section, a comparative analysis is reported so that some changes and tendencies in the children's attitudes toward learning *not only* English *but also* skills related to phonological awareness development during the intervention can be understood. The use of Likert scale questions made it possible to analyse the children's responses by dividing them into three categories: 'Positive,' 'I don't know,' and 'Negative.' Tables 4.15 and 4.16 above summarises descriptive analyses of the responses of all children in the initial and final assessments. It needs to be noted that there was one boy in Group C who answered negatively to almost all question items. Actually, the HRT told the instructor after the initial questionnaire that he was a type of child that liked playing pranks in class and might not answer the questionnaire seriously. However, it was decided to include his responses in the analysis because he attended all sessions seemingly enjoying activities and working on the worksheets very hard and did not appear to be having difficulty in understanding the instructional content. Thus, when there was a response or responses such as 'Not at all' or 'Difficult' in a certain question item, one of them was unquestionably his.

According to Tables 4.15 and 4.16, the children's responses to individual items do not seem to have changed markedly through the intervention. Preferably, the mean scores of individual pair items between the initial and final questionnaires such as ①, ③/④, and ⑥ in the tables (shading for the initial questionnaire) became slightly more positive. However, a significant difference was found only in the following four items: ③/④ in listening ($t(26) = 2.21$, $p < .05$), in reading ($t(26) = 2.58$, $p < .05$), and in writing ($t(26) = 2.21$, $p < .05$), as well as ⑥ in reading ($t(26) = 2.94$, $p < .01$).

Table 4.15: Children's responses to the initial and final questionnaires (1)

	1 Not at all	2 Not so much	3 I don't know	4 Yes, a little	5 Yes, very much	M	SD
①Attitude toward English learning							
I enjoyed it in Grade 4.	3.70% (1)	7.41% (2)	7.41% (2)	33.33% (9)	48.15% (13)	4.15	1.10
I enjoyed it in Grade 5.	3.70% (1)	0.00% (0)	11.11% (3)	18.52% (5)	66.67% (18)	4.44	0.97
[Initial] I am good at English.	18.52% (5)	29.63% (8)	18.52% (5)	22.22% (6)	11.11% (3)	2.78	1.31
[Final] I am good at English.	18.52% (5)	22.22% (6)	7.41% (2)	22.22% (6)	29.63% (8)	3.22	1.55
②Roma-ji skills							
[Initial] I am good at reading it.	14.81% (4)	14.81% (4)	14.81% (4)	25.93% (7)	29.63% (8)	3.41	1.45
[Initial] I am good at writing it.	14.81% (4)	14.81% (4)	18.52% (5)	14.81% (4)	37.04% (10)	3.44	1.50
③Initial interests in four skills							
Listening	11.11% (3)	18.52% (5)	7.41% (2)	29.63% (8)	33.33% (9)	3.56	1.42
Speaking	7.41% (2)	7.41% (2)	11.11% (3)	37.04% (10)	37.04% (10)	3.89	1.22
Reading	11.11% (3)	11.11% (3)	14.81% (4)	29.63% (8)	33.33% (9)	3.63	1.36
Writing	18.52% (5)	14.81% (4)	0.00% (0)	25.93% (7)	40.74% (11)	3.56	1.60
④During the intervention, I enjoyed							
Listening	3.70% (1)	0.00% (0)	14.81% (4)	40.74% (11)	40.74% (11)	4.15	0.95
Speaking	3.70% (1)	3.70% (1)	14.81% (4)	29.63% (8)	48.15% (13)	4.15	1.06
Reading	3.70% (1)	0.00% (0)	14.81% (4)	37.04% (10)	44.44% (12)	4.19	0.96
Writing	0.00% (0)	3.70% (1)	14.81% (4)	40.74% (11)	40.74% (11)	4.15	0.95
⑤Attitude toward learning four skills							
I want to learn listening more.	11.11% (3)	3.70% (1)	14.81% (4)	29.63% (8)	40.74% (11)	3.85	1.32
I want to learn speaking more.	7.41% (2)	7.41% (2)	3.70% (1)	33.33% (9)	48.15% (13)	4.07	1.24
I want to learn reading more.	7.41% (2)	11.11% (3)	11.11% (3)	33.33% (9)	37.04% (10)	3.81	1.27
I want to learn writing more.	7.41% (2)	11.11% (3)	14.81% (4)	14.81% (4)	51.85% (14)	3.93	1.36

Table 4.16: Children's responses to the initial and final questionnaires (2)

	1 Difficult	2 A little difficult	3 I don't know	4 Not so difficult	5 Not difficult at all	M	SD
⑥Difficulty in learning four skills							
[Initial] Listening	14.81% (4)	25.92% (7)	14.81% (4)	22.22% (6)	22.22% (6)	3.11	1.42
[Final] Listening	3.70% (1)	33.33% (9)	18.52% (5)	14.81% (4)	29.63% (6)	3.33	1.33
[Initial] Speaking	18.52% (5)	33.33% (9)	14.81% (4)	18.52% (5)	14.81% (4)	2.78	1.37
[Final] Speaking	11.11% (3)	40.74% (11)	3.70% (1)	7.41% (2)	37.04% (10)	3.19	1.57
[Initial] Reading	29.63% (8)	22.22% (6)	7.41% (2)	14.81% (4)	25.93% (7)	2.85	1.63
[Final] Reading	11.11% (3)	22.22% (6)	14.81% (4)	7.41% (2)	44.44% (12)	3.52	1.53
[Initial] Writing	18.52% (5)	29.63% (8)	18.52% (5)	7.41% (2)	25.93% (7)	2.93	1.49
[Final] Writing	14.81% (4)	22.22% (6)	18.52% (5)	11.11% (3)	33.33% (9)	3.26	1.51

Examining the results of individual items, 81.48% and 85.19% of the children answered that they enjoyed learning English in Grade 4 and in the intervention in Grade 5 respectively (①). It is also encouraging that the rate of the children who thought they were good at English largely increased from 33.33% to 51.85% and that of the children who were not good at English slightly decreased from 48.15% to 40.74%. However, these results show that, including the children who chose 'Neither,' more than half of the children in Class 5-2 had less confidence in their English ability already at the beginning of Grade 5. Especially, it was among the children in Group B and Group C that responses were divided in negative and positive, whereas most children in Group A tended to answer positively to all items. The present results show that, although many children with less English learning experience at least enjoyed the intervention, they tended to think they were not good at English. Thus, cautious treatment may be necessary so that the children with such negative awareness would not come to dislike English learning in the future.

In fact, the tendency that the children's responses were affected by their English learning background (i.e., Group A, B, or C) was found in many items. Specifically, a significant effect of group difference was yielded in eight items as summarised in Table 4.17. It is noticeable that the children's English learning background outside school seems to have influenced their beliefs about their English ability both before and after the intervention.

Table 4.17: The results of Pearson's *Chi*-square tests

	value	df	p
Initial questionnaire			
I'm good at English	18.25	8	.019
Difficulty in reading	18.50	8	.018
Interests in writing	13.18	6	.040
I'm good at Roma-ji	18.25	8	.019
Final questionnaire			
I'm good at English	18.66	8	.017
Difficulty in speaking	24.71	8	.002
Difficulty in writing	19.92	8	.011
I want to learn wrining more	21.04	8	.007

When the opportunity arose, the instructor asked two children who said that they were not good at English why they thought so. RJ14 records the following responses and the instructor's reaction to them:

P16: I don't understand English. It's not clear to me at all. (answering my question of "What do you mean by 'don't understand' or 'not clear'?") I don't know any English words and can't express what I want to say in English.

P30: I cannot remember English words or phrases because they are difficult.

Listening to them, I felt this might be natural to some extent considering that they had hardly been encouraged, or forced, to memorise the expression introduced in class because English is not a proper curricular subject in its own right and no assessment is expected to be done as in other subjects.

Furthermore, regarding the children's thoughts and beliefs about the four macro skills in English, no statistically significant difference among four skills could be found in their initial interests (③), whether they enjoyed learning them (④), whether they want to learn them more (⑤), and difficulty (⑥). With a close look at their responses to the items related to reading skill, it was revealed not only that significantly more children enjoyed learning reading in English during the intervention than those who had interests in it at the beginning, but also that their beliefs about the difficulty in reading were remarkably lowered. Thus, it might be assumed that, because the present intervention aimed to develop the children's early English reading and employed focused activities on it, the children came to feel the enjoyment of reading English words by themselves. Other skills they enjoyed learning more through the intervention than they had been interested included listening and writing. Writing here means the worksheet activities administered to assess their development in phonological awareness skills as well as letter-sound knowledge. It is interesting that the children expressed significantly a more positive attitude toward both component skills of literacy than their initial expectation, whereas the *Course of Study* avoided including them for fear of making English learning more demanding for children.

With regard to the children's awareness about their ability in reading and writing *Roma-ji* (②), similar percentages of the children answered that they were good at reading (55.56%) and writing (51.85%) *Roma-ji* and the percentages of the children who thought they were not good at reading or writing *Roma-ji* were the same (29.62%). Considering that seven out of eight children who answered negatively were in Group C, it could be assumed that familiarity with the alphabet which the children in Group A and B acquired through learning English outside school became an advantage for them to learn to read or write *Roma-ji*.

Table 4.18 and 4.19 illustrate the children's thoughts about their un-

158   *Introducing Phonological Awareness and Early Literacy Instruction*

derstanding, how much they enjoyed, and difficulty in learning the main instructional content for the intervention: Lower-case letters, letter sounds, and simple word reading. Generally, their responses to these items were consistent among content, and no significant difference was found in terms of three perspectives.

Table 4.18: Children's responses to the final questionnaires (1)

	1 Not at all	2 Not so much	3 I don't know	4 Yes, a little	5 Yes, very much	M	SD
⑦**Understanding**							
Lower-case letters	3.70% (1)	11.11% (3)	7.41% (2)	37.04% (10)	40.74% (11)	4.00	1.14
Letter sounds	3.70% (1)	7.41% (2)	7.41% (2)	22.22% (6)	59.26% (16)	4.26	1.13
How to read simple words	3.70% (1)	0.00% (0)	7.41% (2)	37.04% (10)	51.85% (14)	4.37	0.79
⑧**Enjoyment**							
Lower-case letters	3.70% (1)	7.41% (2)	14.81% (4)	29.63% (8)	44.44% (12)	4.04	1.13
Letter sounds	3.70% (1)	3.70% (1)	18.52% (5)	22.22% (6)	51.85% (14)	4.15	1.10
How to read simple words	3.70% (1)	7.41% (2)	14.81% (4)	37.04% (10)	37.04% (10)	3.96	1.09

Table 4.19: Children's responses to the final questionnaires (2)

	1 Difficult	2 A little difficult	3 I don't know	4 Not so difficult	5 Not difficult at all	M	SD
⑨**Difficulty in learning**							
Lower-case letters	3.70% (1)	14.81% (4)	14.81% (4)	22.22% (6)	44.44% (12)	3.89	1.25
Letter sounds	3.70% (1)	14.81% (4)	3.70% (1)	29.63% (8)	48.15% (13)	4.04	1.22
How to read simple words	0.00% (0)	22.22% (6)	3.70% (1)	37.04% (10)	37.04% (10)	3.89	1.15

The similar tendency as other items was found that the children in Group A were generally positive while the children in Group B and C were either positive or negative. However, only in the item of early word reading, one girl (P2) in Group A gave a negative response that she did not enjoy learning it so much and found it a little difficult. With regard to early word reading, 88.89% gave positive responses to the item about their understanding and only one boy (3.70%) answered negatively, whereas more children (22.22%) were rather negative and answered that learning how to read simple words was difficult for them. As demonstrated in the results from the final assessment, their performance on simple word reading was still at the lower level (Section 4.5.1.2). However, the following comments in their reflection sheets were recorded:

P7 (girl, Group B, Session 10): We read a picture book today. It was a little difficult at the beginning but, after practicing several times, I came to be able to read words little by little by myself. So, I was happy. It still takes long for me to read words, but I want to practice more so that I can read them better.

P19 (girl, Group A, Session 10): We learnt how to read an English book today. This was my first time and difficult, but I was happy because I could read some words.

P24 (girl, Group C, Session 12): I enjoyed reading a book very much today. I sometimes got confused by some words I didn't know how to read, but I want to read more books. I hope I will be able to read English well.

On the other hand, there were also some negative comments in the reflection sheets: These were simple and jotted down in a few words:

P29 (boy, Group A, Session 10): That activity to read a book—that's difficult.

P30 (boy, Group C, Session 10): It is difficult to read English.

Thus, it seems safe to say that relatively many children enjoyed activities aiming to apply phonological awareness skills to reading simple English words, although the tasks were new and tough for them. Then, some sense of achievement they felt after the activities might cause them to think that they understood how to read English, while there were some other children who did not feel the same.

Finally, concerning the item about which of four skills the children want to learn more (⑤), the instructor asked the same question during lunch time [audio-recorded]. Some expressed diverse opinions:

P1 (girl, Group A): "I want to learn reading and writing in English at school because I learn them at an English school."

P10 (boy, Group A): "I don't mind if reading and writing begin to be taught in school because they are not so difficult."

P29 (boy, Group A): "Speaking is difficult because I don't know what I have to say, and listening is also difficult because I don't understand what is being said. I like copying English, and learning English reading is fine if it is not too much."

P14 (boy, Group C): "I want to learn writing in English because it is interesting, but don't want to read in English because it is difficult." (answering to the instructor's question "Why do you think it is difficult?") "I don't know, but I

160   *Introducing Phonological Awareness and Early Literacy Instruction*

can't."

P20 (girl, Group C): "I want to read English because I like reading, but writing is difficult and I don't know how to write."

I added some comments to these children's responses:

> Listening to the children's words, the instructor began to think that it was not the reasons on the side of children that decided not to introduce reading and writing into elementary school English education, but policies of adults in administration. As far as children's affection is concerned, there seems to be little problem to begin to learn English literacy. However, what is important it how it is introduced. [RJ15]

4.7. Children's reactions to the reflection sheets

As a reflection sheet was administered in Japanese just after or in the middle of the main activity of the session, it had to be distributed in a noisy atmosphere. Some children appeared to be caught by thoughts of between-classes activities and, therefore, it seems to be a little doubtful whether they answered the questions with their full attention. On the other hand, however, because the children had to fill in the reflection sheet within a short time,

Figure 4.8: Children's reactions to the reflection sheets—General

Session	Enjoyment (1–5)	Effort (0–100)
Session 1: Revision of letter names	3.89	73
Session 2: Activities to get familiar with letters	3.81	74.17
Session 3: Activities to get familiar with letters	4.04	75.83
Session 4: Elkonin cards	4.15	77.23
Session 5: Introduction of V and C sounds	4.11	71.54
Session 6: Introduction of C sounds / Halloween activities	4.56	77.01
Session 7: Expression of 'Do you like ~?'	4.44	80.25
Session 8: Review song / Onset-rime slides / CVC word reading	4.27	78.2
Session 9: Expression of 'What would you like ?'	4.3	77.53
Session 10: Reading aloud simple sentences	4.33	79.65
Session 11: Video activities for phonological awareness skills development	4.04	66.6
Session 12: Introduction of sprit-grapheme rule	4.23	81.85
Session 13: Initial phoneme deletion / Christmas activities	4.44	90.43
Session 14: Letter-sound Karuta	4.41	83.88
Session 15: Phoneme segmentation and categorisation	4.12	81.66
Session 16: Phoneme substitution	4.3	84
Session 17: Introduction of consonant blend / consonant doubling / long vowels	4.3	79.11
Session 18: Introduction of th / Time table	4.63	89.48
Session 19: Initial sound Domino	4.76	91.39
Session 20: Introduction of wh, ck, ch, sh	4.56	92.63
Session 21: Expression of 'Would you like ~?'	4.63	88.84

■ How much I enjoyed this session (1 [Not at all] - 2 - 3 [I don't know] - 4 - 5 [Very much])
■ How much effort I made. Give the mark 0-100.

it might have succeeded in eliciting their intuitive responses to the questions. Thus, it may be worth referring to some findings obtained from these sheets. In all scales, 1 meant the most negative answer to a question while 5 was the most positive (e.g., 1 [I didn't enjoy it at all.] - 2 - 3 [Neither.] - 4 - 5 [I enjoyed it very much.])

Figure 4.8 shows the average of the children's responses to the items of 'how much they enjoyed each session (five-point scale)' and 'the mark they gave to their own efforts in each session (0 ~ 100),' and Figure 4.9 illustrates their reactions to 'the individual phonological awareness activities (five-point scale).'

Figure 4.9: Children's reactions to the reflection sheets—Phonological awareness activities

■ How much I enjoyed this activity (1 [Not at all] - 2 - 3 [I don't know] - 4 - 5 [Very much])

With regard to the enjoyment of the sessions, mean scores for most sessions were higher than 4 and, after Session 6, there was no children who gave negative responses such as 1 or 2. Thus, the children showed overall positive attitudes toward the interventional sessions. The sessions which obtained the mean score of more than 4.5 were Sessions 6, 18, 19, 20, and 21. A common feature among these sessions was that main activities in them were easy for the children to understand and enjoyable. In Sessions 6, 18, and 21, the main activity was a communicative activity based on the content of *Eigo Note 1*, and in Session 19 and 20 it was an activity asking the children to demonstrate their acquired letter-sound knowledge and phonological awareness. Especially, the main activity in Session 19 which yielded the highest mean score was a group competition in 'Initial Phoneme Domino' where the children had to keep connecting a letter with a picture representing a word which has the same letter in its initial position until they finished all letter cards. In fact, the instructor had worried at first that this activity was too difficult for them because all the words were not three-letter CVC and some were even unfamiliar to them. However, the children found it very exciting and, when they could not think of an English word for a picture, they asked other children or teachers about it using the newly learnt expression of 'How do you say ... in English?' Many children were looking for a picture repeating a sound of the letter they wanted like /ppppp/. This was pleasing because the instructor was sure that many of the children learnt to segment the initial phoneme of a word through the intervention. They also appeared to be enjoying the competition among groups (eight groups of four children).

The mark the children gave to efforts made in each session seemed to be positively correlated with how much they enjoyed the session. Even though the instructional content became more complex and demanding for the children as the intervention proceeded, they seemed to enjoy learning them and made more efforts. The differences in the children's responses to activities for phonological awareness and early English reading from those to other curricular content in FLA were not so significant, which may mean that the children generally could enjoy both types of instruction to a similar extent, without feeling uncomfortable in the phonological awareness instruction.

4.8. Summary

The main objective of this chapter was to draw descriptive accounts of interventional sessions in reference to their target instructional content, including the qualitative data such as the instructor's journal and informal interviews. In addition, referring to the results of the initial and final assessment as well as the mini assessment, the children's understanding and development of instructional content was discussed. Moreover, the children's affective reactions to the sessions and the content of intervention were considered based on their responses to the questionnaires and the reflection sheets.

Chapter 5

Discussion

The objective of this study was to examine the feasibility of introducing phonological awareness instruction into Japanese elementary school English classes, as well as the children's reactions to the instruction itself. The results of the intervention adds to the existing but still limited literature on the instruction of phonological awareness in a second or foreign language in that it explored the teachability and learnability of phonological awareness for children whose L1 is phonologically and orthographically different from English in which the facilitative role of phonological awareness in the early reading development has been widely agreed on.

This chapter first gives an overview of significant findings from this research in the light of individual research questions, and then examines these findings with reference to previous research considered in Chapter 2, in order to judge the potential of the phonological awareness instruction for Japanese elementary school children.

5.1. The effectiveness of the phonological awareness instruction in 'Foreign Language Activities'

The intervention aimed to investigate the *effectiveness* of the instruction of phonological awareness and early reading, which will be considered from the following four perspectives: [A] whether the children could achieve the intended learning outcomes and what characteristics could be found in their phonological awareness, [B] whether there are difficulties in developing phonological awareness specific to Japanese children, [C] whether the children and the teachers would appreciate the instruction, and [D] whether the instruction could be well incorporated into FLA. Below, the findings will be discussed in relation to each of these perspectives.

5.1.1. The outcomes of the instruction and the characteristics of the children's phonological awareness and early English reading — RQ-A

The children's development of phonological awareness and early English reading

According to the qualitative observational data, it seems reasonably safe to posit that, through instruction, most of the Japanese children who participated in the intervention could develop not only the letter name and sound knowledge but also phonological awareness and began to apply all these types of knowledge to early English word reading. The quantitative assessment data served as confirming evidence for these findings. Indeed, the mean scores of all tests assessing the children's letter name knowledge, phonological awareness, and early word reading increased from the initial (the average correct response rate of 59.24%) to the final assessment (70.69%). Their knowledge of letter sounds assessed at the end of the intervention (91.73%) was as proficient as that of letter names.

We should note, however, that the intervention was only exploratory and based on the interpretive paradigm, without a control group of children. The development of the children's phonological awareness might be partly the result of their natural cognitive development during the period of the seven-month intervention. Nevertheless, considering the distinctiveness of the target phonological awareness skills necessary for learning to read in English as well as the EFL environment where children would hardly be required to manipulate English speech in their daily lives, it is virtually impossible to imagine they would have developed these skills and knowledge spontaneously without having been taught. Therefore, it should be justifiable to argue that the overall, although small, increase in the test scores was one of the positive outcomes of the intervention.

The characteristics of the children's phonological awareness and early English reading

First, the results suggested that the children had a moderate level of phonological awareness as well as the letter name knowledge at the beginning of the intervention. Specifically, in the initial assessment, the average correct response rates were relatively high in the letter name knowledge test and the set of phonological awareness tests (76.85% and 66.42% respectively), while that in the word reading test was low (19.14%). Moreover, the children's correct response rates in the initial phoneme *recognition* test (74.17% to 85.92%) and the phoneme *recognition & location* test (75.37% to 86.28%) were both approximately 75% at the beginning. These findings might show that the Japanese children had already developed some *phonemic* awareness up to the level of being able to *recognise* and *locate* a target phoneme sound in a word before the intervention. As discussed in Section 2.2.3, phonemic awareness is assumed to appear after the awareness of larger phonological units such as rhymes and syllables in the continuum of the phonological awareness development, as children cognitively develop (Adams, 1990; Anthony et al., 2003; Bowey, 2002; Stanovich, 1992). Moreover, it has been demonstrated in earlier studies that *recognition* is easier than *production* (Vendervelden & Siegel, 1995), and *location* is easier than *segmenting* or *deleting*, which are in turn easier than *manipulation* that requires multiple skills (e.g., substitution) (Chafouleas & Martens, 2002; Schatschneider et al., 1999; Stahl & Murray, 1994; Yopp, 1988). Given the fact that none of the children had experienced a systematic instruction of phonological awareness or phonics before the intervention, it seems justifiable to suppose that these fifth-graders had developed *the beginning* of the higher-level phonological awareness (i.e., phonemic awareness) before the intervention, naturally in the process of their L1 development without being taught. This is consistent with the finding in Mann (1986) that:

> … whereas most Japanese first graders could manipulate syllables but not phonemes, the majority of Japanese children were able to manipulate both syllables and phonemes by the fourth grade, whether or not they had been instructed in the use of an alphabet. Thus, with increasing age and educational experience Japanese children may become more and more capable of manipulating phonemes whether or not they are alphabet-literate (p. 87).

The task of "manipulating" in Mann's (1986) study was counting and deleting, the former of which overlaps with segmenting in the present study to a large extent. Moreover, with regard to "educational experience," *Roma-ji* learning may play an important role in sophisticating the children's awareness of Japanese phonology.

Second, regarding the children's segmenting skill, the observational findings from the intervention revealed a noticeable feature which seems to have not been reported in the previous literature. That is, when orally presented with a three-letter $C_1V_1C_2$ word (e.g., *dog*), many children could say three sounds which correspond to the number of constituent sounds of the target word. However, the sounds pronounced by them were like C_1V_2, V_1, C_2V_3 (e.g., /dʊ/, /o/, and /gʊ/) rather than C_1, V_1, C_2 (e.g., /d/, /o/, and /g/). The sound of V_2 and V_3 was mostly /ʊ/ or /o/ which was reported to be popular epenthetic vowels (Kubozono 2006). In fact, based on the discussion in the literature review chapter, it was expected that the children would segment a $C_1V_1C_2$ word into two sounds of C_1V_1 and C_2V_2 (e.g., /do/ and /gʊ/) by dividing it after the initial C_1V_1 combination because Japanese speakers' speech segmentation is likely to be affected by the moraic procedure (i.e., CV, CV, ...) which is characteristic to Japanese (Cutler & Otake, 1994; Inagaki et al., 2000; Otake et al., 1993), but it did not apply to the children in this study. It should be admitted that, in the early stage of the intervention, Elkonin cards were used for the introduction and practice of segmentation and the number of boxes on the cards might have given the children a clue about the number of the constituent sounds. Nevertheless, without such clues, they soon came to be able to say the initial, middle, or final sound after the instructor's cue. Also in these cases, the initial and final consonant sounds were frequently followed by a vowel sound.

Whereas the children's letter sound knowledge became as high as their letter name knowledge in the final assessment, vowel epenthesis was recognised very frequently in many children's pronunciation throughout the intervention. For example, the word *clip* tended to be pronounced /kʊlip(ʊ)/ presumably under the influence of *katakana* spelling クリップ (*Roma-ji*: *kurippu*). However, when the children were asked to delete a phoneme /k/ from /klip/ in the initial-phoneme deletion task, most could answer /lip(ʊ)/ correctly, not /ulip(ʊ)/. Thus, while they failed in the pronunciation of a single consonant phoneme or consonant clusters without adding a vowel, they could *recognise* the target phoneme accurately and perform well in phonological awareness tasks. Some children did not appear to have noticed that their consonants were followed by a vowel. Generally, the children came to be able to recognise consonant sounds through the instruction but kept struggling in making these sounds correctly by themselves under the influence of their L1 phonology. In fact, this was where *letters* could play an important role of explicitly showing the difference between C and CV. During the intervention, the children appeared to have understood better that there is no vowel sound between consonant sounds comprising a consonant cluster when their difference was demonstrated using letters than when it was only orally explained. Several previous studies reported that many elementary schools teachers felt anxiety about teaching English because they considered that their English ability was not good enough (Allem-Tamai, Tsukada, & Ogawa, 2001; Kanazawa & Ito, 2008; Tsuidou, 1998). Therefore, the use of letters for the purpose of demonstrating sound differences would be easier and more convenient for teachers who have less confidence in their English ability.

A related observation brought out by the frequent appearance of vowel epenthesis is that, for Japanese children, the connection of CV may be stronger than that of VC which is an important intrasyllabic unit for speech segmentation in English phonology (i.e., rimes), as demonstrated in the case of Korean-speaking children (Kim, 2007). In the current study, the results from sound manipulation tests showed that, when asked to delete a consonant phoneme from a cluster, many children deleted the target consonant together with the following vowel, and replaced it with a different vowel such as /ʊ/ (e.g., /sʊp/ after trying to delete /l/ from a word *slip*). Similarly, in a substitution task, they deleted both the target consonant and the following vowel and inserted the new consonant together with a different vowel (e.g., /slʊk/ after substituting /l/ for /t/ in a word *stick*). They might not have intended to delete the following vowel when separating a consonant from a word, but they did tend to insert the new consonant in combination with a vowel sound of /ʊ/ or /o/ which is popular in vowel epenthesis.

With regard to these phenomena, a study in the field of brain science on the phonological development of Japanese infants may provide valuable insight into the rationale for the above discussion. Mazuka, Cao, Dupoux, and Christophe (2011) demonstrated that 14-month-old Japanese infants, in contrast to their French counterparts, failed to discriminate phonetically varied sets of /ɑbnɑ/-type and /ɑbʊnɑ/-type (i.e., /ɑbnɑ/ with vowel epenthesis of /ʊ/ after /b/) words, although 8-month-old Japanese and French infants did not differ significantly from each other. They suggested that, before having acquired many L1 words, Japanese infants have come to break up sequences of consonants with illusory vowels at the age of 14 months. Thus, it might be reasonable to suppose that adding a vowel sound after a consonant is natural in terms of "Japanese phonological grammar" (Mazuka et al., 2011, p. 693). Therefore, in attempting to segment $C_1C_2V_1C_3$ to delete C_2, Japanese children may lose V_1 together with C_2 because C_2 is more attributed to V_1 than to C_1 and V_1 is not so much linked to C_3 under the influence of Japanese phonology. Then, a new C_4 may be inserted after C_1 combined with a following new V_2 which is in many cases /ʊ/ or /o/.

It may even be stated that the above characteristics in the children's segmenting performance seems to have been caused by their poor understanding of letter sounds. However, it was observed that more children tried to read words by blending individual phonemes in the final assessment compared to their performance in the initial assessment where most children kept silent and only a few children attempted to find CV combinations and read them as they do in *Roma-ji*. Moreover, as the HRT told the author as the instructor, some children came to be able to enjoy changing words of the phonic song outside the interventional classes: They could categorise Japanese words according to their initial phonemes and made new songs for it such as "/ɑ/, /ɑ/, /ɑri/ (*ant* in English), /b/, /b/, /bʊtɑ/ (*pig*), /k/, /k/, /kɑerʊ/ (*frog*), /d/, /d/, /dorɑemon/ (name of a popular cartoon character), …." These examples support that many children had developed letter sound knowledge enough to be able to apply it to the newly-learnt phonological awareness tasks during the intervention.

In summary, the results suggested that Japanese children could learn phonological awareness but their learning path is different from that of English-speaking children and the speakers of other alphabetic languages. However, what is important is to teach the children phonological awareness necessary for learning to read in English so that they would minimise the effect of their L1 phonology and orthography in processing English speech, and the development of a special program for Japanese EFL children should be prioritised.

5.1.2. The difficulties in phonological awareness tasks in English for Japanese children — RQ-B

Regarding the difficulty in the four target phonological awareness tasks, the results from the intervention showed that substitution was more difficult for the Japanese children to perform than deletion, consistent with the findings for English-speaking children (Adams, 1990). Then, as to deletion and segmentation, whereas segmentation has been reported to be more difficult for English-speaking children in the earlier studies (Chafouleas & Martens, 2002; Stahl & Murray, 1994), both were generally doable for the Japanese fifth-graders during sessions. However, in segmentation, the isolated consonant sounds were frequently combined with a vowel sound (i.e., vowel epenthesis), and the difficulty in blending was affected by the types of target phonemes. Specifically, the children struggled in blending C_1 and V in a C_1VC_2 word when C_1 was a voiceless plosive (e.g., /p/ and /k/) or a voiceless fricative (e.g., /s/). It has been demonstrated in English L1 studies that consonant clusters such as *st-* and *pl-* (Stahl & Murray, 1994) and C_1V_1 are not especially demanding for children to segment when the initial consonant was a plosive or a fricative because these consonants are less attributed to the following sound (Bouwmeester, van Rijen, & Sijtsma, 2011; Treiman, 1984). Considering this, it could be assumed that the phonological independence of special C_1 from V_1 caused the difficulty for the Japanese children to blend these sounds. Generally, the Japanese children's pronunciation of C_1 sounded accurate when practising to blend it with the following V_1. In contrast, segmenting C_1V_1 was not so demanding for them because they could easily, but wrongly, add a new vowel V_2 after C_1 in trying to separate it from V_1 and make a mora which was easy for them to deal with (i.e., C_1V_2).

Moreover, it was found that the influence of the position of a target phoneme in a word on the difficulty of phonological awareness tasks for the Japanese children was not consistent with the earlier findings with English-speaking children. In English L1 studies, it has been widely demonstrated that a phoneme in the middle position of a word is more difficult than the initial or the final phonemes (Lewkowicz, 1980; Lewkowicz & Low, 1979). Then, concerning the difficulty of the initial or the final phonemes, although there is still some inconsistency in earlier L1 findings, it is generally agreed that the final phonemes are more difficult to manipulate than the initial phonemes (Schreuder & van Bon, 1989; Stanovich, Cunningham, & Cramer, 1984; Marsh & Mineo, 1977; McBride-Chang, 1995). In contrast, the results from the present intervention clearly showed that the final phonemes were easier for the Japanese children to delete or substitute than the initial phonemes: Whereas the advantage of the initial phonemes for English-speaking children could be explained in terms of the preference for the onset-rime unit in segmenting English speech where V is more closely connected to C_2 than C_1 in C_1VC_2, this might not apply to Japanese-speaking children who seem to prefer the moraic segmentation procedure in which V is more closely connected to C_1. Thus, it could be reasonably assumed that consonants which are not combined with vowels are easier to be segmented for manipulation, and such a consonant is C_1 (i.e., the initial phonemes) for English speakers, while it is C_2 (i.e., the final phonemes) for Japanese speakers. The present intervention demonstrated that the influence of Japanese phonology could be recognised in Japanese children's early phonological processing of English speech.

Indeed, the increase in the children's scores for the sound manipulation test in the final assessment may be an outcome of the interventional instruction focusing on the onset-rime unit in a word. However, as described just above, many of the children had still more difficulty in segmenting, blending, deleting, or substituting the word-initial consonant which is an onset, compared with the final consonant. This is another aspect of the influence of Japanese phonology, which Japanese children have to overcome in order to learn to read in English (McBride-Chang, 1995; Lewkowicz, 1980). Therefore, it can be safely claimed that, as long as the negative influence of Japanese phonological and orthographical characteristics could be recognised in the children's early processing of English speech, the preventive instruction of phonological awareness is necessary, and the use of letters would make such instruction more explicit and easier for children to understand and for teachers to conduct.

5.1.3. The reaction of children and elementary school teachers to the instruction — RQ-C

The children's attitudes toward English learning in general

Throughout the intervention, the author as the instructor was pondering that the participating children seemed to have interest in English, but this might not necessarily lead to motivating them to learn. In other words, whereas the initial questionnaire for the children revealed more than 60% of them had interests in learning four skills in English, it was observed during sessions that the majority had little intention to remember what they learnt, which in fact troubled the instructor in giving instructions as planned. This was presumably because English is not yet a proper subject and children know that they will not be officially assessed in FLA. Specifically in reading activities, some children's concentration was low as if they were saying that they did not know why they had to read in English. Indeed, in the first place, the children seemed to have been little convinced of the reason why they learn *English* in FLA.

With regard to children's motivation, it has been demonstrated that intrinsic motivation, which is "motivation to engage in an activity for its own sake" (Pintrich & Schunk, 2002, p. 245), for studying in general declines gradually with age (Corpus, McClintic-Gilbert, & Hayenga, 2009; Harter, 1981; Lepper, Corpus, & Iyengar, 2005; Lepper, Sethi, Dialdin, & Drake, 1997). Applying this perspective to EFL teaching, Carreira (2006) found a developmental decrease in both intrinsic and extrinsic motivation for learning English among Japanese elementary school children, and gave the following interpretation:

This may be happening not only in English learning, but also in their general learning. It has often been said that Japanese pupils tend to lose their goals and become unmotivated with age. This might be a sort of general trend in contemporary Japanese elementary school pupils. (p. 150)

Thus, the significance of "placing learning in meaningful and exciting contexts" (Lepper & Henderlong, 2000, p. 289) was recognised through the observation of the children: They actively participated in singing songs or playing games during the intervention but appeared to consider FLA as 'the period for games,' or just for fun. In fact, what the developmental decline in children's motivation for learning (Carreira, 2006) suggests is that children in upper grades may come to enjoy even fun activities such as songs and games less in their English classes, compared to children in lower grades, and only using popular activities might not be enough for them to achieve the expected outcome. According to Paul (2003), who has extensive experience in teaching English to Japanese children, in order to bring out children's genuine and meaningful desire and need to learn, it is important to ensure that they "first come across new targets inside an activity, and then later they may do some less game-like activities, such as writing sentences in their notebooks" (p. 51).

To recapitulate, it may be claimed that, in order to extend elementary school English education from the level of fun activities to the instruction of specific knowledge and skills such as letters and early reading, it would be necessary to think about how to keep children motivated by promoting and maintaining their intellectual curiosity in learning them as well as English in general as with other curricular subjects. To explain the utilitarian advantage of knowing English explicitly at the beginning of the instruction might be one solution because instructional motivation is thought to emerge at around the age of 11 or 12 (Nikolov, 1999) corresponding to Grade 5 or 6 respectively, where FLA is taught. In other words, in order to incorporate the instruction of phonological awareness and early reading well into FLA, it is necessary not only to make it enjoyable for children but also to make them realise *why* they should acquire these new skills. Indeed, this was attempted throughout the intervention because, as it progressed, the instructor came to think that, as long as the children had little motivation to *learn* new content, the instructional targets would not be effectively taught to these children who would not make any spontaneous efforts to acquire them. Thus, if the instruction of phonological awareness and then early reading is systematically introduced into FLA, children in Grades 5 and 6 would be able to develop *phonological awareness* satisfactorily at the beginning, as demonstrated in the present intervention, considering their cognitive and intellectual abilities. However, before their primary curiosity fades away, it is necessary to make them realise a special *reason* for developing it, by applying it to the higher level of skills such as early reading and spelling (Bus & van IJzendoorn, 1999; Ehri et al., 2001).

The children's reactions to the intervention

Taking all the data from various tools (i.e., questionnaires, reflection sheets, informal interviews, and observational data recorded in the instructor's journal) into consideration, the results show that the reactions of the children to the target instructional content for the intervention were generally positive and not so different from their reactions to the communicative activities including songs and games that are generally recommended for young learners. It should be noted that the children's favourable reactions to the intervention were not for the purpose of flattering the instructor because she constantly reminded them of the fact that she was not the person who could evaluate them.

Moreover, the data clearly suggests that the children's reactions to the intervention were affected by their English learning background. In other words, whereas some children in Group C showed rather negative reactions to learning phonological awareness and early English reading, the children in Group A and B generally enjoyed the intervention and appeared to be more confident and eager to demonstrate their ability in both individual sessions and the assessment. What should be emphasised is that these differences in the children's reactions reflecting their English learning background positively correlated with their achievement through the intervention. The most remarkable finding was the influence of whether the children had been exposed to letters in English lessons outside school. For instance, the results from the initial questionnaire revealed that almost all the children in Group A and B had been taught reading and writing in English lessons outside school. Specifically, in the intervention, greater familiarity with the shapes and names of the alphabet which the children in Group A and B had acquired through such lessons seemed to be a potential advantage for them in learning the target instructional content.

These findings further show that there is a considerable disparity in elementary school children's preliminary knowledge about English, or *readiness* for learning English, which may be further enhanced by a recent burst of enthusiasm for some parents sending their children to English lessons outside school. In addition, it seems unlikely that such diversity in children's English ability would decrease even after the children begin to be exposed to English in Grade 5, due to the lack in the standard for the concrete achievement goals in FLA. Moreover, high motivation to learn English that the children with some English learning experience outside school seems to have lead to acquiring a higher level of ability, extending the disparity of ability in class wider. Therefore, if one of the most remarkable differences among children with different English learning background was the familiarity with English literacy skills, it seems reasonable to claim that a more positive but cautious introduction of these skills into elementary school English education, in addition to spoken skills which are currently focused, might be a potential measure for lowering the possibility of producing children who fail English in elementary school, which is exactly what MEXT aims for. The instruction of phonological awareness should be the first step as it is the precursor to the literacy acquisition (Bryant, 1998; Goswami, 2002; Seymour & Evans, 1994).

The elementary school teachers' reactions
During the intervention, various teachers from the elementary school where the intervention was carried out, an ALT, and volunteer teachers frequently came and observed the sessions. Above all, as described in Section 6.4.1, the HRT was the only teacher that participated in all the sessions and her cooperation played a very important role in the implementation of the intervention.

When the instructor first interviewed the HRT [audio-recorded], she said;

> I'm very interested in your intervention because ..., having been involved in elementary school English education for about seven years, I'm wondering if the current practice, which focuses on songs, games, and communicative activities, will really be beneficial for the children in the future ... I mean, if it will help them learn English when they start learning English ... officially in junior high school.

She also added, "Some knowledge ... or skill instruction should be included in ECA or coming FLA, otherwise it might become a waste of time." Then, throughout the intervention, her reactions were positive and she said she herself enjoyed learning this special instructional content. Even when some demanding content or tasks were introduced and caused difficulty for some children, she did not say that those should not have been introduced but, from the HRT's viewpoint, gave the instructor advice of how she could have presented them to the children so that they would have been able to understand them more easily; for example, including explicit demonstration by the instructor first and then by some children in front of the other children before having all children practice on their own. Thus, gradually, the author as the instructor came to think that the cognitive demand or difficulty of a task might be lowered if an alternative introduction is adopted. Moreover, her comments after each session convinced the author that she had acknowledged the merit of the phonological awareness instruction as well as the children's ability to develop it. Indeed, some regret was frequently expressed that the intervention for the children was only for the two terms in Grade 5 and no such instruction would be held in Grade 6.

Similarly, as to the teachers' appreciation of the phonological awareness instruction, about five months after the intervention, the author gave a lecture on the significance of introducing letters into FLA by incorporating them into the phonological awareness instruction, as well as the EFL literacy development of Japanese children, in the one-day seminar for 56 elementary school teachers. Generally, their reactions to the lecture expressed in the comment sheet were positive and a female teacher came up after the seminar and said;

> I had felt that children could benefit from letters in learning English with no solid ground, just because they showed a genuine interest in them. But your talk today gave the answer. I didn't know how to present letters so that children would be able to not only enjoy learning them but also make use of them for learning English. I will try to practice what I learnt today in my school. [audio-recorded]

Thus, it appeared that, presented with the demonstration of phonological awareness through various tasks, the teachers generally came to realise its importance for their pupils presumably based on their own English learning experience. On the other hand, many of them said that it would be too demanding for them to teach phonological awareness because they had had no special training before, and this also suggests the necessity of providing teachers more training opportunities in this field.

5.1.4. Problems related to the instruction — RQ-D

As the intervention progressed, the instructor felt more confidence in the children's potential to develop phonological awareness and early English reading. However, at the same time, it was also realised that there might be some difficulty, or issues, in introducing such an instruction straightaway into current FLA. Below, the reasons for this assumption will be given from two perspectives that could be related to the effectiveness of the phonological awareness instruction in FLA.

The delivery of the instruction
　　The more children there are in one classroom, the more diverse characteristics which could affect the instruction there may be. In fact, how to deal with those 32 children with a variety of English-learning backgrounds was one of the difficulties the instructor felt throughout the intervention. For example, during a chorus reading, she ran her eye over the children to see how confidently they were making a sound of each letter or word. However, honestly, it was almost impossible to do so while some children with ability were leading the chorus at their pace. She focused on the children who appeared to be struggling, but different children would have difficulty at different points. Similarly, she recorded the following in RJ, referring to the difference in the extent of children's participation in sessions:

> The instructional content was relatively easy for the children in Group A, who shouted the correct answer for my question while other children were still thinking. Even when I told them not to say an answer but wait until I called a name of a child who was to answer, boys couldn't stop it. What is worse, it appears that my asking them not to say an answer discourages the children who can work out an answer by themselves. In contrast, most children in Group B and C, especially those who are slow learners, are not willing to say an answer even when asked to do so. They get nervous as they have less confidence in their answers. I've decided to join these children and do a task together, but it is very difficult to do this for all individual children within a limited amount of time in each session. [RJ17]

The author gradually came to agree with the earlier findings that phonological awareness could be better instructed in a smaller group than in a big classroom like mine (Bus & van IJzendoorn, 1999; Ehri et al., 2001) because, in a small group, an instructor could make sure that all individual children understood and articulated sounds correctly at a time, on the spot, and adjust the instructional content according to their pace and levels. However, in the current Japanese education system, the number of children per class has been decided to be 'fewer than 35.' Therefore, in order to introduce the phonological awareness instruction into current Japanese elementary school classes, it should be considered in advance how to minimise a negative effect of this relatively large number of children. Some possible suggestions might be, as practised in the intervention, to ask for the help of the HRT or the assistant teachers walking around in the classroom to check the understanding of children who are slow learners, and to offer frequent short-time revision opportunities using the period for morning or classroom activities, in addition to the regular session periods. By doing so, it would become possible for teachers to identify who could correctly say target sounds and who could not, and for children to deepen their understanding of the instructional content.

Hence, it may seem that, if a small class is easier for checking the children's development, tutoring would be more effective as the delivery of the instruction is one to one (Bloom, 1984; Cohen, Kulik, & Kulik, 1982; Pinnell, Lyons, DeFord, Bryk, & Seltzer, 1994; Wasik & Slavin, 1993). However, considering the enjoyment of pair or small-group activities in which children could be encouraged by their peers as observed in the current intervention, the small group instruction also seems to have its own advantage (Blachman et al., 1994; Williams, 1980).

The teaching materials

In order to introduce the instruction of phonological awareness and early reading systematically in FLA, it is also necessary to use or develop materials suitable for this purpose. During the intervention, considering that the phonological awareness instruction in L1 generally begins after children have developed enough oral word recognition ability (Blachman et al., 2000; Blackman & Tangel, 2008; Haager, Dimino, & Windmueller, 2007), it was originally intended to introduce the target content using the words from *Eigo Note 1* as a recommended material for FLA because they were familiar with the children. However, since this textbook was not designed for developing children's English literacy skills, the number of words which are phonologically regular (i.e., words which can be pronounced simply by blending the target letter sounds) or could be used for demonstrating the target spelling rules was very small. As a result, the instructor had to introduce the children some new words to be used for the succeeding phonological awareness instruction by means of picture cards. In these cases, not all children seemed to be able to learn their meaning on the spot. Thus, so that the phonological awareness instruction would be well incorporated into FLA, the revision of the current materials might be necessary in the future.

However, there was an unexpected finding from the observation of the children during sessions that most of them showed tolerance for ambiguity in word meaning while they were practicing phonological awareness skills. That is, they could enjoy blending, deleting, and manipulating constituent phonemes of a word whose meaning they did not seem to have fully understood. Nevertheless, with an aid of picture cards, most children could practice performing target phonological awareness skills just like they were doing a mechanical drill of manipulating sounds in orally-presented unfamiliar words. In other words, they seemed to be enjoying the change in the sound of *not* a resulting meaningful real word *but* a meaningless sound combination after manipulating its constituent phoneme. This is a unique finding because none of the previous EFL studies has considered children's attitudes toward working with unfamiliar words in the phonological awareness instruction. Thus, the author also came to think that it might be acceptable to use unknown words for the practice of sound manipulation under EFL condition as long as the children could enjoy it as a drill. This point seems to be worthy of further research for justification.

The dispute about the assessment

As we have seen earlier, children are not officially assessed in the current FLA and only the HRT's comments on their attitudes and participation in sessions are to be reported. Again, this is for preventing children from being forced to cram knowledge and rules about English in FLA so that they could enjoy communication in English.

However, as discussed above based on the current observation, avoiding assessment could decrease children's motivation and interests in learning English. Regarding this, the HRT said to the instructor, one day after the final assessment [audio-recorded], "You know? After they [the children] were given the individual test ... that interview style of ... and the written test, they got motivated to do revision activities." She referred to the change in the children's attitude as being due to both the written and the oral tests that had been administered as the final assessment before then. Not wanting to make the children feel pressurised through the assessment was one of the most important things the instructor had to be careful about during the intervention. Then, listening to the HRT, she thought that the assessment might be included in the FLA curriculum so that it would motivate them to learn what they were taught in sessions. In fact, after the oral test, some children came to the instructor and said, "That test was very difficult!" or "I couldn't work well on the test," but almost all of them further continued, "I want to try it once more," or "Can you let me do it again?" [RJ for the final assessment]

Moreover, as frequently mentioned in Chapter 5 in relation to the children's reactions to the worksheet activities, many of the children became excited about the test-like activities in which they had to work on the tasks on their own and showed more concentration than in other pair- or group-work activities. This might be another characteristic of Japanese children who have been educated in "a classical approach to learning that places an emphasis on basic knowledge accumulation and testing" (Gordon, 2010, p. 26). Thus, as far as the reactions of the children in this intervention are concerned, it may be claimed that we might not need to worry about the negative influence of the assessment at the present extent.

5.1.5. The learnability and teachability of phonological awareness

One of the primary aims of this study was to see if the children could develop phonological awareness and then apply it to early word reading through the instruction. The significant increase in the children's mean scores in the word reading test may serve as confirming evidence that the children could benefit from the interventional instruction. In other words, the results from the intervention demonstrated that the fifth-graders who participated in the intervention were able to develop early English reading, which seems to have been avoided in Japanese elementary schools for various negative reasons, on the basis of phonological awareness and letter sound knowledge which could also be acquired through the instruction in an incorporated manner. Thus, the learnability of phonological awareness and early English reading was demonstrated in this study.

On the other hand, the results bear out the teachability of phonological awareness to Japanese fifth-graders in FLA. The instruction of phonological awareness usually takes 10 or 15 minutes in each session and needs to be continuously offered for a certain length of period until children come to adopt it to other skills such as reading and spelling. Therefore, by maintaining a balance between regular curricular activities and the content for teaching phonological awareness or making use of the periods for morning and classroom activities, the current intervention demonstrated that phonological awareness could be taught in the current elementary school curriculums. However, in order to introduce it systematically into more elementary schools, it seems necessary to design further materials and communicative activities that would be suitable for the school system and children's characteristics in Japan as well as the EFL context.

5.2. Summary

This chapter discussed the important findings of the present study and considered their significance with reference to individual research questions. It also points out possible contributions the findings of this research make to the future practice of FLA. In the intervention, the participating Japanese children had some difficulty in developing phonological awareness necessary for learning to read in English but showed the sign of its sophistication at the end. Thus, considering the outcomes of the instruction as well as the children's affective reactions to it, it was claimed that phonological awareness could be effectively taught to the Japanese fifth-graders in FLA although the development of materials and methodology specifically for this purpose would be necessary. Moreover, the characteristics of the children's developing phonological awareness suggest the indispensability of explicitly teaching phonological awareness at the early stage of English learning, in order to minimise the influence of their L1 phonology and orthography.

Chapter 6

Conclusion

The notion of this study originally originated from the author's own experience of having been asked *whether or not* or *how* letters should be used in English classes by several Japanese elementary school teachers. How to respond to the teachers' question as to whether letters and literacy-related activities do not have to be introduced into FLA simply because it aims to "form the foundation of pupils communication abilities … familiarizing pupils with the sounds and basic expressions of foreign languages" (*The Course of Study*) was the main concern.

In this conclusion chapter, the important findings of this research will be restated. Following the consideration of the significance and the contributions of this research, some theoretical and practical implications for the research on early EFL literacy development and Japanese elementary school English education will be proposed. Furthermore, the limitations of this research and the recommendations for the future research directions will be considered.

6.1. Main findings of this study

The following are the significant findings of this study:

1. The data from the intervention demonstrated that the characteristics affected by phonology and orthography of Japanese as L1 can be recognised in phonological awareness of Japanese children learning English.
2. The intervention illuminated the effectiveness of the phonological aware-

ness instruction incorporated into the letter instruction for Japanese elementary school children from both qualitative and quantitative perspectives. The data underpinned the *learnability* of phonological awareness for Japanese fifth-graders as well as the *teachability* of phonological awareness in FLA.

Indeed, the scarcity of published research which is based on empirical data about English teaching practices in Japanese elementary schools in terms of letter use and early reading instruction has prompted the author to carry out the intervention. In observing FLA classrooms, there appeared to be no standard for how much children's attention should be drawn on early literacy skills, and most teachers only showed the spellings of the words on the picture cards with no focused instruction. Thus, it was claimed that this lack of guidelines for teaching letters and literacy skills would have caused the confusion among teachers, some of whom expressed positive beliefs about the introduction of English literacy into Japanese elementary schools (Ikeda, 2013).

The theoretical and practical suggestions of this study will be proposed in the following sections.

6.2. Theoretical implications

The result that several characteristics specific to Japanese phonology and orthography can be recognised in the phonological awareness of Japanese children learning English adds to the existing literature on the theories on the development of phonological awareness in a second or foreign language.

First, Japanese children seemed to have developed the onset of the higher-level *phonemic* awareness as their natural cognitive development. Their knowledge about *Roma-ji* learnt in the previous grade might be related to the sophistication of their phonological awareness because some children attempted to read English words referring to this knowledge.

Second, whereas most children generally could *imitate and repeat* individual phoneme sounds accurately and many were even able to segment an English CVC word into three sounds, the consonant sounds they *spontaneously made* in the sound manipulation tasks tended to be followed by a vowel sound (i.e., vowel epenthesis). That is, they seemed to be able to *recognise* consonant sounds correctly but had difficulty in *pronouncing* them accurately without inserting an epenthetic vowel after them. This might be natural in terms of the phonological development of Japanese children

(Mazuka et al., 2011), but will certainly cause difficulty in their literacy acquisition in English.

In addition, in contrast to English-speaking children, Japanese children found the manipulation of the word-final phoneme easier than the word-initial phoneme presumably due to the lack of the intrasyllabic onset-rime unit in Japanese phonology as well as their moraic speech segmentation enhanced by the acquisition of Japanese *kana* characters.

Finally, as for the task difficulty of segmenting and blending, while segmenting is considered to be more challenging for English L1 children who are mostly first or second-graders, it was observed that both tasks were generally doable for the participating Japanese fifth-graders. Furthermore, regarding the influence of target sounds on the task difficulty, while it has been demonstrated that voiceless plosives and voiceless fricatives are difficult for English children to segment, many Japanese children found these sounds difficult to blend but could segment them adding an unnecessary epenthetic vowel sound after them.

Actually, it was possible to assume, based on the previous research, that the fact that the most important phonological unit in Japanese is a mora would have some influence on Japanese children's sound manipulation in English whose smallest sound unit is a phoneme. The theoretical significance of this study was that concrete examples of this influence were obtained from the data on the children's performance in phonological awareness tasks. Moreover, it can be argued that the results also suggest the theoretical hypothesis of the development of phonological awareness by Japanese children learning English proposed in Section 2.6.2.2, in which the acquisition of *kana* characters contributes to enhancing the moraic segmentation and the *Roma-ji* learning may promote the early development of phonemic awareness.

6.3. Practical implications

The aforementioned manifestation of L1-specific characteristics in the developing phonological awareness of Japanese children learning English seems to support the necessity of introducing phonological awareness instruction in the early stages of English language teaching in Japan for preventive purposes. In this way, the current research gave some practical support for the future introduction of literacy-related skills such as letters and early reading into Japanese elementary school English education.

First, written skills, specifically early reading, could be introduced in addition to spoken skills in FLA. The present study found that, whereas FLA focuses on developing the ability for oral communication, the diversity of the children's exposure to English written skills outside school affected their interests in learning not only these skills but also English learning in general. As a result, the children who had little experience in reading and writing English tended to express negative attitudes toward or anxiety for learning literacy skills, and their general achievement in FLA was lower than the other children. Delaying the introduction of reading and writing until junior-high school English education would lead to widening the gap between these children. Thus, if FLA tries to avoid producing children who dislike English learning, the instructional content needs to be selected so that children would be able to demonstrate an equal level of *readiness* for learning English at the entrance of junior-high school where English begins to be taught as a proper subject in the current Japanese education system. The early reading instruction seems to be essential for this purpose, and the intervention demonstrated the positive outcome of its instruction for Japanese fifth-graders.

Second, regarding the most important claim in this study, before the sudden introduction of early reading into FLA, it is important to ensure that children have developed adequate levels of phonological awareness as a potential precursor to learning to read in English. Whereas English requires multiple levels of phonological awareness such as phonemic, onset-rime, and syllable awareness, Japanese speakers cannot be expected to fully develop them spontaneously as they become fluent in their L1. Therefore, phonological awareness needs to be taught intensively, ideally before encouraging reading words and sentences. The information obtained from the current intervention suggested that the fifth-graders were able to develop sophisticated phonological awareness gradually through instruction.

The above point leads to the methodological suggestion that a possible way to introduce letters in Japanese elementary school English education is to incorporate this instruction into phonological awareness instruction. Only making children memorise the shapes and names of individual letters does not seem to develop into the advanced skills of reading and writing, and children may soon find it monotonous. Therefore, the introduction of letters in relation to the phonological awareness in view of the subsequent English reading development will be another important proposal for the future of Japanese elementary school English education.

Moreover, the necessity of teacher training has been realised so that elementary school teachers would have more confidence in teaching early reading as well as enhanced phonological awareness to children. Through the training, teachers would be able to use a wider variety of activities or tasks in FLA. In addition, even the same task could also be taught in a more effective way: The author once observed an English class in a Japanese junior-high school. In that class, the teacher asked students to connect two separate spelling components of a word in order to make one real word and read it aloud. For example, students were presented with a card of *ha* and another of *t*, blended them together, and then sounded out a word *hat*. What should be noted is that the target CVC word was divided in two just after the initial CV combination, presumably under the influence of Japanese phonological unit, a mora. However, if the teacher had had the knowledge about the onset-rime unit which plays an important role in English speech segmentation, she might have divided the word at a different point. That is, as in the sessions of the present intervention, the division can be better made between the initial consonant (i.e., onset) and the rest of the word (i.e., rime) (e.g., *h-at*). In this way, by acquiring good knowledge about teaching English literacy to young children, teachers may come to be able to change an activity which might have been used unintentionally before into a better technique to enhance children's awareness of English phonology.

Finally, the session plans for teaching phonological awareness and early English reading to Japanese fifth-graders that were developed and carried out in the current intervention could be used also in other elementary school English classes. Adding necessary modifications on the basis of the future research findings, these plans will be a model in making a more systematic programme to teach these skills to Japanese children. Then, as to the methodology of teaching phonological awareness to children in the current Japanese elementary school education system, the use of *invented spelling* (i.e., to ask children to express words they hear with letters) could be helpful in checking individual phoneme sounds made by children. It was noted in Section 4.2.4 that, due to the relatively large class size in the Japanese elementary school, it seems difficult to pay attention to each child's pronunciation of the target phonemes or words in a short session period. What was most troubling was the case in which a child did not realise his or her phoneme sounded like a CV combination. In other words, it is assumed that there were some children who might not able to articulate or pronounce a certain English phoneme accurately but could represent it with the right orthographic symbol (i.e., letter) based on their very limited knowledge of grapheme-phoneme correspondence.

Referring to the advantage of *invented spelling*, it has been posited that it follows a predictable developmental sequence and exhibit regularities because their reliance of different levels of phonological and orthographic knowledge is reflected in developmentally common spelling errors (Caravolas, Kesseler, Hulme, & Snowling, 2005; Ehri, 2000; Frith, 1985; Henderson, 1990; Ritchey, Coker, & McCraw, 2010; Treiman, 2004; Weinrich & Fay, 2007). Especially with regard to emerging phonological awareness, it has been argued that a simple spelling measure may be more sensitive to it than many oral language tests because the attempts to *invent* spellings encourage children to use concrete representations of phonemes with letters to think about the sounds in words (Jongejan, Verhoeven, & Siegel; 2007; Mann, Tobin, & Wilson, 1987; Wagner, Torgesen, Rashotte, Hecht, Barker, Burgess, Donahue, & Garon, 1997). From the synchronic point of view, phonological awareness probably plays a central role in spelling in alphabetical languages whether it is in L1 (Bruck & Treiman, 1990; Caravolas, Hulme, & Snowling, 2001; McBride-Chang, 1998, 1999; Ouellette & Sénéchal, 2008a, 2008b) or in L2 (Chiappe, Siegel, & Gottardo, 2002; Chiappe, Siegel, & Wade-Woolley, 2002; He & Wang, 2009; Lipka & Siegel, 2007; McBride-Chang, Cho, Liu, Wagner, Shu, Zhou, Cheuk, & Muse, 2005; Temple et al., 1993, Wade-Wooolley & Siegel, 1997), and invented spelling measures would provide a window into children's developing phonological and orthographic processing skills as well as their knowledge of the alphabet in a particular stage (Frost, 2001; Rathvon, 2004; Tangel & Blachman, 1992, 1995; Torgesen & Davies, 1996). As Read (1975) had already speculated in his pioneering study on invented spelling, "children's spelling has an important kinaesthetic component, that its segmentation corresponds to felt gestures" (p. 57). In other words, children's early spelling attempts reflect the way they feel or sound target words in their mouths. Thus, by utilising this tool of *invented spelling*, a difficulty specific to Japanese education system might be overcome to a certain extent.

6.4. Limitations and future directions

There are some limitations that need to be acknowledged in this study. First, with the research design based on the exploratory interpretive paradigm, the present intervention did not set up a control group, and the findings are essentially suggestive but not conclusive. Future experimental designs aiming to compare the outcome of the instruction with the children's natural cognitive development can help to make the claims more convincing. There is another issue of how far the current findings could be generalised. However, considering the target school's in-house English curriculum following the guidelines for FLA as well as its regional characteristics reflected in the diverse English learning background among the children, it may be argued that the sample of participating children was indicative of the general population of public elementary school children in Japan.

Next, the intervention did not include the perspective of longitudinal observation on not only the children's phonological awareness development but also the long-term effect of the instruction. Although the children could enhance phonological awareness but not so much ability for word reading through the intervention whose length was originally determined to be seven months, they might have been able to demonstrate more sophistication of phonemic awareness and even better early reading performance if more instruction could be conducted. However, to carry out the intervention over two sequential grades was virtually impossible in the present study because the children were to be placed in different classes in Grade 6. Since the phonological awareness instruction has been demonstrated to contribute to the subsequent reading development in L1 (Goswami & Bryant, 1990; Snow, Burns, & Griffin, 1998; Perfetti et al., 1987; Stanovich, 1986), the research design extending over both elementary school and junior-high school English education will be needed in order to investigate the advantage of teaching phonological awareness in Japanese EFL environment by assessing the children's reading skill in junior-high school.

6.5. Concluding statement

The fact that an exploratory intervention was carried out in the real classrooms led to the uniqueness and significance of the present study. To be honest, carrying out the intervention to teach not only phonological awareness but also how to apply it to early English reading in an elementary school in Japan, where the research on introducing written skills in FLA is at present considered taboo, was a difficult challenge for the author that required a lot of courage. Although the L1 literature on early English reading seemed to imply the indispensability of developing phonological awareness for Japanese children learning English to avoid the possible L1 influence on their English reading acquisition, the most important thing was to make sure that Japanese elementary school children would be able to increase the awareness and enjoy this instruction in the current FLA. Therefore, it was such a precious opportunity that the author still profoundly appreciates the understanding and cooperation of the teachers and children in the school. As is known, FLA commenced in 2011 and, as the *Course of Study* is revised about every ten years, it will continue for at least another eight years. The claims and suggestions that have been made from this study should be taken seriously and be considered for the future of Japanese elementary school English education.

After Session 21 in the intervention, the author had an opportunity to interview one teacher who used to be a junior high school English teacher but transferred to the elementary school to take charge of ECA. She said, "I wonder why in elementary school we are not allowed to tell children to write simple English words ten times each in order to memorise them, although we can do so in junior high school. The *Course of Study* says that we should not. But children won't learn English words and expressions if they are not told to learn them by heart." [audio-recorded] To continue, a dilemma was noted that she was in a dilemma as to whether teachers should strictly follow the guidelines for FLA announced by MEXT considering the confusion in classrooms. It seems obvious that children should make some efforts to learn English because it is not realistic for them to acquire it naturally in EFL classes at school in Japan. Thus, only making children have fun and familiarised with English without its systematic and explicit instruction may be more likely to produce children who feel that they are not good at English. Then, if some teachers have realised the potential of introducing letters or early reading into their English classes, nothing entitles them from stopping. It is the teachers' beliefs about what children need to learn that may promote effective curriculum reform.

The success of curriculum reform by introducing new instructional content should depend on the teachers' beliefs about the importance and significance of learning this content for children. Teachers would overcome the difficulty in teaching if an adequate number of opportunities for teacher training are provided. Moreover, the learning demand for children would be lowered by devising methods and materials. As a researcher who claims the necessity of teaching phonological awareness in view of the instruction of letters and subsequent early literacy in English language teaching in the Japanese school system, the author would like to take a positive attitude toward it in the future reform of national curriculm based on what has been discussed in this book. The teachability of phonological awareness in FLA as well as its learnability for the elementary school children, as demonstrated in the present study, makes for persuasive evidence.

References

Abercrombie, D. (1967). *Elements of general phonetics.* Edinburgh, UK: Edinburgh University Press.

Adams, M. J. (1990). *Beginning to read: Thinking and learning about print.* Cambridge, MA: The MIT Press.

Adams, M. J., Foorman, B. R., Lundberg, I., & Beeler, T. (1998). *Phonemic awareness in young children: A classroom curriculum.* Baltimore, MD: Paul H. Brookes Publishing.

Adins, A., & Nunes, T. (2001). The role of different levels of phonological awareness in the development of reading and spelling in Greek. *Reading and Writing: An Interdisciplinary Journal, 14,* 145–177.

Akita, K., & Hatano, G. (1999). Learning to read and write in Japanese. In M. Harris, & G. Hatano (Eds.), *Learning to read and write: Cross-linguistic perspectives* (pp. 214–238). Cambridge, England: Cambridge University Press.

Allem-Tamai, M., Tsukada, T., & Ogawa, H. (2001). Analysis of English activities in a public elementary school (1). *Journal of Bunkyo Gakuin University, 3,* 1, 87–99.

Amano, K. (1986). Acquisition of phonemic analysis and literacy in children. *The Annual Report of Educational Psychology in Japan, 27,* 142–164.

Anderson, S. R. (1985). *Phonology in the twentieth century: Theories of rules and representations.* Chicago, IL: University of Chicago Press.

Anthony, J. L., & Francis, D. J. (2005). Development of phonological awareness. *Current Directions in Psychological Science, 14,* 5, 255–259.

Anthony, J. L., & Lonigan, C. J. (2004). The nature of phonological awareness: Converging evidence from four studies of preschool and early grade school children. *Journal of Educational Psychology, 96,* 1, 43–55.

Anthony, J. L., Lonigan, C. J., Burgess, S. R., Driscoll, K., Phillips, B. M., & Cantor, B. G. (2002). Structure of preschool phonological sensitivity: Overlapping sensitivity to rhyme, words, syllables, and phonemes. *Journal of Experimental Child Psychology, 82*, 65–92.

Anthony, J. L., Lonigan, C. J., Driscoll, K., Phillips, B. M., & Burgess, S. R. (2003). Phonological sensitivity: A quasi-parallel progression of word structure units and cognitive operations. *Reading Research Quarterly, 38*, 4, 470–487.

Anthony, J. L., Williams, J. M., Aghara, R. G., Dunkelberger, M., Novak, B., & Mukherjee, A. D. (2010). Assessment of individual differences in phonological representation. *Reading and Writing, 23*, 8, 969–994.

Archangeli, D., & Langendoen, L. D. (1997). *Optimality theory: An overview.* Oxford, England: Blackwell.

Asai, A., & Mihara, M. (1999). Letter instruction in elementary school English education: A case study of Nagahara elementary school (*Shōgakkō eigo kyōiku ni okeru moji shidou: Nagahara syōgakkō no kēsu sutadī*). *Shikoku Eigo Kyōiku Gakkai Kiyō, 19*, 21–35.

Babbie, E. R. (1990). *Survey research methods* (2nd ed.). Belmont, CA: Wadsworth Publishing.

Ball, E. W., & Blachman, B. A. (1991). Does phoneme awareness training in kindergarten make a difference in early word recognition and developmental spelling? *Reading Research Quarterly, 26*, 1, 49–66.

Baron, J. (1977). Mechanisms for pronouncing printed words: Use and acquisition. In L. Laberge, & S. J. Samuels (Eds.), *Basic processes in reading: Perception and comprehension* (pp. 175–216). Hillsdale, NJ: Erlbaum.

Barron, R. W. (1986). Word recognition in early reading: A review of the direct and indirect access hypothesis. *Cognition, 24*, 93–119.

Bialystok, E., Majumder, S., & Martin, M. M. (2003). Developing phonological awareness: Is there a bilingual advantage? *Applied Psycholinguistics, 24*, 27–44.

Blachman, B. A. (1991). Phonological awareness: Implications for pre-reading and early reading instruction. In S. A. Brady, & D. P. Shankweiler (Eds.), *Phonological processing in literacy* (pp. 29–36). Hillsdale, NJ: Lawrence Erlbaum.

Blachman, B. A. (Ed.). (1997). *Foundation of reading acquisition and dyslexia.* Mahwah, NJ: Lawrence Erlbaum Associates.

Blachman, B. A., Ball, E. W., Black, R. S., & Tangel, D. M. (1994). Kindergarten teachers develop phoneme awareness in low-income, inner-city classrooms: Does it make a difference? *Reading and Writing: An Interdisciplinary Journal, 6*, 1–17.

Blachman, B. A., Ball, E. W., Black, R., & Tangel, D. M. (2000). *Road to the code: A phonological awareness program for young children.* Balimore, MD: Paul H. Brookes.

Blachman, B. A., & Tangel, D. M. (2008). *Road to reading: A program for preventing and remediating reading difficulties.* Baltimore, MD: Paul H. Brookes.

Blaiklock, K. E. (2004). The importance of letter knowledge in the relationship between phonological awareness and reading. *Journal of Research in Reading, 27*, 36–57.

Bloom, B. (1984). The 2 sigma problem: The search for methods of group instruction as effective as one-to-one tutoring. *Educational Researcher, 13*, 6, 4–16.

Bloomfield, L. (1933). *Language*. New York, NY: H. Holt & Company.

Borg, S. (1998). Talking about grammar in the foreign language classroom. *Language Awareness, 7*, 159–175.

Borg, S. (2003). Teacher cognition in language teaching: A review of research on what language teachers think, know, believe, and do. *Language Teaching, 36*, 81–109.

Borg, S. (2006). *Teacher cognition and language education: Research and practice*. London, England: Continuum.

Borg, S. (2009). Introducing language teacher cognition. Retrieved from http://www.education.leeds.ac.uk/people/staff.php?staff=29

Bos, C., Mather, N., Dickson, S., Podhajski, B., & Chard, D. (2001). Perceptions and knowledge of preservice and inservice educators about early reading instruction. *Annals of Dyslexia, 51*, 97–120.

Bouwmeester, S., van Rijen, E. H. M., & Sijtsma, K. (2011). Understanding phoneme segmentation performance by analyzing abilities and word properties. *European Journal of Psychological Assessment, 27*, 2, 95–102.

Bowey, J. A. (1994). Phonological sensitivity in novice readers and nonreaders. *Journal of Experimental Child Psychology, 58*, 134–159.

Bowey, J. A. (2002). Reflections on onset-rime and phoneme sensitivity as predictors of beginning word reading. *Journal of Experimental Child Psychology, 82*, 29–40.

Bowey, J. A., & Francis, J. (1991). Phonological analysis as a function of age and exposure to reading instruction. *Applied Psycholinguistics, 12*, 91–121.

Bowey, J. A., Vaugham, L., & Hansen, J. (1998). Beginning readers' use of orthographic analogies in word reading. *Journal of Experimental Child Psychology, 28*, 2, 108–133.

Bradley, L. (1988). Making connections in learning to read and to spell. *Applied Cognitive Psychology, 2*, 3–18.

Bradley, L., & Bryant, P. E. (1983). Categorizing sounds and learning to read: A causal connection. *Nature, 301*, 419–421.

Brady, S. A., & Shankweiler, D. P. (Eds.). (1991). *Phonological processing in literacy*. Hillsdale, NJ: Lawrence Erlbaum.

Brady, S., Gillis, M., Smith, T., Lavalette, M. E., Liss-Bronstein, L., Lowe, E., North, W., Russo, E., & Wilder, T. D. (2009). First grade teachers' knowledge of phonological awareness and code concepts: Examining gains from an intensive form of professional development and corresponding teacher attitudes. *Reading and Writing, 22*, 4, 425–455.

Breen, M. P., Hird, B., Milton, M., Oliver, R., & Thwaite, A. (2001). Making sense of language teaching: Teachers' principles and classroom practice. *Applied Linguistics, 22*, 4, 470–501.

Brown, G. D., & Deavers, R. P. (1999). Units of analysis in non-word reading: Evidence from children and adults. *Journal of Experimental Child Psychology, 73*, 208–242.

Bruck, M., & Genesee, F. (1995). Phonological awareness in young second language learners. *Journal of Child Language, 22*, 307–324.

Bruck, M., & Treiman, R. (1990). Phonological awareness and spelling in normal children and dyslexics: The case of initial consonant clusters. *Journal of Experimental Child Psychology, 50*, 156–178.

Bryant, P. (1998). Sensitivity to onset and rhyme does predict young children's reading: A comment on Muter, Hulme, Snowling, and Taylor (1997). *Journal of Experimental Child Psychology, 71*, 29–37.

Bryant, P. E., Bradley, L., Maclean, M., & Crossland, J. (1989). Nursery rhymes, phonological skills and reading. *Journal of Child Language, 16*, 407–428.

Bryant, P. E., Maclean, M., Bradley, L., & Crossland, J. (1990). Rhyme, alliteration, phoneme detection and learning to read. *Developmental Psychology, 26*, 3, 429–438.

Bryman, A. (2006). Integrating quantitative and qualitative research: How is it done? *Qualitative Research, 6*, 1, 97–113.

Bryman, A. (2008). *Social research methods* (3rd ed.). Oxford, England: Oxford University Press.

Burgess, S. R. (2002). The influence of speech perception, oral language ability, the home literacy environment, and pre-reading knowledge on the growth of phonological sensitivity: A one-year longitudinal investigation. *Reading and Writing, 15*, 7–8, 709–737.

Burgess, S. R., & Lonigan, C. J. (1998). Bidirectional relations of phonological sensitivity and prereading abilities: Evidence from a preschool sample. *Journal of Experimental Child Psychology, 70*, 117–141.

Bus, A. G., & van IJzendoorn, M. H. (1999). Phonological awareness and early reading: A meta-analysis of experimental training studies. *Journal of Educational Psychology, 91*, 3, 403–414.

Butler-Goto, Y. (2005). *English language education in Japanese elementary school: Analysis and suggestions based on East Asian perspectives.* Tokyo: Sanseido.

Byrne, B. (1996). The learnability of the alphabetic principle: Children's initial hypotheses about how print represents spoken language. *Applied Psycholinguistics, 17*, 401–426.

Byrne, B. (1998). *The foundation of literacy: The child's acquisition of the alphabetic principle.* East Sussex, England: Psychology Press.

Byrne, B., & Fielding-Barnsley, R. (1989). Phonemic awareness and letter knowledge in the child's acquisition of the alphabetic principle. *Journal of Educational Psychology, 81*, 3, 313–321.

Byrne, B., & Fielding-Barnsley, R. (1991). Evaluation of a program to teach phonemic awareness to young children. *Journal of Educational Psychology, 83*, 4, 451–455.

Byrne, B., & Fielding-Barnsley, R. (1993). Evaluation of a program to teach phonemic awareness to young children: A 1-year follow-up. *Journal of Educational Psychology, 85*, 1, 104–111.

Byrne, B., & Fielding-Barnsley, R. (1995). Evaluation of a program to teach phonemic awareness to young children: A 2- and 3-year follow-up and a new preschool trial. *Journal of Educational Psychology, 87*, 3, 488–503.

Byrne, B., Fielding-Barnsley, R., & Ashley, L. (2000). Effects of preschool phoneme identity training after six years: Outcome level distinguished from rate of response. *Journal of Educational Psychology, 92*, 4, 659–667.

Campbell, R., & Sais, E. (1995). Accelerated metalinguistic (phonological) awareness in bilingual children. *British Journal of Developmental Psychology, 13*, 61–68.

Caravolas, M., & Bruck, M. (1993). The effect of oral and written language input on children's phonological awareness: A cross-linguistic study. *Journal of Experimental Child Psychology, 55*, 1–30.

Caravolas, M., Hulme, C., & Snowling, M. J. (2001). The foundations of spelling ability: Evidence from a 3-year longitudinal study. *Journal of Memory and Language, 45*, 751–774.

Caravolas, M., Kesseler, B., Hulme, C., & Snowling, M. (2005). Effects of orthographic consistency, frequency, and letter knowledge on children's vowel spelling development. *Journal of Experimental Child Psychology, 92*, 307–321.

Carreira, J. M. (2006). Motivation for learning English as a foreign language in Japanese elementary schools. *JALT Journal, 28*, 2, 158–157.

Carroll, J. M. (2004). Letter knowledge precipitates phoneme segmentation, but not phoneme invariance. *Journal of Research in Reading, 27*, 212–225.

Carlisle, J. F., Correnti, R., Phelps, G., & Zeng, J. (2009). Exploration of the contribution of teachers' knowledge about reading to their students' improvement in reading. *Reading and Writing, 22*, 4, 457–486.

Carney, E. (1994). *A survey of English spelling*. New York, NY: Routledge.

Carroll, J. M., Snowling, M. J., Hulme, C., & Stevenson, J. (2003). The development of phonological awareness in preschool children. *Developmental Psychology, 39*, 913–923.

Carson, J., & Leki, I. (Eds.). (1993). *Reading in the composition classroom: Second language perspectives*. Boston, MA: Heinle and Heinle Publishers.

Castles, A., & Coltheart, M. (2004). Is there a causal link from phonological awareness to success in learning to read? *Cognition, 91*, 77–111.

Chafouleas, S. M., & Martens, B. K. (2002). Accuracy-based phonological awareness tasks: Are they reliable, efficient, and sensitive to growth? *School Psychology Quarterly, 17*, 2, 128–147.

Chan, A. Y. W. (2006). Strategies used by Cantonese speakers in pronouncing English initial consonant clusters: Insights into the interlanguage phonology of Cantonese ESL learners in Hong Kong. *International Review of Applied Linguistics in Language Teaching, 44*, 331–355.

Chen, X., Anderson, R. C., Li, W., Hao, M., Wu, X., & Shu, H. (2004). Phonological awareness of bilingual and monolingual Chinese children. *Journal of Educational Psychology, 96*, 142–151.

Cheung, H. (1999). Improving phonological awareness and word reading in a later learned alphabetic script. *Cognition, 70*, 1–26.

Chiappe, P., & Siegel, L. S. (1999). Phonological awareness and reading acquisition in English- and Punjabi-speaking Canadian children. *Journal of Educational Psychology, 91*, 1, 20–28.

Chiappe, P., Siegel, L. S., & Gottardo, A. (2002). Reading-related skills of kindergarteners from diverse linguistic backgrounds. *Applied Psycholinguistics, 23*, 95–116.

Chiappe, P., Siegel, L. S., & Wade-Woolley, L. (2002). Linguistic diversity and the development of reading skills: A longitudinal study. *Scientific Studies of Reading, 6*, 369–400.

Cho, J.-R., & McBride-Chang, C. (2005). Levels of phonological awareness in Korean and English: A 1-year longitudinal study. *Journal of Educational Psychology, 97*, 4, 564–571.

Chomsky, N., & Halle, M. (1968). *The sound pattern of English*. New York, NY: Harper & Row.

Cisero, C. A., & Royer, J. M. (1995). The development of cross-language transfer of phonological awareness. *Contemporary Educational Psychology, 20*, 275–303.

Clements, G. N., & Keyser, S. J. (1983). *CV phonology: A generative theory of the syllable*. Cambridge, MA: The MIT Press.

Clay, M. M. (1979). *The early detection of reading difficulties* (3rd ed.). Portsmouth, NH: Heinemann.

Cohen, P., Kulik, J., & Kulik, C. (1982). Educational outcomes of tutoring: A meta-analysis of findings. *American Educational Research Journal, 19*, 237–248.

Cohen, L., Manion, L., & Morrison, K. (2007). *Research methods in education* (6th ed.). New York, NY: Routledge.

Comeau, L., Cormier, P., Grandmaison, É., & Lacroix, D. (1999). A longitudinal study of phonological processing skills in children learning to read in a second language. *Journal of Educational Psychology, 91*, 1, 29–43.

Cook, V. (1997). Orthographic processes in L2 users. Unpublished article. Retrieved from http://homepage.ntlworld.com/vivian.c/Writings/Papers/OrthProcesses..htm

Cook, V. (1999). Teaching spelling. Unpublished article. Retrieved from http://homepage.ntlworld. com/vivian.c/Writings/Papers/TeachingSpelling.htm

Corbin, J., & Strauss, A. (2008). *Basics of qualitative research: Techniques and procedures for developing grounded theory* (3rd ed.). Thousand Oaks, CA: Sage Piblications.

Corpus, J. H., McClintic-Gilbert, M. S., & Hayenga, A. O. (2009). Within-year changes in children's intrinsic and extrinsic motivational orientations: Contextual predictors and academic outcomes. *Contemporary Educational Psychology, 34*, 154–166.

Cresswell, J. W. (2009). *Research design: Qualitative, quantitative, and mixed methods approaches*. Thousand Oaks: CA, Sage Publications.

Cummins, J. (1978). Bilingualism and the development of metalinguistic awareness. *Journal of Cross-Cultural Psychology, 9*, 2, 131–149.

Cummins, J. (1979). Linguistic interdependence and the educational development of bilingual children. *Review of Educational Research, 49*, 221–251.

Cunningham, A. (1990). Explicit vs. implicit instruction in phonemic awareness.

Journal of Experimental Child Psychology, 50, 429–444.
Cunningham, A. E., Perry, K. E., Stanovich, K. E., & Share, D. L. (2002). Orthographic learning during reading: Examining the role of self-teaching. *Journal of Experimental Child Psychology, 82,* 185–199.
Cunningham, A. E., Perry, K. E., Stanovich, K. E., & Stanovich, P. J. (2004). Disciplinary knowledge of K-3 teachers and their knowledge calibration in the domain of early literacy. *Annals of Dyslexia, 54,* 139–167.
Cunningham, A. E., & Stanovich, K. E. (1990). Assessing print exposure and orthographic processing skill in children: A quick measure of reading experience. *Journal of Educational Psychology, 82,* 4, 733–740.
Cunningham, A. E., & Stanovich, K. E. (1993). Children's literacy environments and early word recognition skills. *Reading and Writing: An Interdisciplinary Journal, 5,* 2, 193–204.
Cunningham, A. E., Zibulsky, J., & Callahan, M. D. (2009). Starting small: Building preschool teacher knowledge that supports early literacy development. *Reading and Writing, 22,* 4, 487–510.
Cutler, A., & Butterfield, S. (1992). Rhythmic cues to speech segmentation: Evidence from juncture misperception. *Journal of Memory & Language, 31,* 218–236.
Cutler, A., & Carter, D. M. (1987). The predominance of strong initial syllables in the English vocabulary. *Computer Speech & Language, 2,* 133–142.
Cutler. A., Mehler, J., Norris, D. G., & Segui, J. (1986). The syllable's differing role in the segmentation of French and English. *Journal of Memory and Language, 25,* 385–400.
Cutler, A., & Norris, D. G. (1988). The role of strong syllables in segmentation for lexical access. *Journal of Experimental Psychology: Human Perception & Performance, 14,* 113–121.
Cutler, A., & Otake, T. (1994). Mora or phoneme? Further evidence for language-specific listening. *Journal of Memory and Language, 33,* 824–844.
D'Angiulli, A., Siegel, L. S., & Serra, E. (2001). The development of reading in English and Italian bilingual children. *Applied Psycholinguistics, 22,* 479–507.
Deal, D., & White, C. S. (2006). Voices from the classroom: Literacy beliefs and practices of two novice elementary teachers. *Journal of Research in Childhood Education, 20,* 4, 313–329.
De Cara, B., & Goswami, U. (2003). Phonological neighbourhood density: Effects in a rhyme awareness task in five-year-old children. *Journal of Child Language, 30,* 695–710.
DeKeyser, R. (2000). The robustness of critical period effects in second language acquisition. *Studies in Second Language Acquisition, 22,* 4, 499–533.
DeKeyser, R. (2003). Implicit and explicit learning. In C. Doughty, & J. Williams (Eds.), *Handbook of second language acquisition* (pp. 313–349). Malden, MA: Blackwell.
DeKeyser, R. M., & Juffs, A. (2005). Cognitive considerations in L2 learning. In E. Hinkel (Ed.), *Handbook of research in second language teaching and learning* (pp. 437–454). Mahwah, NJ: Lawence Erlbaum Associates.

DeKeyser, R., & Larson-Hall, J. (2005). What does the critical period really mean? In J. Kroll, & A. De Groot (Eds.), *Handbook of bilingualism: Psycholinguistic approaches* (pp. 88–108). Oxford, England: Oxford University Press.

Denton, C. A., Hasbrouck, J. E., Weaver, L. R., & Riccio, C. A. (2000). What do we know about phonological awareness in Spanish? *Reading Psychology, 21*, 4, 335–352.

Denzin, N. K., & Lincoln, Y. S. (Eds.). (2005). *The SAGE handbook of qualitative research* (3rd ed.). Thousand Oaks, CA: Sage Publications.

Dey, I. (1993). *Qualitative data analysis: A user-friendly guide for social scientists.* London, England: Routledge.

Dodd, B. J., So, L. K. H., & Lam, K. K. C. (2008). Bilingualism and learning: The effect of language pair on phonological awareness abilities. *Australian Journal of Learning Difficulties, 13*, 2, 99–113.

Dörnyei, Z. (2007). *Research methods in applied linguistics: Quantitative, qualitative, and mixed methodologies.* Oxford, England: Oxford University Press.

Dörnyei, Z. (2009a). *Questionnaires in second language research: Construction, administration, and processing* (2nd ed.). New York, NY: Routledge.

Dörnyei, Z. (2009b). *The psychology of second language acquisition.* Oxford, England: Oxford University Press.

Dowker, A. (1989). Rhyme and alliteration in poems elicited from young children. *Journal of Child Language, 16*, 181–202.

Downing, S. M., & Haladyna, T. M. (Eds.). (2006). *Handbook of test development.* Mahwah, NJ: Erlbaum.

Durgunoğlu, A. Y., & Nagy, W. E., & Hancin-Bhatt, B. J. (1993). Cross-language transfer of phonological awareness. *Journal of Educational Psychology, 85*, 3, 453–465.

Duncan, L. G., & Johnston, R. S. (1999). How does phonological awareness relate to non-word reading amongst poor readers? *Reading and Writing: An Interdisciplinary Journal, 11*, 405–439.

Ehri, L. C. (1979). Linguistic insight: Threshold of reading acquisition. In T. Waller, & G. Mackinnon (Eds.), *Reading research: Advances in theory and practice* (pp. 63–114). New York, NY: Academic Press.

Ehri, L. C. (1998). Research on learning to read and spell: A personal-historical perspective. *Scientific Studies of Reading, 2*, 2, 97–114.

Ehri, L. C. (2000). Learning to read and learning to spell: Two sides of a coin. *Topics in Language Disorders, 20*, 3, 19–49.

Ehri, L. C. (2005). Learning to read words: Theory, findings, and issues. *Scientific Studies of Reading, 9*, 2, 167–188.

Ehri, L. C., Nunes, S. R., Willows, D. M., Schuster, B. V., Yaghoub-Zadeh, Z., & Shanahan, T. (2001). Phonemic awareness instruction helps children learn to read: Evidence from the National Reading Panel's Meta-Analysis. *Reading Research Quarterly, 36*, 3, 250–287.

Ehri, L. C., & Robbins, C. (1992). Beginners need some decoding skill to read words by analogy. *Reading Research Quarterly, 27*, 12–25.

Ehri, L. C., & Snowling, M. J. (2004). Developmental variation in word recognition. In C. Addison Stone, E. R. Silliman, B. J. Ehren, & K. Apel (Eds.), *Handbook of language and literacy development and disorders* (pp. 433–460). New York: Guilford Press.

Ehri, L. C., & Wilce, L. S. (1980). *Applied Psycholinguistics, 1*, 371–385.

Eisenstein-Ebsworth, M., & Schweers, C. W. (1997). What researchers say and practitioners do: Perspectives on conscious grammar instruction in the ESL classrooms. *Applied Language Learning, 8*, 237–260.

Ellis, R. (1994). *The study of second language acquisition.* Oxford, England: Oxford University Press.

Ellis, R. (2009). Implicit and explicit learning, knowledge and instruction. In R. Ellis, S. Loewen, C. Elder, R. Erlam, J. Philip, & H. Reinders, *Implicit and explicit knowledge in second language learning, testing and teaching* (pp. 3–25). Bristol, England: Multilingual Matters.

Engen, L., & Hoien, T. (2002). Phonological Skills and Reading Comprehension. *Reading and Writing: An Interdisciplinary Journal, 15*, 613–631.

Ernest, P. (1989). The knowledge, beliefs and attitudes of the mathematics teacher: A model. *Journal of Education for Teaching, 15*, 1, 13–33.

Fang, Z. (1996). A review of research on teacher beliefs and practices. *Educational Research, 38*, 1, 47–65.

Fielding-Barnsley, R., & Purdie, N. (2005). Teachers' attitude to and knowledge of metalinguistics in the process of learning to read. *Asia-Pacific Journal of Teacher Education, 33*, 1, 65–76.

Fletcher, J. M., Shaywitz, S. E., Shankweiler, D. P., Katz, L., Liberman, I. Y., Stuebing, K. K., Francis, D. J., & Fowler, A. E. (1994). Cognitive profiles of reading disability: Comparisons of discrepancy and low achievement definitions. *Journal of Educational Psychology, 86*, 1, 6–23.

Foorman, B. R., & Francis, D. J. (1994). Exploring connections among reading, spelling, and phonemic segmentation during first grade. *Reading and Writing, 6*, 65–91.

Fowler, F. J. (2008). *Survey research methods* (4th ed.). Thousand Oaks, CA: Sage Publications.

Foorman, B. R., Chen, D.-T., Carlson, C., Moats, L., David, J. F., & Jack, M. F. (2003). The necessity of the alphabetic principle to phonemic awareness instruction. *Reading & Writing, 16*, 289–324.

Fox, B., & Routh, D. (1975). Analyzing spoken language into words, syllables, and phonemes: A developmental study. *Journal of Psycholinguistic Research, 4*, 331–342.

Fox, B., & Routh, D. K. (1976). Phonemic analysis and synthesis as word-attack skills. *Journal of Educational Psychology, 68*, 70–74.

Freeman, D. (1993). Renaming experience/reconstructing practice: Developing new understandings of teaching. *Teaching and Teacher Education, 9*, 485–497.

Frith, U. (1985). Beneath the surface of developmental dyslexia. In K. E. Patterson, J. C. Marshall, & M. Coltheart (Eds.), *Surface Dyslexia: Neuropsychological and*

cognitive studies of phonological reading (pp. 201–220). Hillsdale, NJ: Erlbaum.
Frost, J. (2001). Phonemic awareness, spontaneous writing, and reading and spelling development from a preventive perspective. *Reading and Writing: An Interdisciplinary Journal, 14*, 487–513.
Frost, R., Katz, L., & Bentin, S. (1987). Strategies for visual word recognition and orthographical depth: A multilingual comparison. *Journal of Educational Psychology: Human Perception and Performance, 13*, 1, 104–115.
Frost, R., & Katz, L. (Eds.). (1992). *Advances in Psychology 94 Orthography, Phonology, Morphology, and Meaning*. Amsterdam, The Netherlands: North-Holland.
Fudge, E. C. (1969). Syllables. *Journal of Linguistics, 5*, 2, 253–286.
Gentry, J. R. (2000). A retrospective on invented spelling and a look forward. *The Reading Teacher, 54*, 3, 318–332.
Geudens, A., Sandra, D., & van den Broeck, W. (2004). Segmenting two-phoneme syllables: Developmental differences in relation with early reading skills. *Brain and Language, 90*, 338–352.
Geva, E., & Siegel, L. S. (2000). Orthographic and cognitive factors in the concurrent development of basic reading skills in two languages. *Reading and Writing: An Interdisciplinary Journal, 12*, 1–30.
Geva, E., & Wang, M. (2001). The development of basic reading skills in children: A cross-language perspective. *Annual Review of Applied Linguistics, 21*, 182–204.
Geva, E., Wade-Woolley, L., & Shany, M. (1997). Development of reading efficiency in first and second languages. *Scientific Studies of Reading, 1*, 119–144.
Gillon, G. T. (2004). *Phonological awareness. From research to practice*. New York, NY: Guilford Press.
Gipstein, M., Brady, S. A., & Fowler, A. E. (2000). Questioning the role of syllables and rimes in early phonological awareness. In N. Badian (Ed.), *Prediction and prevention of reading failure* (pp. 179–216). Timonium, MD: York Press.
Goetry, V., Urbain, S., Morais, J., & Kolinsky, R. (2005). Paths to phonemic awareness in Japanese: Evidence from a training study. *Applied Psycholinguistics. 26*. 285–309.
Gonzalez, J. E. J., & Garcia, D. R. H. (1995). Effects of word linguistic properties on phonological awareness in Spanish children. *Journal of Educational Psychology, 87*, 2, 193–201.
Goldstein, D. M. (1976). Cognitive-linguistic functioning and learning to read in preschoolers. *Journal of Educational Psychology, 68*, 6, 680–688.
Gordon, J. A. (2010). *Challenges to Japanese education: Economics, reform, and human rights*. New York, NY: Teachers College Press.
Goswami, U. (1993). Toward an interactive analogy model of reading development: Decoding vowel graphemes in beginning reading. *Journal of Experimental Child Psychology, 56*, 443–475.
Goswami, U. (1994). Reading by analogy: Theoretical and practical perspectives. In M. Snowling (Ed.), *Reading development and dyslexia* (pp. 18–30). London, England: Whurr.
Goswami, U. (2002). Phonology, reading development, and dyslexia: A cross-linguis-

tic perspective. *Annals of dyslexia, 52*, 141–163.

Goswami, U., & Bryant, P. (1990). *Phonological skills and learning to read.* Hillsdale, NJ: Lawrence Erlbaum Associates.

Goswami, U., Gombert, J. E., & de Barrera, L. F. (1998). Children's orthographic representations and linguistic transparency: Nonsense word reading in English, French, and Spanish. *Applied Psycholinguistics, 19*, 19–52.

Goswami, U., Porpodas, C., & Wheelwright, S. (1997). Children's orthographic representations in English and Greek. *European Journal of Psychology of Education, 3*, 273–292.

Gottardo, A., Yan, B., Siegel, L., & Wade-Woolley, L. (2001). Factors related to English reading performance in children with Chinese as a first language: More evidence of cross-language transfer of phonological processing. *Journal of Educational Psychology, 93*, 3, 530–542.

Green, D. W., & Meara, P. (1987). The effects of script on visual search. *Journal of Language Research, 3*, 102–117.

Gregory, E. (1996). *Making sense of a new world: Learning to read in a second language.* Thousand Oaks, CA: Sage Publications.

Haager, D., Dimino, J., & Windmueller, M. P. (2007). *Interventions for reading success.* Baltimore, MD: Paul H. Brookes Publishing.

Haraguchi, S. (1996). Syllable, mora and accent. In T. Otake, & A. Cutler (Eds.), *Phonological structure and language processing: Cross-linguistic studies* (pp. 45–75). New York, NY: Mouton de Gruyter.

Harter, S. (1981). A new self-report scale of intrinsic versus extrinsic orientation in the classroom: Motivational and informational components. *Developmental Psychology, 17*, 300–312.

Hatcher, P. J., Hulme, C., & Ellis, A. (1994). Ameliorating early reading failure by integrating the teaching of reading and phonology. *Child Development, 65*, 1, 41–57.

Hatcher, P. J., & Hulme, C. (1999). Phonemes, rhymes, and intelligence as predictors of children's responsiveness to remedial reading instruction: Evidence from a longitudinal study. *Journal of Experimental Child Psychology, 72*, 130–153.

Hatta, T. (1992). The effects of Kanji attributes on Kanji attributes on visual field differences: Examination with lexical decision, naming, and semantic clarification tasks. *Neuropsychologia, 30*, 361–371.

He, T., & Wang, W. (2009). Invented spelling of EFL young beginning writers and its relation with phonological awareness and grapheme-phoneme principles. *Journal of Second Language Writing, 18*, 44–56.

Helfer, K. S., & Huntley, R. A. (1991). Aging and consonant errors in reverberation and noise. *Journal of Acoustical Society of America, 90*, 1786–1795.

Henderson, E. H. (1990). *Teaching spelling* (2nd ed.). Orlando, FL: Houghton Mifflin.

Higuchi, T., Kanamori, T., & Kunikata, T. (Eds.). (2005). *Elementary school English education from now on: Theory and practice (Korekara no shōgakkō eigo kyōiku: Riron to jissen).* Tokyo: Kenkyusha.

Hindman, A. H., & Wasik, B. A. (2008). Head start teachers' beliefs about language and literacy instruction. *Early Childhood Research Quarterly*, *23*, 479-492.

Ho, C. S., & Bryant, P. (1997). Phonological skills are important in learning to read Chinese. *Developmental Psychology*, *33*, 946-951.

Høien, T., Lundberg, I., Stanovich, K. E., & Bjaalid, I. (1995). Components of phonological awareness. *Reading and Writing*, *7*, 171-188.

Huang, H. S., & Hanley, J. R. (1995). Phonological awareness and visual skills in learning to read Chinese and English. *Cognition*, *54*, 73-98.

Huang, H. S., & Hanley, J. R. (1997). A longitudinal study of phonological awareness, visual skills, and Chinese reading acquisition among first-graders in Taiwan. *Journal of Behavioral Development*, *20*, 2, 249-268.

Hulme, C., Hatcher, P. J., Nation, K., Brown, A., Adams, J., & Stuart, G. (2002). Phoneme awareness is a better predictor of early reading skill than onset-rime awareness. *Journal of Experimental Child Psychology*, *82*, 2-28.

Iizuka, N. (1997). *A book for growing up together in English (Eigo de issho ni sodatsu hon)*. Tokyo: Zenken-Honsya.

Ijima Elementary School (2003). *The report of 'English Language Activities' in Okayama-municipal Ijima Elementary School (Okayama shiritu Ijima shōgakkō 'eigo katsudō' houkokusho)*.

Ikeda, C. (2013). Teachers' beliefs and principles about the introduction of letters and early reading into Japanese elementary school English education. *The Bulletin of the Graduate School of International Cultural Studies, Aichi Prefectural University*, *14*, 1-21.

Ikeda, C. (2014). Teacher beliefs about the introduction of letters and early literacy into Foreign Language Activities: Comparative study of elementary and junior high school teachers. *Annual Review of English Language Education in Japan*, *25*, 17-32.

Imura, M. (2003). *The 200 years of English language education in Japan (Nihon no eigo kyōiku 200 nen)*. Tokyo: Taishukan.

Inagaki, K., Hatano, G., & Otake, T. (2000). The effect of kana literacy acquisition on the speech segmentation unit used by Japanese young children. *Journal of Experimental Child Psychology*, *75*, 70-91.

International Reading Association. (1988). Phonemic awareness and the teaching of reading. A position statement from the board of directors of the International Reading Association. Retrieved from http://www.reading.org/Libraries/Position_Statements_and_Resolutions/ps 1025_phonemic.sflb.ashx

Jakobson, R., & Halle, M. (1971). *Foundation of language*. The Hague: Mouton.

JASTEC Kanto-Koshinetsu Branch: Second Research Project Team. (1999). The usefulness of letters in the acquisition of English language by Japanese children. *JASTEC Journal*, *18*, 37-53.

JASTEC Kanto-Koshinetsu Branch: Second Research Project Team. (2000). The usefulness of letters in the acquisition of English language by Japanese children: Basic study version. *JASTEC Journal*, *19*, 35-44.

Johnson, K. E. (1992). The relationship between teachers' beliefs and practices during literacy instruction for non-native speakers of English. *Journal of Reading*

Behavior, *24*, 1, 83–108.
Johnston, R. S., Anderson, M., & Holligan, C. (1996). Knowledge of the alphabet and explicit awareness of phonemes in pre-readers: The nature of the relationship. *Reading and Writing*, *8*, 3, 217–234.
Jongejan, W., Verhoeven, L., & Siegel, L. S. (2007). Predictors of reading and spelling abilities in first- and second-language learners. *Journal of Educational Psychology*, *99*, 4, 835–851.
Jusczyk, P. (1992). Developing phonological categories from the speech signal. In C. Ferguson, L. Menn, & C. Stoel-Gammon (Eds.), *Phonological development: Models, research, implications* (pp. 17–64). Timonium, MD: York Press.
Jusczyk, P. W., Goodman, M. G., & Baumann, A. (1999). Nine-month-olds' attention to sound similarities in syllables. *Journal of Memory and Language*, *40*, 62–82.
Kagan, D. M. (1992). Professional growth among preservice and beginning teachers. *Review of Educational Research*, *62*, 2, 129–169.
Kager, R. (1999). *Optimality theory*. Cambridge, England: Cambridge University Press.
Kageura, M. (Ed.). (1997). *The guideline for elementary school English education (Shōgakkō eigo kyōiku no tebiki)*. Tokyo: Meiji-Tosho.
Kageura, M. (2000). *Elementary school English—Complete information on the practice of 66 schools for research development (Syōgakkō eigo—66 kenkyūkaihatsu gakkō no torikumi zenjōhō)*. Tokyo: Meiji-Tosho.
Kan, M. (2010). *Everybody can easily teach with 'Eigo Note': Grade 5 (Dare demo dekiru! 'Eigo Note' de rakuraku jugyō: 5 nensei you)*. Tokyo: Gyousei.
Kanazawa, N., & Ito, M. (2008). A survey on the attitudes of public elementary school teachers to 'English Language Activities': The ability of instructors and teacher training in elementary school English ('Eigo katsudō' ni kansuru kritsu syōgakkō kyōin no ishiki chōsa: Shōgakkō eigo no shidōsha no shishitsu to shidōsha kensyū nit suite). *JES Bulletin*, *8*, 61–68.
Katada, F. (1990). On the Representation of Moras: Evidence from a Language Game. *Linguistic Inquiry*, *21*, 4, 641–646.
Katagiri, T. (1985). The importance and methods of 'reading' instruction. *JASTEC Journal*, *4*, 13–21.
Kazama, K., Ueno, Y., Matsumura, K., & Machida, K. (2004). *Linguistics: An introduction* (2nd ed.). Tokyo: University of Tokyo Press.
Kessler, B., & Treiman, R. (1997). Syllable structure and the distribution of phonemes in English syllables. *Journal of Memory and Language*, *37*, 295–311.
Keung, Y-C., & Ho, C., S-H. (2009). Transfer of reading-related cognitive skills in learning to read Chinese (L1) and English (L2) among Chinese elementary school children. *Contemporary Educational Psychology*, *34*, 103–112.
Kim, Y. S. (2007). Phonological awareness and literacy skills in Korean: An examination of the unique role of body-coda units. *Applied Psycholinguistics*, *28*, 1, 69–94.
Kim, Y. S. (2009). Crosslinguistic influence on phonological awareness for Korean-English bilingual children. *Reading and Writing: An Interdisciplinary Journal*,

22, 843-861.
Kirtley, C., Bryant, P., MacLean, M., & Bradley, L. (1989). Rhyme, rime, and the onset of reading. *Journal of Experimental Child Psychology, 28*, 224-245.
Koda, K. (1989). Effects of L1 orthographic representation on L2 phonological coding strategies. *Journal of Psycholinguistic Research, 18*, 201-222.
Koda, K. (1998). The role of phonemic awareness in second language reading. *Second Language Research, 14*, 2, 194-215.
Koda, K. (1999). Development of L2 intraword orthographic sensitivity and decoding skills. *Modern Language Journal, 83*, 51-64.
Koda, K. (2000). Cross-linguistic variations in L2 morphological awareness. *Applied Psycholinguistics, 21*, 297-320.
Koda, K. (2008). Impacts of prior literacy experience on second-language learning to read. In K. Koda, & A. M. Zehler (Eds.), *Learning to read across languages. Cross-linguistic relationships in first- and second-language literacy development* (pp. 68-96). New York, NY: Routledge.
Kolen, M. J., & Brennan, R. L. (2004). *Test equating, scaling, and linking*. New York, NY: Springer.
Kosuga, A. (1998). From the classroom of junior high school (Chūgakkō no genba kara). *Modern English Teaching (Gendai Eigo Kyōiku), July*, 28-29.
Krashen, S, D. (1989). *Language acquisition and language education: Extensions and applications*. New York, NY: Prentice Hall.
Krashen, S. D. (2004). *The power of reading: Insights from the research* (2nd ed.). Portsmouth, NH: Heinemann.
Krashen, S, D., & Terrell, T. D. (1983). *The natural approach: Language acquisition in the classroom*. Oxford, England: Pergamon.
Kubozono, H. (1989). The mora and syllable structure in Japanese: Evidence from speech errors. *Language and Speech, 32*, 3, 249-278.
Kubozono, H. (1995). *Gokeisei to onin kouzou*. Tokyo: Kurosio Syuppan.
Kubozono, H. (1999). Mora and syllable. In N. Tsujimura (Ed.), *The handbook of Japanese linguistics* (pp. 31-61). Oxford, England: Basil Blackwell Publishing.
Kubozono, H. (2006). The phonetic and phonological organization of speech in Japanese. In M. Nakayama, R. Mazuka, & Y. Shirai (Eds.), *The handbook of east Asian psycholinguistics. Volume II: Japanese* (pp. 191-200). Cambridge, England: Cambridge University Press.
Kubozono, H., & Homma, T. (2002). *Onsetsu to mora*. Tokyo: Kenkyusha.
Kubozono, H., & Ota, S. (1998). *Phonological structure and accents*. Tokyo: Kenkyusha.
Kuno, Y. (1996). Teaching materials, learning methods, and children (Kyōzai, gakusyū hōhō to kodomo). *The English Teachers' Magazine, 45*, 8, 29-31.
Kuno, Y. (1999a). *Advice room on Child English when in trouble (Komatta toki no kodomo eigo soudan sitsu)*. (revised ed.). Tokyo: Pearson Education.
Kuno, Y. (1999b). Dos & Don'ts in early English teaching (Sōki eigo kyōiku no Dos & Don'ts). *The English Teacher's Magazine, 48*, 8, 17-19.
Kuo, L., & Anderson, R. C. (2008). Conceptual and methodological issues in com-

paring metalinguistic awareness across language. In K. Koda, & A. M. Zehler (Eds.), *Learning to read across languages. Cross-linguistic relationships in first- and second-language literacy development* (pp. 39–67). New York, NY: Routledge.

Ladd, D. R. (2011). Phonetics in Phonology. In J. A. Goldsmith, J. Riggle, & A. C. L. Yu (Eds.), *The handbook of phonological theory* (2nd ed.) (pp. 348–373). Wiley-Blackwell.

Lee, J. S., & Ginsburg, H. P. (2007). Preschool teachers' beliefs about appropriate early literacy and mathematics education for low- and middle-socioeconomic status children. *Early Education and Development, 18*, 1, 111–143.

Leong, C. K., & Haines, C. F. (1978). Beginning readers' analysis of words and sentences. *Journal of Reading Behavior, 10*, 393–407.

Lepper, M. R., & Henderlong, J. (2000). Turning "play" into "work" and "work" into "play": 25 years of research on intrinsic versus extrinsic motivation. In C. Sansone, & J. M. Harackiewicz (Eds.), *Intrinsic and extrinsic motivation: The search for optimal motivation and performance* (pp. 257–372). San Diego, CA: Academic Press.

Lepper, M. R., Corpus, J. H., & Iyengar, S. S. (2005). Intrinsic and extrinsic motivational orientations in the classroom: Age differences and academic correlates. *Journal of Educational Psychology, 97*, 2, 184–196.

Lepper, M. R., Sethi, S., Dialdin, D., & Drake, M. (1997). Intrinsic and extrinsic motivation: A developmental perspective. In S. S. Luthar, J. A. Burack, D. Cicchetti, & J. R. Weisz (Eds.), *Developmental psychology: Perspectives on adjustment, risk, and disorder* (pp. 23–50). New York: Cambridge University Press.

Lesaux, N. K., Rupp, A. A., & Siegel, L. S. (2007). Growth in reading skills of children from diverse linguistic backgrounds: Findings from a 5-year longitudinal study. *Journal of Educational Psychology, 99*, 4, 821–834.

Lewkowicz, N. K. (1980). Phonemic awareness training: What to teach and how to teach it. *Journal of Educational Psychology, 72*, 5, 686–700.

Lewkowicz, N. K., & Low, L. Y. (1979). Effects of visual aids and word structure on phoneme segmentation. *Contemporary Educational Psychology, 4*, 3, 238–252.

Liberman, I. Y. (1983). A language-oriented view of reading and its disabilities. In H. R. Myklebust (Ed.), *Progress in learning disabilities, Vol. 5* (pp. 81–101). New York, NY: Grune & Stratton.

Liberman, I. Y., Shankweiler, D., Fischer, F. W., & Carter, B. (1974). Explicit syllable and phoneme segmentation in the young child. *Journal of Experimental Child Psychology, 18*, 201–212.

Liberman, I. Y., Shankweiler, D., Liberman, A. M., Fischer, F. W., & Fowler, C. (1977). Phonetic segmentation and recording in the beginning reader. In Reber, A. S., & Scarborough, D. (Eds.). *Toward a Psychology of Reading* (pp. 207–225). Hillsdale, NJ: Lawrence Erlbaum.

Liberman, I. Y., Shankweiler, D., & Liberman, A. M. (1989). The alphabetic principle and learning to read. In D. Shankweiler, & I. Y. Liberman (Eds.), *Phonology and reading disability: Solving the reading puzzle. International academy of re-*

search on learning disabilities monograph series (pp. 1–33). Ann Arbor, MA: University of Michigan Press.

Lim, C., & Torr, J. (2007). Singaporean early childhood teachers' beliefs about literacy development in a multilingual context. *Asia-Pacific Journal of Teacher Education, 35,* 4, 409–434.

Lindsey, K. A., Manis, F. R., & Bailey, C. E. (2003). Prediction of first-grade reading in Spanish-speaking English-language learners. *Journal of Educational Psychology, 95,* 3, 482–494.

Liow, S. J. R., & Poon, K. K. L. (1998). Phonological awareness in multilingual Chinese children. *Applied Psycholinguistics, 19,* 339–362.

Lipka, O., & Siegel, L. S. (2007). The development of reading skills in children with English as a second language. *Scientific Studies of Reading, 11,* 2, 105–131.

Loizou, M., & Stuart, M. (2003). Phonological awareness in monolingual and bilingual English and Greek five-year-olds. *Journal of Research in Reading, 26,* 1, 3–18.

Lonigan, C. J., Burgess, S. R., Anthony, J. L., & Barker, T. A. (1998). Development of phonological sensitivity in two- to five-year-old children. *Journal of Educational Psychology, 90,* 294–311.

Lonigan, C. J., Burgess, S. R., & Anthony, J. L. (2000). Development of emergent literacy and early reading skills in preschool children: Evidence from a latent-variable longitudinal study. *Developmental Psychology, 26,* 5, 596–613.

Lundberg, I. L., Frost, J., & Peterson, O-L. (1988). Effects of an extensive program for stimulating phonological awareness in preschool. *Reading Research Quarterly, 23,* 3, 263–284.

Lundberg, I., Olofsson, A., & Wall, S. (1980). Reading and spelling skills in the first school years predicted from phonemic awareness skills in kindergarten. *Scandinavian Journal of Psychology, 21,* 159–173.

Lynch, J. (2009). Preschool teachers' beliefs about children's print literacy development. *Early Years, 29,* 2, 191–203.

MacCarthy, J. J. (1979). On stress and syllabification. *Linguistic Inquiry, 10,* 443–466.

Macalister, J. (2010). Investigating teacher attitudes to extensive reading practices in higher education: Why isn't everyone doing it? *RELC Journal, 41,* 1, 59–75.

MacKay, D. G. (1972). The Structure of words and syllables: Evidence from errors in speech. *Cognitive Psychology, 3,* 210–227.

Maclean, M., Bryant, P., & Bradley, L. (1987). Rhymes, nursery rhymes, and reading in early childhood. *Merrill-Palmer Quarterly, 33,* 3, 255–281.

Macmillan, B. M. (2002). Rhyme and reading: A critical review of the research methodology. *Journal of Research in Reading, 25,* 1, 4–42.

Mann, V. A. (1986). Phonological awareness: The role of reading experience. *Cognition, 24,* 65–92.

Mann, V. A. (1991). Are we talking too narrow a view of the conditions for development of phonological awareness? In S. A. Brady, & D. P. Shankweiler (Eds.), *Phonological processing in literacy* (pp. 55–64). Hillsdale, NJ: Lawrence Erlbaum.

Mann, V. A. (1993). Phoneme awareness and future reading ability. *Journal of Learning Disabilities, 26*, 4, 259–269.

Mann, V. A., & Liberman, I. Y. (1984). Phonological awareness and verbal short-term memory: Can they presage early reading problems? *Journal of Learning Disabilities, 17*, 592–599.

Mann, V. A., Tobin, P., & Wilson, R. (1987). Measuring phonological awareness through the invented spelling of kindergarten children. *Merrill-Palmer Quarterly, 33*, 3, 365–391.

Marsh, G., & Mineo, R. J. (1977). Training preschool children to recognize phonemes in words. *Journal of Educational Psychology, 69*, 748–753.

Martins, M. A., & Silva, C. (2006). The impact of invented spelling on phonemic awareness. *Learning and Instruction, 16*, 41–56.

Mather, N., Bos, C., & Babur, N. (2001). Perceptions and knowledge of preservice and inservice teachers about early literacy instruction. *Journal of Learning Disabilities, 34*, 5, 472–482.

Mazuka, R., Cao, Y., Dupoux, E., & Christophe, A. (2011). The development of a phonological illusion: A cross-linguistic study with Japanese and French infants. *Developmental Science, 14*, 4, 693–699.

McBride-Chang, C. (1995). What is phonological awareness? *Journal of Educational Psychology, 87*, 2, 179–192.

McBride-Chang, C. (1998). The development of invented spelling. *Early Education & Development, 9*, 2, 147–160.

McBride-Chang, C. (1999). The ABCs of the ABCs: The development of letter-name and letter sound knowledge. *Merill-Palmer Quarterly, 45*, 2, 285–308.

McBride-Chang, C., Bialystok, E., Chong, K. K. Y., & Li, Y. P. (2004). Levels of phonological awareness in three cultures. *Journal of Experimental Child Psychology, 89*, 93–111.

McBride-Chang, C., Cho, J-R., Liu, H., Wagner, R. K., Shu, H., Zhou, A., Cheuk, C. S-M., & Muse, A. (2005). Changing models across cultures: Associations of phonological awareness and morphological structure awareness with vocabulary and word recognition in second graders from Beijing, Hong Kong, Korea, and the United States. *Journal of Experimental Child Psychology, 92*, 140–160.

McBride-Chang, C., Tong, X., Shu, H., Wong, A. M.-Y., Leung, K., & Tardif, T. (2008). Syllable, phoneme, and tone: Psycholinguistic units in early Chinese and English word recognition. *Scientific Studies of Reading, 12*, 2, 171–194.

McCutchen, D., Abbott, R. D., Green, L. B., Beretvas, S. N., Cox, S., Potter, N. S., Quiroga, T., & Gray, A. L. (2002). Beginning literacy: Links among teacher knowledge, teacher practice, and student learning. *Journal of Learning Disabilities, 35*, 1, 69–86.

McCutchen, D., Green, L., Abbot, R. D., & Sanders, E. A. (2009). Further evidence for teacher knowledge: Supporting struggling readers in grades three through five. *Reading and Writing, 22*, 4, 401–423.

McCutchen, D., Harry, D. R., Cunningham, A. E., Cox, S., Sidman, S., & Covill, A.

E. (2002). Reading teachers' knowledge of children's literature and English phonology. *Annals of Dyslexia, 52,* 207-228.

McDonough, J., & McDonough, S. (1997). *Research methods for English language teachers.* London, England: Arnold.

McGuiness, D. (2004). *Early reading instruction: What science really tells us about how to teach reading.* Cambridge, MA: The MIT Press.

McQueen, J. M., Norris, D. G., & Cutler, A. (1994). Competition in spoken word recognition: Spotting words in other words. *Journal of Experimental Psychology: Learning, Memory & Cognition, 20,* 621-638.

Mehler, J., Dommergues, J.-Y., Frauenfelder, U., & Segui, J. (1981). The syllable's role in speech segmentation. *Journal of Verbal Learning and Verbal Behavior, 20,* 298-305.

Meijer, P. C., Verloop, N., & Beijaard, D. (1999). Exploring language teachers' practical knowledge about teaching reading comprehension. *Teaching and Teacher Education, 15,* 59-84.

Metsala, J. L. (1999). Young children's phonological awareness and non-word repetition as a function of vocabulary development. *Journal of Educational Psychology, 91,* 3-19.

MEXT. (2001). *The guideline for the practice of elementary school English language activities (Shōgakkō eigo katsudō jissen no tebiki).* Tokyo: Kairyūdo.

MEXT. (2002). A strategy to cultivate *Japanese with English abilities*

MEXT. (2004). The summary of the survey on the attitudes toward English education in elementary schools. Retrieved from http://www.mext.go.jp/b_menu/shingi/chukyo/chukyo3/015/gijiroku/05032201/004/001/002.pdf

MEXT. (2006). The summary of the survey on the practice of elementary school English language activities 2005. Retrieved from http://www.mext.go.jp/b_menu/shingi/chukyo/chukyo3/015/siryo/06032708/003/006.htm

MEXT. (2007). The summary of the survey on the practice of elementary school English language activities 2006. Retrieved from http://www.mext.go.jp/b_menu/shingi/chukyo/chukyo3/029/siryo/07090310/004/003.htm

MEXT. (2008a). *The commentary on the course of study for elementary schools.* Retrieved from http://www.mext.go.jp/component/a_menu/education/micro_detail/__icsFiles/afieldfile/2009/06/16/1234931_012.pdf

MEXT. (2008b). *The course of study for elementary schools.* Retrieved from http://www.mext.go.jp/a_menu/shotou/new-cs/youryou/syo/gai.htm

MEXT. (2008c). The summary of the survey on the practice of elementary school English language activities 2007. Retrieved from http://www.mext.go.jp/b_menu/houdou/20/03/08031920/002.htm

MEXT. (2009a). *Eigo Note 1.* Tokyo: Kyoiku-shuppan.

MEXT. (2009b). *Eigo Note 2.* Tokyo: Kyoiku-shuppan.

MEXT. (2009c). *The guidebook for teacher training in Foreign Language Activities in elementary schools (Shōgakkō gaikokugo katsudō kenshū gaido bukku).* Tokyo: Obunsha.

MEXT. (2010). The summary of the statistic survey of school teachers (Gakkou

Kyōin Toukei Chōsa). Retrieved from http://www.mext.go.jp/b_menu/toukei/chousa01/kyouin/1268573.htm

MEXT. (2011). The summary of school basic survey (Gakkou Kihon Chōsa). Retrieved from http://www.mext.go.jp/b_menu/toukei/chousa01/kihon/kekka/1268046.htm

MEXT. (2012a). *Hi, friends! 1*. Tokyo: Tokyo-shoseki.

MEXT. (2012b). *Hi, friends! 2*. Tokyo: Tokyo-shoseki.

Mishra, R., & Stainthorp, T. (2007). The relationship between phonological awareness and word reading accuracy in Oriya and English: A study of Oriya-speaking fifth-graders. *Journal of Research in Reading, 30*, 1, 23–37.

Moats, L. (2009). Knowledge foundations for teaching reading and spelling. *Reading and Writing, 22*, 4, 379–399.

Moats, L. E., & Foorman, B. R. (2003). Measuring teachers' content knowledge of language and reading. *Annals of Dyslexia, 53*, 23–45.

Morais, J. (1991). Constraints on the development of phonemic awareness. In S. A. Brady, & D. P. Shankweiler (Eds.), *Phonological processing in literacy* (pp. 5–27). Hillsdale, NJ: Lawrence Erlbaum.

Morais, J., Cary, L., Alegria, J., & Bertelson, P. (1979). Does awareness of speech as a sequence of phones arise spontaneously? *Cognition, 7*, 323–331.

Moran-Ellis, J., Alexander, V. D., Cronin, A., Dickinson, M., Fielding, J., Sleney, J., & Thomas, H. (2006). Triangulation and integration: Processes, claims and implications. *Qualitative Research, 6*, 1, 45–59.

Morgan, D. L. (1998). Practical strategies for combining qualitative and quantitative methods: Applications for health research. *Qualitative Health Research, 8*, 362–376.

Muljani, D., Koda, K., & Moates, D. R. (1998). The development of word recognition in a second language. *Applied Psycholinguistics, 19*, 1, 99–114.

Mumtaz, S., & Humphreys, G. W. (2001). The effects of bilingualism on learning to read English: Evidence from the contrast between Urdu-English bilingual and English monolingual children. *Journal of Research in Reading, 24*, 2, 113–134.

Muter, V., Hulme, C., Snowling, M., & Stevenson, J. (2004). Phonemes, rimes and language skills as foundations of early reading development: Evidence from a longitudinal study. *Developmental Psychology, 40*, 663–681.

Muter, V., Hulme, C., Snowling, M., & Taylor, S. (1998). Segmentation, not rhyming, predicts early progress in learning to read. *Journal of Experimental Child Psychology, 71*, 3–27.

Muter, V., & Snowling, M. (1998). Concurrent and longitudinal predictors of reading: The role of metalinguistic and short-term memory skills. *Reading Research Quarterly, 33*, 3, 320–337.

Näslund, J. C., & Schneider, W. (1996). Kindergarten letter knowledge, phonological skills, and memory processes: Relative effects on early literacy. *Journal of Experimental Child Psychology, 62*, 30–59.

Nakagawa, A. (1994). Visual and semantic processing in reading Kanji. *Journal of Experimental Psychology: Human Perception and Performance, 20*, 864–875.

Nakata, R. (1993). *How to teach English for children—An instruction of development of English speaking ability (Kōshite oshieru kodomo no eigo: Hanaseru eigo no shidō)*. Tokyo: Kyobundo.

Naoshima Elementary School (1996). *The practical report of schools for research development, 1996. Naoshima-town Naoshima Elementary School (Heisei 8 nendo kenkyūkaihatsukō jisshi hōkokusho)*. Kagawa-ken Naoshima-chōritsu Naoshima shōgakkō.

Naoyama, Y. (2001). English Language Activities with 'letter reading activities' in public elementary schools: The practice lessons in upper grades (Moji no yomi shidō o toriireta shōgakkō no eigo katsudō: Shōgaku kōgakunen no jissen jugyō). *STEP Bulletin, 13*, 156–164.

Nation, K., & Hulme, C. (1997). Phonemic segmentation, not onset-rime segmentation, predicts early reading and spelling. *Reading Research Quarterly, 32*, 2, 154–167.

Nespor, J. (1987). The role of beliefs in the practice of teaching. *Journal of Curriculum Studies, 19*, 317–328.

Nikolov, M. (1999). Why do you learn English? Because the teacher is short: A study of Hungarian children's foreign language learning motivation. *Language Teaching Research, 3*, 33–56.

Nolen, P. A., McCutchen, D., & Berninger, V. (1990). Ensuring tomorrow's literacy: A shared responsibility. *Journal of Teacher Education, 41*, 3, 63–72.

Norris, J. M., & Ortega, L. (2000). Effectiveness of L2 instruction: A research synthesis and quantitative meta-analysis. *Language Learning, 50*, 3, 417–528.

Oka, H., & Kanamori, T. (Eds.). (2009) *English education in elementary schools for communication (Shōgakkō eigo kyōiku no susume kata: Kotoba no kyōiku to shite)* (revised ed.). Tokyo: Seibido.

Omura, Y. (Ed.). (1980). *Eigo kyouikushi shiryou: Eigo kyouiku katei no hensen. Vol. 1*. Tokyo: Tokyo Hourei.

Osgood, C. E., Suci, G. S., & Tannenbaum, P. H. (1957). *The measurement of meaning*. Urbana, IL: University of Illinois Press.

O'Sullivan, J., & Pressley, M. (1984). The completeness of instruction and strategy transfer. *Journal of Experimental Child Psychology, 38*, 275–288.

Oppenheim, A. N. (1992). *Questionnaire design, interviewing and attitude measurement* (new ed.). New York, NY: Continuum.

Otaka, H. (2009). *Phonetics and phonology of moras, Feet, and geminate consonants in Japanese*. Lanham: ML. University Press of America.

Otake, T. (2006). Speech segmentation by Japanese Listeners: Its language-specificity and language-universality. In M. Nakayama, R. Mazuka, & Y. Shirai (Eds.), *The handbook of east Asian psycholinguistic. Volume II: Japanese* (pp. 201–207). Cambridge, England: Cambridge University Press.

Otake, T., Hatano, G., Cutler, A., & Mehler, J. (1993). Mora or Syllable? Speech Segmentation in Japanese. *Journal of Memory and Language, 32*, 258–278.

Otake, T., Hatano, G., & Yoneyama, K. (1996). Speech segmentation by Japanese listeners. In T. Otake, & A. Cutler (Eds.), *Phonological structure and language processing: Cross-linguistic studies* (pp. 183–201), New York, NY: Mouton de Gruyter.

Otake, T., & Imai, Y. (2001). Awareness of subsyllabic structure by Japanese preschool children and its universality. *Phonological Studies, 4*, 81–88.

Otake, T., & Yoneyama, K. (2000). Phonological units in mental lexicon and their awareness. *Phonological studies, 3*, 21–28.

Ouellette, G., & Sénéchal, M. (2008a). Pathways to literacy: A study of invented spelling and its role in learning to read. *Child Development, 79*, 4, 899–913.

Ouellette, G., & Sénéchal, M. (2008b). A window into early literacy: Exploring the cognitive and linguistic underpinnings of invented spelling. *Scientific Studies of reading, 12*, 2, 195–219.

Pajares, M. K. (1992). Teachers' beliefs and educational research: Cleaning up a messy construct. *Review of Educational Research, 62*, 3, 307–332.

Paul, D. (2003). *Teaching English to children in Asia*. Hong Kong: Longman Asia ELT.

Perfetti, C. A., Beck, I., Bell, L., & Hughes, C. (1987). Phonemic knowledge and learning to read are reciprocal: A longitudinal study of first grade children. *Merrill-Palmer Quarterly, 33*, 283–319.

Piaget, J. (1923). *The Language and Thought of the Child*. New York, NY: Harcourt Brace and World.

Pinnell, G., Lyons, C., DeFord, D., Bryk, A., & Seltzer, M. (1994). Comparing instructional models for the literacy education of high-risk first graders. *Reading Research Quarterly, 29*, 1, 9–39.

Pinter, A. (2006). *Teaching Young Language Learners*. Oxford, England: Oxford University Press.

Pintrich, P. R., & Schunk, D. H. (2002). *Motivation in education: Theory, research, and application* (2nd ed.). Upper Saddle River, NJ: Merrill Prentice Hall.

Prince, A., & Smolensky, P. (2004). *Optimality theory in phonology. A reader.* Oxford, England: Blackwell.

Pufraff, L. A. (2009). A developmental continuum of phonological sensitivity skills. *Psychology in the Schools, 46*, 7, 679–691.

Rathvon, N. (2004). *Early reading assessment. A practitioner's handbook*. New York, NY: Guilford Press.

Read, C. (1971). Pre-school children's knowledge of English phonology. *Harvard Educational Review, 41*, 1, 1–34.

Read, C. (1975). *Children's categorization of speech sounds in English (NCTE Research Report No. 17)*. Urbana, IL: National Council of Teachers of English.

Read, C., Zhang, Y., Nie, H., & Ding, B. (1986). The ability to manipulate speech sounds depends on knowing alphabetic writing. *Cognition, 24*, 31–44.

Redford, M., & Diehl, R. L. (1999). The relative perceptual distinctiveness of initial and final consonants in CVC syllables. *Journal of the Acoustical Society of America, 106*, 3, 1555–1565.

Richards, J. C. (1998). What's the use of lesson plans? In J. C. Richards (Ed.), *Beyond Training: Perspectives on Language Teacher Education* (pp. 103–121).

Cambridge, England: Cambridge University Press.
Richards, J. C., & Lockhart, C. (1994). *Reflective teaching in second language classrooms.* Cambridge, England: Cambridge University Press.
Rixon, S. (2007). Cambridge ESOL YLE tests and children's first steps in reading and writing in English. *Research Notes* (pp. 7-14). Cambridge ESOL.
Richgels, D. J. (1995). Invented spelling ability and printed word learning in kindergarten. *Reading Research Quarterly, 30*, 96-109.
Ritchey, K. D., Coker, Jr., D. L., & McCraw, S. B. (2010). A comparison of metrics for scoring beginning spelling. *Assessment for Effective Intervention, 35*, 2, 78-88.
Roach, P. (1982). On the distinction between 'stress-timed' and 'syllable-timed' languages. In D. Crystal, *Linguistic Controversies* (pp. 73-79). London, England: Hodder Arnold.
Rubin, H., Turner, A., & Kantor, M. (1991). Fourth grade follow-up of reading and spelling skills of French immersion students. *Reading and Writing: An Interdisciplinary Journal, 3*, 63-73.
Rubin, H., & Turner, A. (1989). Linguistic awareness skills in grade one children in a French immersion setting. *Reading and Writing: An Interdisciplinary Journal, 1*, 73-86.
Saito, E. (1996). *The foundation for the level-up of English classes (Eigo jugyō reberu appu no kiso).* Tokyo: Taishukan.
Saito, H. (2006). Orthographic processing. In M. Nakayama, R. Mazuka, & Y. Shirai (Eds.), T*he handbook of east Asian psycholinguistic. Volume II: Japanese* (pp. 233-240). Cambridge, England: Cambridge University Press.
Santa, C. M., & Hoien, T. (1999). An assessment of Early Steps: A program for early intervention of reading problems. *Reading Research Quarterly, 34*, 54-79.
Sasaki, S. (2004). A tentative plan of activities with letters in elementary school English Conversation Activities—in view of the linkage with junior high school English (Shōgakkō eigo katsudō ni okeru moji o atsukatta katsudō no shian: Chūgakkō eigo tono renkei o shiya ni irete). *TELES Bulletin, 24*, 155-167.
Savage, R. S., & Carless, S. (2005). Phoneme manipulation but not onset-rime manipulation is a unique predictor of early reading. *Journal of Child Psychology and Psychiatry and Allied Disciplines, 46*, 1297-1308.
Scarborough, H. S., Ehri, L. C., Olson, R. K., & Fowler, A. E. (1998). The fate of phonemic awareness beyond the elementary school years. *Scientific Studies of Reading, 2*, 115-142.
Scharlach, T. D. (2008). These kids just aren't motivated to read: The influence of preservice teachers' beliefs on their expectations, instruction, and evaluation of struggling readers. *Literacy Research and Instruction, 47*, 3, 158-173.
Schatschneider, C., Francis, D. J., Foorman, B. R., Fletcher, J. M., & Mehta, P. (1999). The dimensionality of phonological awareness: An application of item response theory. *Journal of Educational Psychology, 91*, 3, 439-449.
Schmidt, R. (1990). The role of consciousness in second language learning. *Applied Linguistics, 11*, 129-158.

Schreuder, R., & van Bon, W. H. J. (1989). Phonemic analysis: Effects of word properties. *Journal of Research in Reading, 12*, 59–78.

Seymour, P. H., & Evans, H. M. (1994). Levels of phonological awareness and learning to read. *Reading and Writing: An Interdisciplinary Journal, 6*, 221–250.

Shafiullah, M., & Monsell, S. (1999). The cost of switching between kanji and kana while reading Japanese. *Language and Cognitive Processes, 14*, 567–607.

Share, D. L. (1995). Phonological recoding and self teaching: *Sine qua non* of reading acquisition. *Cognition, 55*, 151–128.

Share, D. L. (1999). Phonological recoding and orthographic learning: A direct test of the self-teaching hypothesis. *Journal of Experimental Child Psychology, 72*, 95–129.

Share, D. L. (2004). Knowing letter names and learning letter sounds: A causal connection. *Journal of Experimental Child Psychology, 88*, 3, 213–233.

Share, D. L., Jorm, A. F., Maclean, R., & Matthews, R. (1984). Sources of individual differences in reading acquisition. *Journal of Educational Psychology, 76*, 6, 1309–1324.

Shibahara, N., Zorzi, M., Hill, M. P., Wydell, T., & Butterworth, B. (2003). Semantic effects in word naming: Evidence from English and Japanese kanji. *The Quarterly Journal of Experimental Psychology, 56A*, 2, 263–286.

Shim, S-Y., & Herwig, J. E. (1997). Korean teachers' beliefs and teaching practices in Korean early childhood education. *Early Child Development and Care, 132*, 1, 45–55.

Silverman, D., & Marvasti, A. (2008). *Doing qualitative research: A comprehensive guide*. Thousand Oaks, CA: Sage Publications.

Singleton, D., & Muñoz, C. (2011). Around and beyond the critical period hypothesis. In E. Hinkel (Ed.), *Handbook of research in second language teaching and learning, Vol. 2* (pp. 444–454). New York, NY: Routledge.

Singleton, D., & Ryan, L. (2004). *Language acquisition: The age factor* (2nd ed.). Clevedon, UK: Multilingual Matters.

Siok, W. T., & Fletcher, P. (2001). The role of phonological awareness and visual-orthographic skills in Chinese reading acquisition. *Developmental Psychology, 37*, 6, 886–899.

Sirois, P., Boisclair, A., & Giasson, J. (2008). Understanding of the alphabetic principle through invented spelling among hearing-impaired children learning to read and write: Experimentation with a pedagogical approach. *Journal of Reading in Reading, 31*, 4, 339–358.

Slocum, T. A., O'Connor, R. E., & Jenkins, I. R. (1993). Transfer among phonological manipulation skills. *Journal of Educational Psychology, 85*, 618–630.

Snider, V. A. (1995). A primer on phonemic awareness: What it is, why it's important, and how to teach it. *School Psychology Review, 24*, 3, 443–455.

Snow, C. E., Burns, M. S., & Griffin, P. (Eds.). (1998). *Preventing reading difficulties in young children*. Washington, DC: National Academy Press.

Snowling, M. (2000). *Dyslexia: A cognitive developmental perspective* (2nd ed.) Oxford, England: Basil Blackwell.

Spagnoletti, C., Morais, J., Alegria, J., & Dominicy, M. (1989). Metaphonological abilities of Japanese children. *Reading and Writing*, *2*, 221-244.

Spear-Swerling, L., & Brucker, P. O. (2003). Teachers' acquisition of knowledge about English word structure. *Annals of Dyslexia*, *53*, 72-103.

Spear-Swerling, L., & Brucker, P. O. (2005). Teacher's literacy-related knowledge and self-perceptions in relation to preparation and experience. *Annals of Dyslexia*, *55*, 2, 266-296.

Spear-Swerling, L., & Brucker, P. O. (2004). Preparing novice teachers to develop basic reading and spelling skills in children. *Annals of Dyslexia*, *54*, 2, 332-364.

Stage, S. A., & Wagner, R. K. (1992). Development of young children's phonological and orthographic knowledge as revealed by their spellings. *Developmental Psychology*, *28*, 287-296.

Stahl, S. A., & Murray, B. A. (1994). Defining phonological awareness and its relationship to early reading. *Journal of Educational Psychology*, *86*, 221-234.

Stanovich, K. E. (1986). Matthew effects in reading: Some consequences of individual differences in the acquisition of literacy. *Reading Research Quarterly*, *21*, 4, 360-407.

Stanovich, K. E. (1992). Speculations of the causes and consequences of individual differences in early reading acquisition. In P. B. Gough, L. C. Ehri, & R. Treiman (Eds.), *Reading Acquisition* (pp. 307-342). Hillsdale, NJ: Erlbaum.

Stanovich, K. E., Cunningham, A. E., & Cramer, B. B. (1984). Assessing phonological awareness of kindergarten children: Issues of task comparability. *Journal of Experimental Psychology*, *38*, 175-190.

Stanovich, K. E., Cunningham, A. E., & Feeman, D. J. (1984). Intelligence, cognitive skills, and early reading progress. *Reading Research Quarterly*, *19*, 3, 278-303.

Stevenson, H. W., & Newman, R. W. (1986). Long-term prediction of achievement and attitudes in mathematics and reading. *Child Development*, *57*, 646-659.

Sulzby, E. (1986). Writing and reading: Signs of oral and written language organization in the young child. In W. H. Teale, & E. Sulzby (Eds.), *Emergent literacy: Reading and writing* (pp. 50-87). Norwood, NJ: Ablex.

Sulzby, E., & Teale, W. (1991). Emergent literacy. In R. Barr, M. Kamil, P. Mosenthal, & P. D. Pearson (Eds.), *Handbook of reading research, Vol. 2* (pp. 727-758). New York, NY: Longman.

Suzuki, T. (1990). *Closed Japanese, and the word of Japanese (Tozasareta nihongo, nihongo no sekai)*. Tokyo: Sinchosha.

Tamaoka, K., & Terao, Y. (2004). Mora or syllable? Which unit do Japanese use in naming visually presented stimuli? *Applied Psycholinguistics*, *25*, 1-17.

Tamaoka, K., & Makioka, S. (2009). Japanese mental syllabary and effects of mora, syllable, bi-mora and word frequencies on Japanese speech production. *Language and Speech*, *52*, 1, 79-112.

Tangel, D. M., & Blachman, B. A. (1992). Effect of phoneme awareness instruction on kindergarten children's invented spelling. *Journal of Reading Behavior*, *24*, 233-261.

Tangel, D. M., & Blachman, B. A. (1995). Effect of phoneme awareness instruction on the invented spelling of first-grade children: A one-year follow-up. *Journal of Reading Behavior, 27*, 153–185.

Tashakkori, A., & Teddlie, C. (Eds.). (2003). *Handbook of mixed methods in social & behavioural research*. Thousand Oaks, CA: Sage Publications.

Teale, W. H., & Sulzby, E. (Eds.). (1986). *Emergent literacy: Writing and reading*. Norwood, NJ: Ablex.

Temple, C., Nathan, R., Burris, N., & Temple, F. (1993). *The beginnings of writing* (3rd ed.). Needham, MA: Allyn and Bacon.

Terrell, T. D. (1982). The natural approach to language teaching: An update. *Modern Language Journal, 66*, 2, 121–132.

Teshima, R. (1997). The initial period of Junior high school English: Techniques for instructing 'spelling and pronunciation' to read words (Chūgaku nymonki: Tango o yomaseru 'tsuzuri to hatsuon' no sidouhō). *Modern English Teaching (Gendai Eigo Kyōiku), July*, 6.

Torgesen, J. K., & Davies, C. (1996). Individual difference variables that predict response to training in phonological awareness. *Journal of Experimental Child Psychology, 63*, 1–21.

Torgesen, J. K., & Mathes, P. G. (2000). *A Basic guide to understanding, assessing, and teaching phonological awareness*. Austin, TX: Pro-Ed.

Torgesen, J. K., Wagner, R. K., & Rashotte, C. A. (1994). Longitudinal studies of phonological processing and reading. *Journal of Learning Disabilities, 27*, 276–286.

Torgesen, J. K., Wagner, R. K., & Rashotte, C. A. (1997). The prevention and remediation of severe reading disabilities: Keeping the end in mind. *Scientific Studies of Reading, 1*, 217–234.

Trask, R. L. (1996). *A dictionary of phonetics and phonology*. Abingdon, England: Routledge.

Treiman, R. (1984). On the status of final consonant clusters in English syllables. *Journal of Verbal Learning and Verbal Behavior, 23*, 343–356.

Treiman, R. (1985). Onsets and rimes as units of spoken syllables: Evidence from children. *Journal of Experimental Child Psychology, 39*, 161–181.

Treiman, R. (1993). *Beginning to spell: A study of first-grade children*. New York, NY: Oxford University Press.

Treiman, R. (1993). *Beginning to spell*. New York, NY: Oxford University Press.

Treiman, R., & Baron, J. (1981). Segmental analysis ability: Development and relation to reading ability. In G. E. MacKinnon, & T. G. Waller (Eds.), *Reading research: Advances in theory and practice* (pp. 159–197). New York, NY: Academic Press.

Treiman, R., & Baron, J. (1983). Phonemic-analysis training helps children benefit from spelling-sound rules. *Memory & Cognition, 11*, 4, 382–389.

Treiman, R., & Bourassa, D. (2000). The development of spelling skill. *Topics in Language Disorders, 20*, 1–18.

Treiman, R., & Weatherston, S. (1992). Effects of linguistic structure on child's ability to isolate initial consonants. *Journal of Educational Psychology, 84*, 174–181.

Treiman, R., & Zukowski, A. (1991). Levels of phonological awareness. In S. A. Brady, & D. P. Shankweiler (Eds.), *Phonological processes in literacy* (pp. 67-83). Hillsdale, NJ: Lawrence Erlbaum.

Treiman, R., & Zukowski, A. (1996). Children's sensitivity to syllables, onsets, rimes, and phonemes. *Journal of Experimental Child Psychology*, *61*, 193-215.

Trubetzkoy, N. S. (1969). *Principles of phonology* (C. A. L. Baltaxe, Trans.). Los Angeles, CA: University of California Press. (Original work published 1936).

Tsuidou, K. (1996). Some hints from students with difficulty (Tsumazuku seito kara no hassō). *Modern English Teaching (Gendai Eigo Kyōiku), December*, 6-9.

Tsuidou, K. (1998). A basic study on letter instruction in teaching English to children (Jidō eigo ni okeru moji shidō ni kansuru kiso teki kōsatsu). *English education and English study (Eigo kyōiku to eigo kenkyū)*, *16*, 21-33.

Tunmer, W. E., Herriman, M. L., & Nesdale, A. R. (1988). Metalinguistic abilities and beginning reading. *Reading Research Quarterly*, *23*, 2, 134-158.

Tunmer, W. E., & Nesdale, A. R. (1985). Phonemic segmentation skill and beginning reading. *Journal of Educational Psychology*, *77*, 417-427.

Udo Elementary School (1996). *The practical report of schools for research development, 1996. Udo-municipal Udo Elementary School (Heisei 8 nendo kenkyūkaihatsukō jisshi hōkokusho)*. Kumamoto-ken Udo-shi Udo shōgakkō.

Umemoto, M. (2000). Letter instruction in English learning in elementary schools: A survey on children's attitudes (Shōgakkō eigo kyōiku deno moji shidō: Kodomo no ishiki chōsa kara). *JES Bulletin*, *1*, 17-22.

Ure, C., & Raban, B. (2001). Teachers' beliefs and understandings of literacy in the pre-school: Pre-school literacy project stage 1. *Contemporary Issues in Early Childhood*, *2*, 2, 157-168.

Vance, T. J. (2008). *The Sounds of Japanese*. Cambridge: England. Cambridge University Press.

Vandervelden, M. C., & Siegel, L. S. (1995). Phonological recoding and phoneme awareness in early literacy: A developmental approach. *Reading Research Quarterly*, *30*, 854-875.

Verhoeven, L. T. (1994). Transfer in bilingual development: The linguistic interdependence hypothesis revisited. *Language Learning*, *44*, 3, 381-415.

Wade-Woolley, L., & Siegel, L. S. (1997). The spelling performance of ESL and native speakers of English as a function of reading skills. *Reading and Writing*, *9*, 387-406.

Wagner, R. K., & Torgesen, J. K. (1987). The nature of phonological processing and its causal role in the acquisition of reading skills. *Psychological Bulletin*, *101*, 2, 192-212.

Wagner, R. K., Torgesen, J. K., Laughon, P., Simmons, K., & Rashotte, C. A. (1993). Development of young readers' phonological processing abilities. *Journal of Educational Psychology*, *85*, 1, 83-103.

Wagner, R. K., Torgesen, J. K., & Rashotte, C. A. (1994). Development of reading-related phonological processing abilities: New evidence of bidirectional causality from a latent variable longitudinal study. *Developmental Psychology*, *30*, 73-87.

Wagner, R. K., Torgesen, J. K., Rashotte, C. A., Hecht, S. A., Barker, T. A., Burgess, S. R., Donahue, J., & Garon, T. (1997). Changing causal relations phonological processing abilities and word-level reading as children Develop from beginning to fluent readers: A five-year longitudinal study. *Developmental Psychology, 33*, 3, 468–479.

Walley, A. C., Smith, L. B., & Jusczyk, P. W. (1986). The role of phonemes and syllables in the perceived similarity of speech sounds for children. *Memory & Cognition, 14*, 3, 220–229.

Walton, P. D. (1995). Rhyming ability, phoneme identity, letter-sound knowledge, and the use of orthographic analogy by pre-readers. *Journal of Educational Psychology, 87*, 587–597.

Wang, M., Koda, K., & Perfetti, C. A. (2003). Alphabetic and nonalphabetic L1 effects in English word identification: A comparison of Korean and Chinese English L2 learners. *Cognition, 87*, 129–149.

Wang, M., Perfetti, C. A., & Liu, Y. (2005). Chinese-English biliteracy acquisition: Cross language and writing system transfer. *Cognition, 97*, 67–88.

Wasik, B., & Slavin, R. (1993). Preventing early reading failure with one-to-one tutoring: A review of five programs. *Reading Research Quarterly, 18*, 2, 179–200.

Weinrich, B., & Fay, E. (2007). Literacy predictors of spelling abilities for first-grade children. *Contemporary Issues in Communication Science and Disorders, 34*, 94–100.

White, C. (1999). Expectations and emergent beliefs of self-instructed language learners. *System, 27*, 443–457.

Whitehurst, G. J., & Lonigan, C. J. (1998). Child development and emergent literacy. *Child Development, 69*, 3, 848–872.

Williams, J. (1980). Teaching decoding with an emphasis on phoneme analysis and phoneme blending. *Journal of Educational Psychology, 72*, 1, 1–15.

Wimmer, H., Landerl, K., Linortner, R., & Hummer, P. (1991). The relationship of phonemic awareness to reading acquisition: More consequence than precondition but still important. *Cognition, 40*, 219–249.

Wise, B. W., Ring, J., & Olson, R. K. (1999). Training phonological awareness with and without explicit attention to articulation. *Journal of Experimental Child Psychology, 72*, 271–304.

Wood, C., & Terrell, C. (1998). Poor readers' ability to detect speech rhythm and perceive rapid speech. *British Journal of Developmental Psychology, 16*, 297–413.

Wood, C. (2006). Metrical stress sensitivity in young children and its relationship to phonological awareness and reading. *Journal in Research in Reading, 29*, 3, 270–287.

Woods, D. (1996). *Teacher cognition in language teaching.* Cambridge, England: Cambridge University Press.

Wydell, T. N., & Butterworth, B. (1999). A case study of an English-Japanese bilingual with monolingual dyslexia. *Cognition, 70*, 273–305.

Wydell, T. N., & Kondo, T. (2003). Phonological deficit and the reliance on orthographic approximation for reading: A follow-up study on an English-Japanese bilingual with monolingual dyslexia. *Journal of Research in Reading*, *26*, 1, 33–48.

Yamada, J. (2004). An L1-script-transfer-effect fallacy: A rejoinder to Wang et al. (2003). *Cognition*, *93*, 127–132.

Yin, R. K. (2009). *Case study research: Design and methods* (4th ed.). Thousand Oaks, CA: Sage Publications.

Yopp, H. K. (1988). The validity and reliability of phonemic awareness tests. *Reading Research Quarterly*, *23*, 159–177.

Ziegler, J. C., & Goswami, U. (2005). Reading acquisition, developmental dyslexia, and skilled reading across languages: A psycholinguistic grain size theory. *Psychological Bulletin*, *131*, 1, 3–29.

Appendices

Appendix 1.1: The Chapter of 'Foreign Language Activities'
in the *Course of Study for Elementary Schools* enacted in the academic year of 2011
(Available from the website of MEXT: http://www.mext.go.jp/component/a_menu/education/micro_detail/_icsFiles/afieldfile/2009/04/21/1261037_12.pdf)

Chapter 4 Foreign Language Activities

I. OVERALL OBJECTIVES
To form the foundation of pupils' communication abilities through foreign languages while developing the understanding of languages and cultures through various experiences, fostering a positive attitude toward communication, and familiarizing pupils with the sounds and basic expressions of foreign languages.

II. CONTENT
[Grade 5 and Grade 6]
1. Instructions should be given on the following items in order to help pupils actively engage in communication in a foreign language:
   (1) To experience the joy of communication in the foreign language.
   (2) To actively listen to and speak in the foreign language.
   (3) To learn the importance of verbal communication.
2. Instructions should be given on the following items in order to deepen the experiential understanding of the languages and cultures of Japan and foreign countries:
   (1) To become familiar with the sounds and rhythms of the foreign language, to learn its differences from the Japanese language, and to be aware of the interesting aspects of language and its richness.
   (2) To learn the differences in ways of living, customs and events between

Japan and foreign countries and to be aware of various points of view and ways of thinking.
(3) To experience communication with people of different cultures and to deepen the understanding of culture.

III. LESSON PLAN DESIGN AND HANDLING THE CONTENT
1. In designing the syllabus, consideration should be given to the following:
    (1) In principle English should be selected for foreign language activities.
    (2) Taking into account the circumstances of pupils and the local community, each individual school should establish objectives of foreign language activities for each grade in an appropriate manner and work to realize them over the period of two school years.
    (3) With respect to the instructions on the content mainly concerning language and culture listed in Subsection II-2, teachers should make them link with the content mainly concerning communication listed in Subsection II-1. In doing so, teachers should try to have pupils understand language and culture experientially, avoiding giving too detailed explanations or engaging pupils in rote learning.
    (4) The instructions on the content and activities should be in line with pupils' interest. Effort should be made to increase the effectiveness of teaching by, for example, taking advantage of what pupils have learnt in other subjects, such as the Japanese language, music and arts and handicrafts.
    (5) Homeroom teachers or teachers in charge of foreign language activities should make teaching programs and conduct lessons. Effort should be made to get more people involved in lessons by inviting native speakers of the foreign language or by seeking cooperation from local people who are proficient in the foreign language, depending on the circumstances of the local community.
    (6) When dealing with sounds, teachers should make active use of audio-visual materials such as CDs and DVDs. The audio-visual materials should be selected according to the actual circumstances of the pupils, school and local community.
    (7) Based on the objectives of moral education listed in Subsections I and II of Chapter 1 "General Provisions" and in Subsection I of Chapter 3 "Moral Education", instructions concerning the content listed in Subsection II of Chapter 3 "Moral Education" should be given appropriately. The instructions should be in accordance with the characteristics of foreign language activities and should be related to the period for moral education.
2. In the handling of the content listed in Subsection II, consideration should be given to the following:
    (1) Consideration should be given to the following points when giving instructions over the period of two school years:
        A. When giving pupils opportunities to experience communication in the foreign language, teachers should select appropriate expressions, giving consideration to the developmental stages of the pupils and set communication situations familiar to them.

B. When giving pupils opportunities to experience communication in the foreign language, teachers should focus on the foreign language sounds and use letters of the alphabet and words as supplementary tools for oral communication, in effort not to give too much burden to pupils.
C. Since non-verbal communication is also an essential means of communication, teachers should adopt gestures etc. and help pupils understand their functions.
D. Teachers should enable pupils to deepen their understanding not only of the foreign language and culture, but also of the Japanese language and culture through foreign language activities.
E. When giving pupils opportunities to experience communication in the foreign language, teachers should mainly set the communication situations and functions listed in the following examples:

[Examples of Communication Situations]
 (a) Situations where fixed expressions are often used
  ・ Greeting ・ Self-introduction ・ Shopping
  ・ Having meals ・ Asking and giving directions
  etc.
 (b) Situations that are likely to occur in pupils' lives
  ・ Home life ・ Learning and activities at school
  ・ Local events ・ Childhood play
  etc.

[Examples of Functions of Communication]
 (a) Improving the relationship with a communication partner
 (b) Expressing emotions
 (c) Communicating facts
 (d) Expressing opinions and intentions
 (e) Stimulating a communication partner into action

(2) Consideration should be given to the following points when giving instructions to each grade, taking the learning level of pupils into account:
A. Activities in Grade 5
Considering that pupils learn the foreign language for the first time, teachers should introduce basic expressions about familiar things and events and engage pupils in communication activities where they experience interactions with one another. Teachers should engage pupils mainly in the activities where the pupils may become familiar with the foreign language or in the activities which are related to their daily lives or school lives.
B. Activities in Grade 6
Based on the learning in Grade 5, teachers should engage pupils in communication activities, focused on interactions with one another, including intercultural exchange activities, in addition to activities related to pupils' daily lives or school lives.

Appendix 3.1: The structure of *Eigo Note 1*

Lesson 1 Let's learn "Hello" around the world. [*Hello.*]			
	content	main expressions etc.	main vocabulary
1	To know there are various greetings around the world.	Hello.	hello, meet, name, you
2	To know the manners of greeting, positively exchange greetings, and say their own names.	Hello. My name is Ken.	
3	To exchange greetings with friends and exchange name cards which they made.	Hello. My name is Ken. What's your name? Nice to meet you. Thank you. Good-bye.	
Lesson 2 Let's make gestures. [*I'm happy*]			
1	To learn words expressing various feelings and situations, and make gestures of them.	Happy / Fine / Hungry / Sleepy.	fine, happy, hungry, sleepy
2	To understand the importance of gestures and tell their feelings with gestures.	Hello. How are you? I'm [happy / fine / hungry / sleepy].	
3	To greet others positively with gestures.		
4	To express and tell their feelings and situations with gestures.		
Lesson 3 Let's play with numbers. [*How many?*]			
1	To know there are various gestures around the world and say the numbers from 1 to 10.	Rock, scissors, paper. One, two, three. one, two, three, four, five, six, seven, eight, nine, ten	ear, eight, eighteen, eleven, eye, fifteen, five, four, fourteen, head, knee, mouth, nine, nineteen, nose, one, paper, rock, scissors, seven, seventeen, shoulder, six, sixteen, ten, thirteen, three, toe, twelve, twenty, two
2	To understand there are various gestures around the world and say the numbers from 1 to 20.	eleven, twelve, thirteen, fourteen. fifteen, sixteen, seventeen, eighteen, nineteen, twenty	
3	To ask how many and answer with the numbers from 1 to 20.	Hello. Rock, scissors, paper. One, two, three. Five. Thank you.	
4	To play games dealing with numbers with friends.	Hello, Ken. How many? Five. See you.	
Lesson 4 Let's do self-introduction. [*I like apples.*]			
1	To listen to and understand likes and dislikes.	apple, banana, pineapple, strawberry, carrot, ice cream, milk, juice, cat, dog, bird, fish, rabbit, baseball, soccer, swimming, skiing Do you like dogs? Yes, I do. / No, I don't.	apple, banana, dog, ice cream, like, milk, no, rabbit soccer, swimming, yes
2	To tell others about their likes and dislikes.		
3	To ask friends about likes and dislikes.	I like cats.	
4	To introduce themselves including their likes and dislikes.	Hello. My name is Ken. I like cats. I like apples. I like baseball. Thank you.	
Lesson 5 Let's learn about various clothes. [*I don't like blue.*]			
1	To know there are various clothes around the world and learn the ways of describing clothes.	red, blue, yellow, orange, pink, green, black, white	bag, big, black, blue, cap, cool, cute, dress, green, heart, nice, orange, pants, pink, red, shoe(s), skirt, sock(s), star, sweater, T-shirt, white, yellow
2	To realise the importance of telling their opinion clearly and learn expressions for buying clothes.	T-shirt, sweater, pants, shorts, skirt, socks, shoes, cap I like blue. I don't like red.	
3	To tell their preferences clearly and speak to people so that they can do shopping comfortably.	Do you have a red cap? Here you are. Thank you.	
4	To do a presentation so that listeners can understand what they bought correctly.	Hello. My name is Ken. I have a blue T-shirt and a white cap. I like blue. I don't like yellow. Thank you.	

	Lesson 6 Let's learn loan words. [*What do you want?*]		
1	To realise the difference in pronunciation between loan words and their original words and pronounce them carefully.	tomato, lemon, donut, cake, pudding, salad, pizza, soup, steak, cabbage, gorilla, koala, TV, camera Hamburger, please.	basketball, bear, *bibimbap*, bird, cabbage, cake, calendar, camera, cat, cream puff, donut, elephant, fish, giraffe, glove, gorilla, gratin, guitar, juice, kangaroo, kimchi, koala, lemon, lion, omelette, panda, piano, pizza, please, pudding, salad, sheep, soccer ball, soup, spaghetti, steak, sukiyaki, sushi, tomato, TV, want
2	To ask for what they want when asked by people.		
3	To make a fruit parfait for a friend by asking and requiring what he/she wants.	What do you want? Strawberries, please. Here you are. Thank you. [kiwi, peach, grape, melon, cherry]	
4	To present the fruit parfait which they made.		
	Lesson 7 Let's hold a quiz match. [*What's this?*]		
1	To realise the interesting formation of *kanji* characters through the differences between English and Japanese.	starfish, lobster, jellyfish, octopus, butterfly, bird, pencil, ruler, eraser, pencil case, book, yacht	book, pen, pencil case
2	To understand what they are asked about when spoken to with the question of "What's this?" and answer it.		
3	To ask by using "What's this?"	What's this? It's a pencil.	
4	To enjoy the quiz match by mutually asking and answering questions with friends.		
	Lesson 8 Let's make a timetable. [*I study Japanese.*]		
1	To know what subjects are learnt in foreign primary schools and learn the expressions for subjects.	China, Australia, Japan Japanese, math, science, social studies, P.E., music, home economics, arts and crafts, English Sunday, Monday, Tuesday, Wednesday, Thursday, Friday, Saturday I study math on Friday.	arts and crafts, English, Friday, home economics, Japanese, math, Monday, music, P.E., Saturday, science, sing, social studies, study, Sunday, swim, teach, Thursday, Tuesday, Wednesday
2	To attend the games dealing with subject names and days of a week positively.		
3	To tell about the original timetable for days of a week which they made to friends.		
4	To present the timetable which was made in group work.		
	Lesson 9 Let's make a lunch menu. [*What would you like?*]		
1	To know what people have for breakfast is different between in Japan and in foreign countries.	Korea, America, Japan, France rice, miso soup, *natto*, bread, sandwich, yogurt, curry and rice	bread, cereal, croissant, eat, fruit, kimchi, miso soup, morning, *namul*, *natto*, orange juice, rice, sausage, yogurt
2	To learn words expressing foods and dishes.	What would you like? I'd like rice and miso soup. Here you are. Thank you. You're welcome.	
3	To ask and tell what they want with polite expressions.		
4	To present the original lunch set which was made in groups.		

- based on MEXT. (2009). *The guidebook for teacher training in Foreign Language Activities in elementary schools*. Tokyo: Obunsha.
- 'Content' were translated by the author.

Appendix 3.2: The summary of the plans for the information gathering at both the initial and final stages of the intervention

Tests

	Initial Assessment & Final Assessment
1	**Letter name knowledge** Children hear a letter name and asked to select the corresponding letter out of five options. [Purpose] To investigate how much children have acquired this knowledge through *Roma-ji* learning and daily exposure to the alphabet letters **Test item** (target letter names underlined): 1. t o v y <u>u</u> 11. f r h <u>l</u> x 2. n e u w <u>m</u> 12. u <u>n</u> r m z 3. d <u>w</u> m u n 13. p <u>g</u> q b k 4. e <u>q</u> <u>p</u> d k 14. i k h g <u>y</u> 5. b u z <u>v</u> d 15. y <u>j</u> a w i 6. d s <u>z</u> e v 16. v <u>b</u> d p g 7. <u>d</u> v b z q 17. h <u>k</u> f l y 8. <u>i</u> s y <u>e</u> r 18. l v s <u>r</u> c 9. z u e <u>c</u> t 19. w <u>x</u> y m v 10. <u>h</u> f x <u>e</u> k 20. q <u>b</u> v <u>g</u> p
2	**Sound categorisation** Children three monosyllabic CVC words spoken aloud and are asked to identify the odd word that does not sound similar the other two. [adapted from Kirtley, Bryant, MacLean, & Bradley (1989)] [Purpose] To investigate children's phonemic awareness including the awareness of onset in a CVC word, as well as their intrasyllabic awareness (i.e., rime awareness) **Practice items** (odd words in italics): 　1. page, pain, *line*　　　　3. *seed*, hid, lid 　2. page, *pet*, pain　　　　4. tip, *hid*, lip **Test items [Part 1]** (odd words in italics): 　1. beak, leek, *tip* [ES/C2]　　8. *cap*, light, line [ES/C3]　　15. peg, pen, *pale* [OS/C3] 　2. *cot*, doll, dog [OS/C4]　　9. rail, *hole*, tale [ES/C3]　　16. tail, *hid*, nail [ES/C2] 　3. hid, *tip*, lid [ES/C4]　　10. lap, lamb, *cat* [OS/C4]　　17. pet, *lamb*, pain [OS/C1] 　4. pen, *dot*, peg [OS/C2]　　11. *life*, lap, lad [OS/C3]　　18. rock, sock, *hop* [ES/C4] 　5. *kid*, lead, bead [ES/C3]　　12. *pain*, rail, tail [OS/C4]　　19. light, *lamb*, line [OS/C3] 　6. *deaf*, peg, pen [OS/C4]　　13. dog, den, *page* [OS/C1]　　20. *beak*, lip, hop [ES/C1] 　7. nail, *top*, coal [ES/C1]　　14. *nail*, bowl, coal [ES/C3] **Test items [Part 2]** (odd words in italics): 　1. doll, *can*, deaf [OS/C1]　　8. *bowl*, week, rock [ES/C1]　　15. hop, *bead*, seed [ES/C2] 　2. mop, hop, *whip* [ES/C3]　　9. line, *lad*, dot [OS/C1]　　16. lap, *lad*, pet [OS/C2] 　3. can, cap, *cot* [OS/C3]　　10. tip, *top*, lip [ES/C3]　　17. lead, *week*, bead [ES/C4] 　4. mop, *lead*, whip [ES/C1]　　11. leek, sock, *hid* [ES/C1]　　18. page, pain, *tail* [OS/C4] 　5. *deck*, cap, cough [OS/C1]　　12. *deaf*, page, pain [OS/C2]　　19. lid, *rock*, kid [ES/C2] 　6. bowl, hole, *week* [ES/C2]　　13. hop, mop, *rock* [ES/C4]　　20. doll, *cap*, dog [OS/C2] 　7. den, *dog*, deaf [OS/C3]　　14. deck, *pet*, den [OS/C4] 　　　OS = Opening sound oddity task　ES = End sound oddity task　C = Condition 　　　　<u>　</u> = words which were assumed to be unfamiliar words for children in the initial assessment 　　　　　 = words to which children might be unfamiliar at the time of the initial assessment but later used in the intervention

3	**Initial phoneme recognition** Children are asked to listen for a particular sound and had to decide if the initial sound in a presented word is that particular sound or not. [adopted from Jongejan, Verhoeven, & Siegel (2007)] [Purpose] To investigate children's phonemic awareness with a simpler task **Practice item:** /s/: *sock, fat, soup* **Test items:** 1. /s/: *sock, fat, soup, meat* 5. /b/: *cook, hot, boot, beard* 8. /p/: *dime, cup, duck, top* 2. /m/: *milk, map, paint, cake* 6. /k/: *kiss, kite, bad, gate* 9. /h/: *farm, hip, head, gas* 3. /f/: *head, foot, stick, face* 7. /p/: *duck, put, plant, black* 10. /g/: *gum, boat, goat, cup* 4. /t/: *pen, take, top, duck*
4	**Phoneme recognition and location** Children are asked to listen for a particular sound and then decide if that particular sound was in the first part of a presented word, the second part, or not in the presented word. [adopted from Jongejan, Verhoeven, & Siegel (2007)] [Purpose] To investigate children's phonemic awareness with a more demanding task **Practice item:** 1. /s/: snake, mess 2. /k/: park, ten **Test item:** 1. /s/: *neck, sun, class, grass, sick, pen* 6. /k/: *milk, fat, kill, sick, toe, cup* 2. /m/: *milk, ham, sit, pen, moan, comb* 7. /p/: *soap, neck, ape, grass, pill, pen* 3. /f/: *girl, calf, fat, fruit, knife, class* 8. /d/: *milk, mad, dog, dip, ride, class* 4. /t/: *sit, top, milk, grass, tub, cat* 9. /g/: *gum, dog, cab, bag, girl, nose* 5. /b/: *bike, milk, cab, bus, tub, nose*
5	**Phoneme deletion and substitution** Children are asked to either remove a sound from the presented words or change a sound in the words. [adopted from Jongejan, Verhoeven, & Siegel (2007)] [Purpose] To investigate children's phonemic awareness with a more complex task such as manipulation **Practice items:** 1. *doll* (remove /d/) 2. *doll* (change /d/ to /w/) **Three subtasks:** **(1) Initial:** remove or change the initial phoneme in the words 1. *fill* (remove /f/) 2. *cup* (remove /c/) 3. *bat* (remove /b/) 4. *fill* (change /f/ to /b/) 5. *cup* (change /c/ to /p/) 6. *bat* (change /b/ to /s/) **(2) Final:** remove or change the final phoneme in the words 1. *goat* (remove /t/) 2. *make* (remove /k/) 3. *seal* (remove /l/) 4. *fill* (change /l/ to /t/) 5. *cup* (change /p/ to /t/) 6. *bite* (change /t/ to /k/) **(3) Blend:** remove or change one of the middle phonemes in the words 1. *slip* (remove /l/) 2. *stick* (remove /t/) 3. *nest* (remove /s/) 4. *crest* (change /s/ to /p/) 5. *slip* (change /l/ to /n/) 6. *stick* (change /t/ to /l/)

6	Word spelling
	  Children are asked to spell real words and nonwords they hear.
	  [Purpose] To evaluate children's achievement of the target skill of the intervention
	    Test items: [real words] *yes, six, name, five, cute, home, black, jellyfish, this, thank, sandwich, what, green, cool, book, octopus, study* / [nonwords] *yag, sed, wib, cof, puz, hul, qun, yage, sede, wibe, cofe, puze, chax, tock, shem, rith, whov, jeen, koot* **[Original]**

7	Word reading
	  Children are visually presented with real words and nonwords and asked to read them aloud.
	  [Purpose] To evaluate children's achievement of the target skill of the intervention
	    Test items: [real words] *yes, six, name, five, cute, home, black, jellyfish, this, thank, sandwich, what, green, cool, book, octopus, study* / [nonwords] *yag, sed, wib, cof, puz, hul, qun, yage, sede, wibe, cofe, puze, chax, tock, shem, rith, whov, jeen, koot* **[Original]**

Appendix 4.1: The timetable of the introduction, activities, and tasks for target content

	Instructional Targets	Session	Activities and Tasks
Phonological awareness skills	Blending	4	Elkonin card without letters > to blend sounds of a word looking at a card with a picture the word represents and boxes which gives the idea of how many letters it comprises (i.e., Elkonin card)
		11	Revision: (1) Adding sounds > to blend sounds looking at the screen showing the phoneme structure of a word as 'C+V+C'
	Segmenting	4	Elkonin card without letters > to segment sounds of word looking at Elkonin cards
		4	Elkonin card *Karuta* game > Children find a letter card which represents the sound in the target place of a word orally presented
		15	Pair work: Phoneme segmentation and categorisation > A pair work to segment sounds of a pair of words and categorise them according to the place of a sound which is common between them
	Deletion	13	Introduction of initial / final phoneme deletion > The researcher demonstrated that a word changes into a new word by deleting the initial / final phoneme.
	Substitution	15	Recognition of phoneme substitution > to categorise a pair of words according to the place of a substituted sound
		17	Phoneme substitution > Children were asked to say a new word which could be made by substituting a a sound in the target word.
		16	Demonstration of phoneme substitution > The researcher demonstrated to segment a pair of words and make a new word by substituting a sound (initial, middle, or final)
		16	Phoneme substitution > A worksheet activity to segment a pair of words and recognise the place where substituting occurred (initial, middle, or final)
	Onset-rime	8	Onset-rime slides > to recite words by blending an onset and a rime
		11	Revision: (6) Speed Reading > to recite a set of words with a common rime (Blending at the onset-rime level)
		18	Rime Identification > to categorise words according to the common rimes and then identify the onset of individual words
Sound categorises	Letter sounds	5	Introduction of short vowel sounds > Children were first asked to recite the words which were represented by the picture cards and had a common sound. Then, the researcher explained that the common sound is represented by a particular vowel letter.
		5, 6	Introduction of consonant sounds > Children were first asked to recite the words which were represented by the picture cards and had a common sound. Then, the researcher explained that the common sound is represented by a particular consonant letter.

	Instructional Targets	Session	Activities and Tasks
Sound categorises	Phoneme recognition / identification	5	Letter-sound *Karuta* > Children find a letter card which represents the sound in the target place of a orally presented word.
		8, 14, 15	Review song [Also used for morning activities with HRT] > A phonic video song to make children familiarise with letter sounds
		9, 10	*abc* song > to sing a song of 'abc' with letter sounds
		11	Revision: (5) Phoneme recognition > Children were orally presented two words which differ only in the middle phoneme and then asked to show one or two fingers according to whether the orally presented target was the same with the first one or the second.
		11	Revision: (3) Phoneme identification > to identify the letter which represents the middle sound of a orally presented CVC word
		11	Revision: (4) Phoneme identification > to identify the letters which represents the initial and final sounds of an orally presented CVC word.
		12	Worksheet: Identification of a vowel letter in the middle position > to identify the letter which represents the middle sound of a orally presented CVC word
		13	Worksheet: Final phoneme identification & Initial / final phoneme identification > to identify the letters which represents the initial and final sounds of an orally presented CVC word.
		14	Initial-sound *Karuta* > Children find a letter card which represents the initial sound of a word visually presented by the researcher.
		19	Initial sound *Domino* > to make a domino by combining a letter and a word which has the letter in the initial position.
		7, 8, 12, 14, 15, 16, 17, 18, 19, 20, 21	Revision (and morning activities with HRT) > The researcher randomly showed children letter cards, saying 'Name' or 'Sound.' Children answered names or sounds of the letters according to the cue.
	Digraph	18	Introduction of *th* > Children were first asked to recite the words which were represented by the picture cards and had a common sound. Then, the researcher explained that the common sound is represented by a particular digraph.
		20	Introduction of *wh, th, ck, ch, sh* > Children were first asked to recite the words which were represented by the picture cards and had a common sound. Then, the researcher explained that the common sound is represented by a particular digraph.
		20	Worksheet: Write a digraph! > A worksheet activity to write a digraph which is included in a orally presented word.
		20	Digraph roulette > to blend the sounds including a digraph in three roulettes to say a whole word

	Instructional Targets	Session	Activities and Tasks
Sound categorises		20	Digraph *Bingo* > A bingo activity using words with a digraph
		21	Revision > to recite words including a digraph
	Long vowels	18	Introduction > Children were explained how to pronounce words including long vowels such as *cool* and *green*.
		19, 20, 21	Revision > to recite words including a long vowel
Spelling rules	Split-grapheme (V-*e*) rule	12	Introduction > The researcher explained how the pronunciation of CVC changes when a final-*e* is added.
		13, 14, 15, 16, 18, 19, 20, 21, 22	Revision (and morning activities with HRT) > to recite a CVC word and the corresponding CVC*e* word repeatedly
	Consonant doubling	17	Introduction > Children were explained that consonant doubling in English does not make a glottal stop as it does in *Roma-ji* but shows that the preceding vowel is a short vowel.
		18, 19, 20, 21	Revision > to recite words including consonant doubling
	Consonant cluster	13, 17	Introduction > Children were visually shown a consonant blend and practiced to pronounce it.
		18, 19, 20, 21	Revision > to recite words including consonant blend
Adopted skills	CVC word reading	8, 9	Word card reading > to recite three-letter CVC words
		11	Revision: (2) Word reading > to recite three-letter CVC words on the screen
		9	Revision > to recite three-letter CVC words on randomly presented word cards
	Sentence reading	10	Phonic story reading > to recite simple sentences in a phonic story
		12	Picture book reading: *Top Cat Nap* > to recite simple sentences in a phonic story
Others	Letter names	1, 2, 3	Revision > to recite names of the letters on cards
		1	Alphabet pairs matching game > match the pairs of alphabet letters
		2	Join Alphadots > to draw a line between the alphabet letters as they were read by the researcher
		3	Pair worksheet: What letters do you have? > A pair work to ask what letters the partner has. The letters comprises a word.

* Some activities and task require multiple skills
  (e.g., CVC word reading needs skills such as phoneme segmentation and blending.)

Appendix 4.2: Description of *the new content instruction* and *phonological awareness activities* in each session

Session	The target new content and phonological awareness instruction (i.e., excluding "Greeting," "Reflection sheet," and "Curricular content (*Eigo Note 1*)")
1	**4. Recitation of alphabet names** [*Method*] 1. T shows Ps lower-case alphabet letter cards in a random order and pronounces their names. 2. Ps repeat letter names after T. T consistently uses the expression, "What is the name of this letter?" 3. Showing Ps alphabet letter cards, T asks them to say their names by themselves. T uses the expression, "What is the *name* of this letter?" consistently. (reference to *Roma-ji* when possible, asking where Ps have seen them) [*Target letters*] a-z
	5. Alphabet pairs matching game [*Method*] Ps do a jigsaw puzzle of both upper-case and lower-case letters. [*Target letters*] a-z, A-Z
2	**4. Revision of alphabet names** [*Method*] The same as in "Recitation of alphabet names" in Session 1. [*Target letters*] a-z
	5. Join Alphadots (*Primary Activity Box*, CUP, 2001) [*Method*] Ps join the letters in alphabetical order by drawing a line between the dots beside the letters. [*Target letters*] a-z, A-Z
	6. 'What letters do you have?' Introduction [*Method*] Introduction of the expression "What letters do you like?" and demonstration of the activity which will be held in Session 3. [*Target words*] bag, red, lip, quiz, victory
3	**2. Revision of alphabet names** [*Method*] The same as in "Recitation of alphabet names" in Session 1. [*Target letters*] a-z
	3. 'What letters do you have?' Pair-worksheet [*Method*] 1. In pairs, P1 asks P2 to tell the spelling of the words by using the expression "What letters do you have?" 2. Ps tells the spelling of the words by saying constituent letter names. [*Target words*] bike, tape, fox, watch, happy, hungry, popcorn, bus, desk, fish, rabbit, fine, sleepy, sandwich
4	**2. Elkonin cards without letters** [*Method*] A. Phonological awareness training [blending] 1. T puts up picture cards of words which has already introduced to Ps. 2. T explains the task by saying, "Let's do math. Add the sounds you hear to make a word you know."

	3. (For example,) T says /m/, /a/, /p/.
	4. Ps raise their hand when they recognise the word.
	5. Ps say the word together and check the answer. Ps repeat the word after T.
	B. Phonological awareness training [segmenting]
	   1. T shows an Elkonin card (e.g,. dog) and say the word extending each sound (e.g., /ddddd/, /ooooo/, /ggggg/) and pointing each box.
	   2. T explains that each box means one sound and the number of boxes on the card represents that of sounds which make up the word.
	   3. T shows another card and asks Ps to guess the sound for each box.
	   4. While T points to boxes from left to right, Ps say each sound extending it.
	[*Target words*]
	  > [words which will be used for introducing short vowel and consonant sounds in Session 5] *bat, bag, cab, can, cat, fan, ham, hat, jam, jar, map, man, mat, pan, rat, tap, wax, bed, hen, jet, leg, pen, red, ten, pen, pet, net, vet, web, yes, big, hit, sit, kid, lip, pin, pig, six, zip, box, boy, dog, dot, fox, hop, hot, job, log, not, top, toy, pot, mop, bus, bug, cut, fun, hug, mug, nut, run, sun, tub*
	  > [phonologically regular words from *Eigo Note 1*, Lesson 1, 2, and 3] *Ken, ten*

	3. Elkonin card *Karuta* game [*Method*] T (or P1) selects a letter and names it, and Ps look for the Elkonin word card whose initial letter is the same as the one read by T (or P1). T may ask Ps to guess the pronunciation of the word on the card. [*Target words*] *ant, bus, cat, dog, egg. fox, gum, hat, ink, job, kid, lip, map, net, oil, pen, quiz, run, sun, top, up, vet, web, (x-box), yes, zip*
5	**2. Revision of words introduced in Session 4** [*Method*] T shows the Elkonin cards and Ps say the words for them.

	3. Introduction of vowel-sound letters
	[*Method*]
	   1. T shows a picture card with a CVC word whose V is *i* and pronounces it. Ps repeat after T.
	     [T starts with i, e, and o first, then a, and finally u because the difference between /a/ and /u/ should be taught explicitly.]
	   2. T points the vowel letter *a* and asks Ps its name.
	   3. T takes out another picture card with a CVC word whose V is *e* and pronounces it. Ps repeat after T.
	   4. T points the vowel letter in the CVC word and asks Ps its name.
	     [T repeats this with picture cards with CVC words whose Vs are *o* and *a*.]
	   5. T explains that letter sounds are different from letter names and that Ps have already been familiar with some vowel letter sounds in *Roma-ji*. T writes *ba, bi, be,* and *bo* on the blackboard. (ignoring S's pointing out that *bu* is missing).
	   6. T shows a picture card with a CVC word whose V is *u* and pronounces it. Ps repeat after T.
	   7. When Ps notice that the sound of the letter *u* is /ʌ/, T explains it explicitly.
	   8. Practice (T asks Ps to pronounce them and sometimes sounds and names of the words in turn. Then, do the same in pairs.)
	[*Target words*]
	/a/: *bat, bag, hat, map, mat, man, tap*
	/e/: *bed, pen, ten, pet, net*
	/i/: *big, hit, sit, kid, pin, pig*
	/o/: *dog, hop, hot, top, mop, dot*
	/u/: *bus, bug, nut, tub, sun, hug*

	4. Introduction of consonant-sound letters (1) [*Method*] 1. T shows a target CVC word card with picture (e.g., *bag*) pronounce it. Ps repeat after T.

	2. T pronounces the word stretching the initial consonant sound (e.g., /bbbbbb/). Ps close eyes and raise right hands when they hear combination of sounds like /bu/, and left hands when /b/. [T explains the difference between /b/ and the sound of *Roma-ji* /bu/.] 3. T asks Ps to imitate /bbbbbb/. 4. T shows another picture card of the same initial consonant and pronounce it. Ps repeat after T. 5. T pronounces the word stretching the initial consonant (e.g., /bbbbbb/), and asks Ps to imitate it. 6. T points the initial consonant letter in the CVC word and asks Ps its name. 7. T explains that the sounds of consonant letters are also different from their names and that Ps have already been familiar with some consonant letter sounds in *Roma-ji*. T writes *ma*, *mi*, *me*, and *mo* on the blackboard. 8. T shows other CVC word cards whose initial consonants are *m* asks children to guess their pronunciation [T introduces other consonant sounds in the same way, revising when necessary.] [6~8: Do these with *ta*, *ti*, *tu*, *te*, and *to*, and let Ps notice the differences between /ti/ and *chi*, and /tu/ and *tsu*.] *Alternatively* 1. T puts all target three-letter CVC word cards on the blackboard. 2. T asks S1 to select a letter in the initial position by saying its name. 3. T picks up the word card with the letter P1 pointed out, and pronounce the word. Ps repeat after T. 4. T asks Ps to guess the sound for the letter. 5. When the right sound is answered*, T shows Ps other words with the same initial consonant. T pronounces them and Ps repeat after T. [T introduces other consonant sounds in the same way, revising when necessary.] *If P1 answers the initial sound with the following vowel sound (e.g. /bi/ for *big*), T picks up other word cards including the same initial consonant (e.g. *bag*, *bed*, *bug*). After asking Ps to pronounce them several times, T gives P1 another chance to answer. T encourages P1 and other Ps to separate the initial sound as small as possible from the word. [*Target consonants*] /b/, /d/, /g/, /h/, /k/, /m/, /n/, /p/, /d/, /t/, /z/ [*Target words*] [words used for vowel sound introduction] *bat*, *bag*, *hat*, *map*, *mat*, *man*, *pan*, *tap*, *bed*, *pen*, *ten*, *pet*, *net*, *big*, *hit*, *sit*, *kid*, *pin*, *pig*, *dog*, *ham*, *hat*, *hen*, *hop*, *hot*, *top*, *man*, *mop*, *mug*, *dot*, *bus*, *bug*, *nut*, *tub*, *sun*, *hug* / [supplementary] *kiss*, *king*, *zip*, *zigzag*, *zebra* / [words needed for later introduction of V-e rule in Session 10] *not*
	5. Letter-sound *Karuta* [*Method*] 1. In groups, Ps place letter card face up. 2. S1 pulls out a picture card and Ps read it. Then, P1 tells which position of letters is the target by reading the word on the back of the card (i.e., initial, medial, or final). Other Ps listen to it and find a card on which the letter is written. S who took the card first keeps it. 3. Continue until all cards are read. 4. Evaluation. Ps read aloud the cards which they have kept and compete with others in number. [At first, T may play a role of S1.] [*Target words*] *Initial letter*: cat, fox (fish), hat, jet (job), kid, leg (lemon?), quiz, red (rabbit), vet, web, zip *Medial letter*: mat, pen (ten), pin, dot, sun *Final letter*: tub, bed, dog (log), jam, can, mop, bus, net, box, boy (toy)
6	**2. Revision of words and letter sounds introduced in Session 5** [*Method*] T shows the Elkonin cards or lower-case letter cards and Ps say the words or letter sounds for them.

	3. Introduction of consonant-sound letters (2)
	[*Method*]
	    The same as in "Introduction of consonant-sound letters (1)" in Session 5.
	[*Target consonants and words*]
	    /c/: cat, cab, can, cut, cool, carrot, cute, cream, curry
	        [T explains that the sound for basic sounds for letters *c* and *k* is the same /k/.]
	    /f/: fan, fat, fox, fun, fine, four, five, fish
	    /j/: jam, jar, jet, job, juice, jump, just
	    /l/: lip, like, leg, log
	    /q/: quiz, queen
	    /r/: run, rat, rock, rabbit, red, ruler
	    /v/: vet, vest, van
	    /w/: web, wax, watch
	    /y/: yes, yellow, boy, toy
	    /x/: box, fox, six	

7	**2. Revision of words and letter sounds introduced**
	[*Method*]
	    T shows the Elkonin cards or lower-case letter cards and Ps say the words or letters for them.
	[*Target words*]
	    >[words used for introducing short vowel and consonant sounds] *bat, bag, cab, can, cat, fan, ham, hat, jam, jar, map, man, mat, pan, rat, tap, wax, bed, hen, jet, leg, pen, red, ten, pen, pet, net, vet, web, yes, big, hit, sit, kid, lip, pin, pig, six, zip, box, boy, dog, dot, fox, hop, hot, job, log, not, top, toy, pot, mop, bus, bug, cut, fun, hug, mug, nut, run, sun, tub*	

8	**2. ♪ Review Song of letter sounds**
	[*Method*]
	    Ps watch the video and sing the phonic song; e.g., "/ɑ/, /ɑ/, ant, /b/, /b/, bee, /c/, /c/, cold, ..."
	[*Target letter sounds*]
	    /ɑ/ - /z/	

	3. Revision of words and letter sounds introduced [*Method*] T shows the Elkonin cards or lower-case letter cards and Ps say the words or letter sounds for them.	

	4. Onset-rime slides
	[*Method*]
	    Ps read the word by combining the new onset which appears in the window and the rime.
	[*Target rimes*]
	    -ad, -ag, -am, -an, -ask, -and, -ank, -ant, -ap, -ed, -en, -est, -et, -id, -end, -in, -it, -ink, -ip, -it, -ob, -op, -ot, -ub, -ug, -um, -un, -ut	

	5. Word card reading
	[*Method*]
	    T shows some word cards and Ps pronounce them.
	[*Target words*]
	    > bag, cat, map, bed, pen, net, dog	

9	**2. ♪ abc Song**
	[*Method*]
	    Ps sing the "abc Song" with letter sounds, not letter names.
	[*Target words*]
	    /ɑ/ - /z/	

	3. Reading aloud of CVC-letter words on the word cards [*Method*] T shows the word cards and Ps pronounce them.	

	[Target words] > [words used for introducing short vowel and consonant sounds] bat, bag, cab, can, cat, fan, ham, hat, jam, jar, map, man, mat, pan, rat, tap, wax, bed, hen, jet, leg, pen, red, ten, pen, pet, net, vet, web, yes, big, hit, sit, kid, lip, pin, pig, six, zip, box, boy, dog, dot, fox, hop, hot, job, log, not, top, toy, pot, mop, bus, bug, cut, fun, hug, mug, nut, run, sun, tub
10	**2. ♪ abc Song** [Method] Ps sing the "abc Song" with letter sounds, not letter names.
	3. Reading aloud simple English sentences [*Fun Phonic Readers 1*: Story 1 & 2] [Method] T shows Ps a simple phonic reader and Ps tries to read it. [Sample sentences] An ant is in a pot. An ant is in a box. An ant is in a bag.
11	**3. Revision:** **(1) Adding sounds** [Method] Ps look at the video that shows blending of $C_1 + V + C_2$ and repeat after the demonstration. [Target words] bag, pen, pig, box, cup **(2) Word reading** [Method] Ps read aloud the words projected on the screen one by one. [Target words] bag, cat, hat, jam, man, ten, men, bed, red, pen, pig, big, sit, six, pin, box, hot, stop, mom, top, cup, sun, sun, bus, cut **(3) Phoneme identification [middle vowel], (4) Phoneme identification [middle vowel]** **(5) Phoneme recognition [initial or final phoneme]** [Method (3)] Ps listen to a pair of words (e.g., 1. *map* / 2. *mop*). Looking at the worksheet which has the pictures for these words, Ps decide which is "No.1" or "No. 2" and show their finger(s) corresponding to the number. [Target words] map / mop, hat / hot, bag / bug, bed / bad, man / men **(6) Speed reading (Onset-rime level)** [Method] Ps read aloud groups of three words, as quickly as possible. Ps clap hands each time after reading three words. [Target words] sad, bad, dad / not, pot, hot / wit, sit, hit / red, bed, Ted / top, hop, pop / run, sun, fun
12	**3. Worksheet: Identification of a vowel letter in the middle position** [Method] Ps listen to a word (e.g., *hat*) and circle a letter which represents the middle vowel sound of the word (e.g., *a* or *u*) on the worksheet. [Target words] hat (distractor: *u*), run (*a*), jam (*e*), bed (*i*), six (*o*), hot (*a*), sit (*e*), mop (*u*), big (*e*), ten (*i*)
	4. Revision of vowel sounds [Method] T show Ps lower-case vowel letter cards randomly and Ps said their sounds. [Target words] a, e, i, o, u
	5. Introduction of Split-grapheme rule [Method] 1. T asks Ps to write the following words in English (saying each constituent sound, if necessary): *rat, pin, hop, not, cut, tub* 2. T adds the letter *e* to the end of these words and asks Ps how to pronounce them.

	3. T explains 'Magic e rule.'[*Target words*] a-e: **tap**e, **hat**e, name, (gate, date, lake, bake, make, take, rate, safe, late, same, fade, rake) i-e: **pin**e, **tim**e, (like, fine, nine, bike, nine, wide, ride, pipe, side, five, rice, bite, ride, hide, Mike) o-e: **hop**e, **not**e (nose, hole, rope, bone, joke, pole, tone, vote, cone, robe, mole) u-e: **cut**e, **tub**e (cube, rule, tune, mute, fuse, mule, rude, dune) e-e: (eve, Pete) Additional: slide, slope, frame, flame, flute, shade, choke, Steve
	6. Picture book reading *Top Cat Nap* [*Method*] T shows a simple phonic story book and Ps tries to read it. [*Sample sentence*] Top Cat had a nap in a cap.
13	**2. Worksheet: Final phoneme identification & initial / Final phoneme recognition** [*Method*] [Final phoneme identification] Ps listen to a word presented by T and choose a letter that represents the initial phoneme of it. [Initial / Final phoneme recognition] Ps listen to a word presented by T and write a letter for the initial and final phonemes respectively. [*Target words*] [Final phoneme identification] *hat, bus, pen, gum, quiz, pig, cap, kid* [Initial / Final phoneme recognition] *mat, tub, fox, bed, big*
	3. Revision of Split-grapheme rule [*Method*] T shows Ps the cards of words with V-*e*, and Ps recite them. [*Target words*] The words used in the introduction.
	4. Introduction of initial / final phoneme deletion [*Method*] T shows Ps two groups of words: (1) words before the initial or final phoneme was deleted, and (2) words after the initial or final phoneme was deleted. After reciting the words, T asks Ps what the difference between the two groups is. [*Target words*] [Initial] clip / lip, clock / lock, ski / key, snail / nail, stop / top, train / rain, swing / wing [Final] date / day, note / no, belt / bell, rose / row, seat / sea, train / tray
	5. Short introduction of consonant cluster [*Method*] During the introduction of initial / final phoneme deletion, T attracted Ps' attention to consonant clusters included in the target words, and Ps recite them. [*Target words*] The words with consonant cluster used to introduce initial / final phoneme deletion.
14	**2. letter-sound *Review Song*** [*Method*] Ps sing the phonic song introduced in Session 8 (and practiced in the morning activities).
	3. Revision of letter sounds (and names) [*Method*] T shows Ps lower-case letter cards randomly saying, "Name" or "Sound," and Ps say their name or sound according to the cue. [*Target words*] a-z, /ɑ/ - /z/
	4. Revision of Split-grapheme rule [*Method*] T shows Ps the cards of words with V-*e*, and Ps recite them. [*Target words*] The words used in the introduction.

	5. Recitation of words for *Karuta*
	 [*Method*]
	    T show Ps picture cards without spellings, and Ps recite the words for the cards.
	 [*Target words*]
	    The same as in Initial-sound Karuta.

	6. Word *Karuta*
	 [*Method*]
	    In groups. T shows Ps a picture card and Ps say the word for it. Then, on the T's cue of "Initial," "Medial," or "Final," Ps find a letter for the phoneme in that position.
	 [*Target words*]
	    [Initial letter] *cat, fox, hat, jet, kid, leg, queen, rabbit, vet, web, zip*
	    [Medial letter] *mat, pen, pin, dot, sun*
	    [Final letter] *tub, bed, dog, jam, can, mop, bus, net, box, boy*

15	**2. letter-sound *Review Song*** [*Method*] Ps sing the phonic song introduced in Session 8 (and practiced in the morning activities).

	3. Revision of letter sounds (and names)
	 [*Method*]
	    T shows Ps lower-case letter cards randomly saying, "Name" or "Sound," and Ps say their name or sound according to the cue.
	 [*Target words*]
	    a-z, /ɑ/ - /z/

	4. Revision of Split-grapheme rule
	 [*Method*]
	    T shows Ps the cards of words with V-e, and Ps recite them.
	 [*Target words*]
	    The words used in the introduction.

	5. Recognition of Phoneme substitution
	 [*Method*]
	    1. Ps recite the target words and receive a double-picture card each from T.
	    2. Ps think about which sound (initial, medial, or final) is different in the two words that represent the pictures.
	    3. In turn, Ps come to the blackboard, and put the card under the picture of a shark's head (initial), body (medial), or tail (final).
	 [*Target words*]
	    lap / cap, pan / fan, bed / head, pen / ten, bell / shell, pin / fin, hat / cat, rock / lock, lake / cake, fire / tire, house / mouse, shawl / shell, cap / cup, chalk / check, bell / ball, hop / hip, tape / top, sheep / ship, boat / bat, can / cone, bug / bag, boat / boot, map / mop, cane / cave, sing / sink, pet / pen, pig / pin, bat / back, sleep / sleeve

	6. Phoneme segmentation and categorisation
	 [*Method*]
	    In a form of a pair worksheet activity. Ps answer the position of a common sound by putting a double-picture card on one of three boxes representing the initial, middle or final sound.
	 [*Target words*]
	    watermelon / can, heart / card, window / toe, hive / kite, tree / cry, star / saddle, computer / zipper, banana / bike, juice / jar, drum / game, guitar / glue, bird / bat, camel / clown, inch / ant

16	**2. Revision of letter sounds (and names)**
	 [*Method*]
	    T shows Ps lower-case letter cards randomly saying, "Name" or "Sound," and Ps say their name or sound according to the cue.
	 [*Target words*]
	    a-z, /ɑ/ - /z/

	3. Revision of Split-grapheme rule [*Method*] T shows Ps the cards of words with V-*e*, and Ps recite them. [*Target words*] The words used in the introduction.

	4. Demonstration of phoneme substitution
	[*Method*]
	Ps decide which phoneme has been changed by comparing two pictures.
	  1. Taking turns, Ps select the top card from the stack and say the name of each picture (e.g., *cat* and *can*).
	  2. Ps determine what sound has been changed and say those two sounds (i.e., /t/ and /n/).
	  3. Ps state whether the sound change is located at the beginning, middle, or end of the word (i.e., The end sound changed from /t/ to /n/.)
	  4. Ps place an "X" under the correct heading on their student sheets.
	[*Target words*]
	nose / toes, boat / coat, rake / cake, book / hook, feet / meat, mug / bug, bell / ball, dog / dig, map / mop, moon / man, kite / coat, gate / game, hat / ham, seed / seal, dice / dime, cat / can

	6. Phoneme identification
	[*Method*]
	  1. Ps recite the target words looking at double-picture cards.
	  2. In pairs, Ps find what sound (initial, medial, or final) is different between two words, and put the card under the pictures of a shark's head (initial), body (medial), or tail (final).
	[*Target words*]
	heart / card, tree / cry, computer / zipper, drum / game, bird / shirt, carrot / bat, camel / clown, inch / ant, watermelon / can, window / toe, hive / kite, star / saddle, banana / bike, juice / jar, guitar / glue

17	**2. Revision of letter sounds (and names)** [*Method*] T shows Ps lower-case letter cards randomly saying, "Name" or "Sound," and Ps say their name or sound according to the cue. [*Target words*] a-z, /ɑ/ - /z/

	4. Phoneme substitution
	[*Method*]
	  1. On a worksheet, Ps individually look at a picture and listen to the word for it (e.g., *fan*).
	  2. T gives an instruction such as "Change /f/ into /k/."
	  3. Ps find a picture (e.g., *can*) which represents the resulting word out of two options (e.g., *can* and *pan*).
	[*Target words*]
	fan / can (distractor: pan), sock / rock (lock), mop / top (hop), can / cap (cat), pin / pen (pan), bike / book (bake), bat / hat (mat), cane / corn (can), phone / fin (fan), sax / six (socks)

	5. Introduction of consonant cluster
	[*Method*]
	  1. T asks Ps to write the following words of foreign origin with *Roma-ji*: *black, ski, stop, slip, sport, train, cream, speed, strike, dress, friend, green, spring*
	  2. T shows the spellings for the words and asks Ps to compare them with what they wrote.
	  3. T raises children's awareness of consonant blends, and explains that vowel epenthesis often occurs in Japanese pronunciation of English.

	Target Words: [Target words] > [words with consonant blends from *Eigo Note 1*] sleepy, twelve, twenty, many, cream, strawberry, swimming, black, blue, dress, green, skirt, sweater, glove, grape, gratin, spaghetti, steak, strawberries, butterfly, crafts, economics, Friday, studies, study, swim, bread, croissant, France, fruit
	6. Introduction of consonant doubling [Method] 1. T prepare word cards on which double consonants are highlighted. 2. T reads the words showing the cards to them, and Ps repeat after T. 3. T asks Ps how the part of double consonants is pronounced, giving a clue such as "There are two consonants in each word, but they are pronounced as if ~?" 4. When Ps understand how to pronounce them, T reads the words again and Ps repeat after T. [Target words] > [words with consonant doubling from *Eigo Note 1*] hello, happy, apple, apples, carrot, pineapple, rabbit, soccer, strawberry, swimming, dress, yellow, ball, basketball, cabbage, cherry, giraffe, gorilla, omelette, puff, strawberries, butterfly, jellyfish, curry
18	**2. Revision of letter sounds (and names)** [Method] T shows Ps lower-case letter cards randomly saying, "Name" or "Sound," and Ps say their name or sound according to the cue. [Target words] a-z, /ɑ/ - /z/
	3. Revision of consonant cluster or consonant doubling [Method] Ps recite the words with consonant cluster or consonant doubling. [Target words] The words used in the introduction.
	4. Revision of Split-grapheme rule [Method] T shows Ps the cards of words with V-e, and Ps recite them. [Target words] The words used in the introduction.
	5. Introduction of a digraph *th* [Method] T tells Ps that *th* makes a sound of /θ/ and explain its articulation. Then, Ps recite some words with *th*. [Target words] thirsty, Thursday, thank, mouth, math
	6. Rime Identification [Method] Ps match rime picture card to corresponding Rime House. 1. Taking turns, Ps name each picture header card, and segment the onset and rime (e.g., *hat*, /h/ /ɑt/). 2. Ps repeat the rime (i.e., /ɑt/), select the top card, look at the target rime pictures, and place the picture pn the matching Rime House. [Target words] cat, hat, mat, bat, rat, log, fog, jog, frog, bug, rug, hug, jug, plug, hop, top, chop, stop, mop, map, cap, clap, lap, tap, pig, dig, wig, twig, big
	7. Introduction of long vowels [Method] 1. Ps are presented with word cards on which *ee* or *oo* as a long vowel is highlighted in red and asked to recite them after T. 2. T explains what sound *ee* or *oo* make in English. [Target words] [ee] green, sleepy, three, sheep [oo] cool, kangaroo (in contrast to *book* and *good*)

19	**2. Revision of letter sounds (and names)**
	[*Method*]
	   T shows Ps lower-case letter cards randomly saying, "Name" or "Sound," and Ps say their name or sound according to the cue.
	[*Target words*]
	   a-z, /a/ - /z/
	
	3. Revision of Split-grapheme rule
	[*Method*]
	   T shows Ps the cards of words with V-*e*, and Ps recite them.
	[*Target words*]
	   The words used in the introduction.
	
	4. Revision of consonant cluster and doubling, and long vowels
	[*Method*]
	   T shows Ps the target word cards and Ps recite them
	[*Target words*]
	   The words used in the introduction.
	
	6. Introduction of words for initial sound *Domino*
	[*Method*]
	   T shows picture cards for the words used in the following *Domino* activity, and Ps recite them after T.
	[*Target words*]
	   The words used in the *Domino*.
	
	7. Group competition: Initial sound *Domino*
	[*Method*]
	   In groups, Ps complete the *Domino* by connecting a letter with the picture of a word whose initial phoneme is represented by the letter.
	[*Target words*]
	   lamp, *skunk*, *zebra*, *pencil*, *kiss*, *octopus*, *yak*, *wink*, *inch*, *x-ray*, *brush*, *hammer*, *ant*, *tent*, *violin*, *robot*, *grapes*, *monkey*, *cat*, *egg*, *nine*, *quilt*, *dog*, *jacks*, *umbrella*, *fish*

20	**2. Revision of letter sounds (and names)**
	[*Method*]
	   T shows Ps lower-case letter cards randomly saying, "Name" or "Sound," and Ps say their name or sound according to the cue.
	[*Target words*]
	   a-z, /a/ - /z/
	
	3. Revision of Split-grapheme rule
	[*Method*]
	   T shows Ps the cards of words with V-*e*, and Ps recite them.
	[*Target words*]
	   The words used in the introduction.
	
	4. Revision of consonant cluster and blending, and long vowels
	[*Method*]
	   T shows Ps the target word cards and Ps recite them
	[*Target words*]
	   The words used in the introduction.
	
	5. Word card reading
	[*Method*]
	   T shows Ps the word cards that have been introduced in the intervention randomly, and Ps recite them after T.
	[*Target words*]
	   Randomly selected words from those that have been already introduced.
	
	6. Introduction of digraphs *wh*, *th*, *ck*, *ch*, *sh*
	[*Method*]
	   1. T shows Ps digraph cards and Ps recite them after T.
	   2. T demonstrates the segmentation of the words with a digraph and asks Ps to blend them.
	   3. Ps practise to recite the words whose spellings are presented by T.

		[Target words] truck, chick, brush, brick, ship, inch, block, bath, check, duck, fish, clock, lock, chin, dish, rock
		7. Worksheet: Write a digraph! [Method] After reciting the target words looking at the picture cards, Ps fill *ch* or *sh* in the blanks on the worksheet. [Target words] tea(ch)er / (sh)oe / (sh)eep / (ch)air / bea(ch) / kit(ch)en / bru(sh) / fi(sh)ing / di(sh) / wat(ch)
		8. Digraph roulette [Method] Ps blend the initial, medial, and final sounds on the individual roulettes to make a word. [Target letters on the roulettes] [Initial] wh, th, ch, sh, [Medial] o, e, u, a, I, [Final] ck, t, p, m, n
		9. Digraph *Bingo* [Method] Ps write three or four of the target digraphs (*sh*, *th*, *ng*, *ck*, and *ch*) in the 4×4 Bingo card. T randomly shows Ps a picture card which represents a word with a digraph. Ps say the word and find the digraph in their Bingo card and circle it. [Target words] fish, dish, toothbrush, leash, brush, inch, sandwich, couch, ostrich, match, sock, brick, chick, clock, haystack, ring, wing, king, sing, teeth, earth, wreath, bath, fifth
21		**2. Revision of letter sounds (and names)** [Method] T shows Ps lower-case letter cards randomly saying, "Name" or "Sound," and Ps say their name or sound according to the cue. [Target words] a-z, /ɑ/ - /z/
		3. Revision of Split-grapheme rule [Method] T shows Ps the cards of words with V-*e*, and Ps recite them. [Target words] The words used in the introduction.
		4. Revision of consonant cluster and doubling, and long vowels [Method] T shows Ps the target word cards and Ps recite them [Target words] The words used in the introduction.
		5. Revision of digraphs *wh*, *th*, *ck*, *ch*, *sh* [Method] T shows Ps the target word cards with digraphs and Ps recite them [Target words] The words used in the introduction.
22		**2. Letter sound knowledge test (part of the final assessment)** [Method] Ps circle the letter whose sound is orally presented by T. [Target letter sounds] /u/, /m/, /w/, /p/. /v/, /z/, /d/, /e/, /c/, /h/, /l/, /n/, /q/, /y/, /j/, /b/, /f/, /r/, /x/, /g/
		3. Revision of Split-grapheme rule [Method] T shows Ps the cards of words with V-*e*, and Ps recite them. [Target words] The words used in the introduction.

Appendix 4.3: The summary of the statistical significance yielded in the written tests of the initial and final assessments

Initial vs. Final Assessment

			t	df	p
All children	Letter Name Knowledge	Total	26	5.515	**
		d	26	5.701	**
		h	26	2.726	*
		l	26	2.563	*
		n	26	2.726	*
		q	26	3.911	**
		b	26	5.292	**
		g	26	3.017	**
	Sound Categorisation	End sound 3	26	3,114	**
	Initial Phoneme Recognition	Total	26	5.249	**
		/m/	26	2.478	*
		/t/	26	2.642	*
		/k/	26	3.425	**
		/p/	26	2.532	*
		/g/	26	2.565	*
	Phoneme Recognition & Location	Total	26	3.920	**
		/m/	26	4.379	**
		/t/	26	4.602	**
		/k/	26	3.166	**
		/g/	26	3.927	**
Group A	Sound Categorisation	Opening sound 1	9	2.333	*
		End Sound 3	9	2.739	*
	Initial Phoneme Recognition	Total	9	3.424	**
		/h/	9	3.308	**
	Phoneme Recognition & Location	/m/	9	2.283	*
		/t/	9	3.721	**
Group B	Letter Name Knowledge	Total	3	3.286	*
	Sound Categorisation	Opening Sound 1	3	4.700	*
		End Sound 4	3	5.000	*
	Phoneme Recognition & Location	/g/	3	5.196	*
Group C	Letter Name Knowledge	Total	12	6.278	**
		d	12	8.124	**
		h	12	2.309	*
		l	12	3.207	**
		n	12	2.739	*
		q	12	5.196	**
		b	12	6.325	**
		g	12	3.742	**
	Initial Phoneme Recognition	Total	12	3.040	*
		/m/	12	3.411	**
		/k/	12	2.379	*
	Phoneme Recognition & Location	Total	12	3.275	**
		/m/	12	3.941	**
		/t/	12	4.395	**
		/k/	12	3.118	**
		/g/	12	2.551	*

* $p < .05$ ** $p < .01$

Between Groups

			t	df	p
Group A vs. Group B	*Initial Assessment* Letter Name Knowledge	Total	12	2.674	*
		m	12	2.928	*
		q	12	2.928	*
	Final Assessment Sound Categorisation	Opening Sound 1	12	3.407	**
		Opening Sound 2	12	2.268	*
	Phoneme Recognition & Location	/t/	12	2.226	*
Group B vs. Group C	*Initial Assessment* Letter Name Knowledge	*l*	15	2.584	*
		b	15	3.525	**
	Phoneme Recognition & Location	/t/	15	2.357	*
		/b/	15	2.199	*
		/k/	15	2.584	*
		/p/	15	3.050	**
Group A vs. Group C	*Initial Assessment* Letter Name Knowledge	Total	21	5.919	**
		d	21	3.880	**
		e	21	3.264	**
		l	21	3.880	**
		n	21	3.264	**
		q	21	4.532	**
		b	21	3.904	**
		g	21	3.264	**
	Initial Phoneme Recognition	/k/	21	2.363	*
	Phoneme Recognition & Location	Total	21	2.189	*
		/m/	21	2.425	*
		/k/	21	2.283	*
		/g/	21	3.121	**
	Final Assessment Letter Name Knowledge	Total	21	3.206	**
		v	21	2.566	*
	Sound Categorisation	Opening Sound 1	21	2.338	*
	Initial Phoneme Recognition	/p/	21	2.166	*
		/h/	21	2.864	**
	Phoneme Recognition & Location	/g/	21	2.816	*

* $p < .05$ ** $p < .01$

Appendix 4.4: The results of the oral tests in the initial and final assessments — Sound manipulation

				Group A			Group B			Group C			All Children		
				N	Mean	SD	N	Mean	SD	N	Mean	SD	N	Mean	SD
Initial	1	IC_D	fill / ill	10	.30	.48	4	.00	.00	13	.08	.28	27	.15	.36
	2	IC_D	cup / up	10	.30	.48	4	.25	.50	13	.15	.38	27	.22	.42
	3	IC_D	bat / at	10	.30	.48	4	.25	.50	13	.08	.28	27	.19	.40
	4	IC_S	fill / bill	10	.50	.53	4	.75	.50	13	.38	.51	27	.48	.51
	5	IC_S	cup / pup	10	.10	.32	4	.25	.50	13	.08	.28	27	.11	.32
	6	IC_S	bat / sat	10	.00	.00	4	.00	.00	13	.15	.38	27	.07	.27
	7	FC_D	goat / go	10	.40	.52	4	.75	.50	13	.62	.51	27	.56	.51
	8	FC_D	make / ma	10	.70	.48	4	.75	.50	13	.92	.28	27	.81	.40
	9	FC_D	seal / sea	10	.80	.42	4	1.00	.00	13	.46	.52	27	.67	.48
	10	IC_S	fill / till	10	.40	.52	4	.25	.50	13	.08	.28	27	.22	.42
	11	FC_S	cup / cut	10	.70	.48	4	.75	.50	13	.54	.52	27	.63	.49
	12	FC_S	bite / bike	10	.70	.48	4	.75	.50	13	.62	.51	27	.67	.48
	13	ICC_D	slip / sip	10	.10	.32	4	.00	.00	13	.00	.00	27	.04	.19
	14	ICC_D	stick / sick	10	.30	.48	4	.25	.50	13	.00	.00	27	.15	.36
	15	FCC_D	nest / net	10	.70	.48	4	.50	.58	13	.23	.44	27	.44	.51
	16	FCC_S	crest / crept	10	.20	.42	4	.00	.00	13	.08	.28	27	.11	.32
	17	ICC_S	slip / snip	10	.10	.32	4	.50	.58	13	.15	.38	27	.19	.40
	18	ICC_S	stick / slick	10	.30	.48	4	.25	.50	13	.00	.00	27	.15	.36
	Total			10	6.90	3.93	4	7.27	2.22	13	4.62	2.90	27	5.85	3.36
Final	1	IC_D	fill / ill	10	.70	.48	3	.67	.58	13	.62	.51	26	.65	.49
	2	IC_D	cup / up	10	.50	.53	3	.33	.58	13	.31	.48	26	.38	.50
	3	IC_D	bat / at	10	.90	.32	3	.67	.58	13	.38	.51	26	.62	.50
	4	IC_S	fill / bill	10	1.00	.00	3	1.00	.00	13	.69	.48	26	.85	.37
	5	IC_S	cup / pup	10	.60	.52	3	.33	.58	13	.31	.48	26	.42	.50
	6	IC_S	bat / sat	10	.50	.53	3	.67	.58	13	.08	.28	26	.31	.47
	7	FC_D	goat / go	10	1.00	.00	3	1.00	.00	13	.85	.38	26	.92	.27
	8	FC_D	make / ma	10	.90	.32	3	1.00	.00	13	.77	.44	26	.85	.37
	9	FC_D	seal / sea	10	.80	.42	3	.67	.58	13	.62	.51	26	.69	.47
	10	IC_S	fill / till	10	.50	.53	3	.33	.58	13	.46	.52	26	.46	.51
	11	FC_S	cup / cut	10	.60	.52	3	.67	.58	13	.69	.48	26	.65	.49
	12	FC_S	bite / bike	10	1.00	.00	3	1.00	.00	13	.46	.52	26	.73	.45
	13	ICC_D	slip / sip	10	.30	.48	3	.33	.58	13	.08	.28	26	.19	.40
	14	ICC_D	stick / sick	10	.60	.52	3	.33	.58	13	.15	.38	26	.35	.49
	15	FCC_D	nest / net	10	.70	.48	3	.67	.58	13	.38	.51	26	.54	.51
	16	FCC_S	crest / crept	10	.50	.53	3	.00	.00	13	.08	.28	26	.23	.43
	17	ICC_S	slip / snip	10	.30	.48	3	.00	.00	13	.08	.28	26	.15	.37
	18	ICC_S	stick / slick	10	.50	.53	3	.33	.58	13	.08	.28	26	.27	.45
	Total			10	11.90	3.64	3	7.50	5.26	13	7.08	3.01	26	10.46	4.43
FInal		V_S	pet / pat	10	.80	.42	3	1.00	.00	13	.38	.51	26	.62	.50
(Additional)		V_S	mop / mip	10	.70	.48	3	.67	.58	13	.46	.52	26	.58	.50

IC = Initial Consonant   FC = Final Consonant   ICC = Initial Consonant Cluster
FCC = Final Consonant Cluster   V = Vowel   D = Deletion
S = Substitution   IP = Initial Phoneme   FP = Final Phoneme
ICC = Initial Consonant Cluster   FCC = Final Consonant Cluster
MV = Middle Vowel   D = Deletion   S = Substitution

Appendix 4.5: The results of the oral tests in the initial and final assessments —Real word and non-word reading

Initial Assessment (Correct answer: 1, Wrong or No answer: 0)

		Group A			Group B			Group C			All Children		
		N	Mean	SD	N	Mean	SD	N	Mean	SD	N	Mean	SD
1	name	10	.20	.42	4	.00	.00	13	.00	.00	27	.07	.27
2	sed	10	.30	.48	4	.00	.00	13	.08	.28	27	.15	.36
3	yes	10	.90	.32	4	.50	.58	13	.54	.52	27	.67	.48
4	wib	10	.40	.52	4	.00	.00	13	.15	.38	27	.22	.42
5	six	10	.50	.53	4	.75	.50	13	.23	.44	27	.41	.50
6	yag	10	.40	.52	4	.25	.50	13	.08	.28	27	.22	.42
7	five	10	.50	.53	4	.25	.50	13	.15	.38	27	.30	.47
8	cof	10	.70	.48	4	.00	.00	13	.00	.00	27	.26	.45
9	cute	10	.50	.53	4	.25	.50	13	.00	.00	27	.22	.42
10	puz	10	.30	.48	4	.25	.50	13	.00	.00	27	.15	.36
11	home	10	.10	.32	4	.00	.00	13	.00	.00	27	.04	.19
12	hul	10	.30	.48	4	.00	.00	13	.00	.00	27	.11	.32
13	black	10	.70	.48	4	.25	.50	13	.00	.00	27	.30	.47
14	quen	10	.00	.00	4	.00	.00	13	.00	.00	27	.00	.00
15	jellyfish	10	.50	.53	4	.25	.50	13	.08	.28	27	.26	.45
16	yage	10	.30	.48	4	.25	.50	13	.00	.00	27	.15	.36
17	this	10	.40	.52	4	.25	.50	13	.00	.00	27	.19	.40
18	sede	10	.00	.00	4	.00	.00	13	.00	.00	27	.00	.00
19	thank	10	.40	.52	4	.50	.58	13	.00	.00	27	.22	.42
20	wibe	10	.10	.32	4	.00	.00	13	.00	.00	27	.04	.19
21	sandwich	10	.40	.52	4	.25	.50	13	.00	.00	27	.19	.40
22	cofe	10	.10	.32	4	.00	.00	13	.00	.00	27	.04	.19
23	what	10	.60	.52	4	.25	.50	13	.00	.00	27	.26	.45
24	puze	10	.20	.42	4	.00	.00	13	.00	.00	27	.07	.27
25	green	10	.70	.48	4	.50	.58	13	.08	.28	27	.37	.49
26	chax	10	.50	.53	4	.00	.00	13	.08	.28	27	.22	.42
27	cool	10	.40	.52	4	.00	.00	13	.08	.28	27	.19	.40
28	tock	10	.30	.48	4	.25	.50	13	.15	.38	27	.22	.42
29	book	10	.80	.42	4	.25	.50	13	.31	.48	27	.48	.51
30	shem	10	.20	.42	4	.00	.00	13	.00	.00	27	.07	.27
31	octopus	10	.80	.42	4	.50	.58	13	.08	.28	27	.41	.50
32	rith	10	.00	.00	4	.00	.00	13	.00	.00	27	.00	.00
33	study	10	.70	.48	4	.00	.00	13	.00	.00	27	.26	.45
34	whov	10	.20	.42	4	.00	.00	13	.00	.00	27	.07	.27
35	jeen	10	.20	.42	4	.00	.00	13	.00	.00	27	.07	.27
36	koot	10	.00	.00	4	.00	.00	13	.00	.00	27	.00	.00
Total		10	13.6	8.96	4	5.75	7.14	13	2.08	3.12	27	6.89	8.20

Appendices   243

Final Assessment (Correct answer: 1, Wrong or No answer: 0)

		Group A			Group B			Group C			All Children		
		N	Mean	SD	N	Mean	SD	N	Mean	SD	N	Mean	SD
1	name	10	.90	.32	3	.33	.58	13	.31	.48	26	.62	.50
2	sed	10	.40	.52	3	.33	.58	13	.38	.51	26	.58	.50
3	yes	10	1.00	.00	3	1.00	.00	13	.85	.38	26	.54	.51
4	wib	10	.70	.48	3	.67	.58	13	.38	.51	26	.38	.50
5	six	10	.90	.32	3	1.00	.00	13	.69	.48	26	.92	.27
6	yag	10	.60	.52	3	1.00	.00	13	.31	.48	26	.54	.51
7	five	10	.80	.42	3	.33	.58	13	.31	.48	26	.81	.40
8	cof	10	.60	.52	3	.00	.00	13	.23	.44	26	.50	.51
9	cute	10	.60	.52	3	.67	.58	13	.38	.51	26	.50	.51
10	puz	10	.40	.52	3	.00	.00	13	.23	.44	26	.35	.49
11	home	10	.40	.52	3	.00	.00	13	.23	.44	26	.50	.51
12	hul	10	.10	.32	3	.00	.00	13	.23	.44	26	.27	.45
13	black	10	.70	.48	3	1.00	.00	13	.08	.28	26	.27	.45
14	quen	10	.10	.32	3	.00	.00	13	.00	.00	26	.15	.37
15	jellyfish	10	.60	.52	3	.00	.00	13	.08	.28	26	.42	.50
16	yage	10	.40	.52	3	.00	.00	13	.00	.00	26	.04	.20
17	this	10	.60	.52	3	.33	.58	13	.23	.44	26	.27	.45
18	sede	10	.20	.42	3	.33	.58	13	.00	.00	26	.15	.37
19	thank	10	.40	.52	3	.00	.00	13	.08	.28	26	.38	.50
20	wibe	10	.30	.48	3	.00	.00	13	.15	.38	26	.12	.33
21	sandwich	10	.70	.48	3	.67	.58	13	.08	.28	26	.19	.40
22	cofe	10	.20	.42	3	.00	.00	13	.00	.00	26	.19	.40
23	what	10	.60	.52	3	.00	.00	13	.15	.38	26	.38	.50
24	puze	10	.50	.53	3	1.00	.00	13	.23	.44	26	.08	.27
25	green	10	.80	.42	3	.67	.58	13	.15	.38	26	.31	.47
26	chax	10	.50	.53	3	.33	.58	13	.08	.28	26	.42	.50
27	cool	10	.50	.53	3	.00	.00	13	.00	.00	26	.46	.51
28	tock	10	.70	.48	3	1.00	.00	13	.31	.48	26	.27	.45
29	book	10	.70	.48	3	.67	.58	13	.38	.51	26	.19	.40
30	shem	10	.30	.48	3	.00	.00	13	.00	.00	26	.54	.51
31	octopus	10	.80	.42	3	.67	.58	13	.38	.51	26	.54	.51
32	rith	10	.00	.00	3	.00	.00	13	.00	.00	26	.12	.33
33	study	10	.70	.48	3	1.00	.00	13	.15	.38	26	.58	.50
34	whov	10	.20	.42	3	.00	.00	13	.08	.28	26	.00	.00
35	jeen	10	.20	.42	3	.00	.00	13	.00	.00	26	.46	.51
36	koot	10	.00	.00	3	.00	.00	13	.00	.00	26	.12	.33
Total		10	18.1	9.21	3	9.75	6.85	13	7.15	5.06	26	12.04	8.40

Index

adding 22, 70, 72
alphabetic principle 16, 17, 51, 64
alphasyllabary 48
analytic skills 72
assessment of phonological awareness, *see* phonological awareness assessment
authenticity of non-words 93

beliefs
    of teachers 10–11, 174, 188
    of parents 10
blending 22, 28, 40, 62, 65, 66, 68–69, 70, 72, 73, 75, 81

Commentary on the Course of Study for Elementary Schools 1
concrete operational stage 8
consonant 84
    cluster 18–19, 39, 47, 50, 57, 61, 69, 73–74, 84, 93
    doubling 82, 83–84
Course of Study for Elementary Schools 1–5, 9, 56, 157, 181, 188

deleting 22, 34–35, 62, 70, 72–73, 81, 91, 122, 165

digraph 37, 84
double vowel-letters 84
dyslexia 46

Early English reading in elementary schools, significance of 6–8
early literacy 9
early reading 6, 16–17
ECA 3–4
    purpose of 3
    surveys on 10–12
    use of letters 12
effect size 64–66
EFL 5
Eigo Note 1 1, 79, 81–85, 149–151, 153, 220–221
Eigo Note 2 1
Elkonin card 103
emergent literacy 29, 63
English as a curricular subject 1–2, 4, 9
English as a foreign language, *see* EFL
English Conversation Activities, *see* ECA
English education in Japanese elementary schools
    beginning 2–3
    historical summary 2–5

245

explicit learning / instruction   51, 61–63

FLA   1, 217–219
    introduction of   4–5
    main focus of   1
Foreign Language Activities, *see* FLA
formal operational stage   8

grain size   46, 48–49, 57
granularity   45–46, 57
Guidebook for Teacher Training in Foreign Language Activities in Elementary Schools   1, 81, 221
Guidelines for the Practice of Elementary School English Language Activities   6, 12

haiku   41
Hi, friends! 1   1
Hi, friends! 2   1
hiragana   33
hypothesis of granularity and transparency   45, 57

identification   73–74
implicit learning / instruction   62–63
informal approach   83
initial phoneme recognition test   89, 223
inside-out strategy   63
instruction of phonological awareness, *see* phonological awareness instruction
interference, *see* negative transfer
intrasyllabic awareness   19, 50, 60
invented spelling   185–186

Japanese logographic characters, *see kanji*
Japanese syllabic symbols, *see kana*
Japanese
    consonant phonemes of   33
    phonological units of   32

    vowel phonemes of   33

kana   33, 56
kana matrix   35–57, 114, 124
kana plus one strategy   35
kanji   8, 33, 56
katakana   33, 166
knowledge of the alphabet, *see* letter knowledge

large-unit hypothesis   23–24
letter knowledge   28
    influence on phonological awareness development   28–30
letter name   9, 28
letter name knowledge test   87, 222
letter sound   9, 28
letter-sound correspondence   9, 39, 56–57
linguistic status hypothesis   71, 73
literacy skills   6, 12
location   91, 165
lower-case letter   1

Magic-*e* rule, *see* split-grapheme rule
manipulation   22, 26, 38, 71, 75
memory   72
    short-term   68
meta-analysis   64
mora / moras   15, 32–35
    and syllables in a single hierarchical phonological structure   50
    types of   32–33, 49
mora awareness   44
mora-timed   41
moraic rhythm, *see* rhythm
moraic segmentation   42–44, 57, 59
motivation
    extrinsic   170
    intrinsic   170

Index   247

non-word, letter combination of   93–94

oddity task   22, 31
onset   19
onset-rime   17, 23–26, 60, 68–69, 84
onset-rime awareness   18–19
onset-rime slide   116
orthographic regularity   93–94
orthographic transparency   45, 49, 53
    influence on phonological awareness transfer   52
orthographic unit, *see* grain size
orthography, deep   63
orthography, influence on learning to read   45–46
orthography, shallow   53, 56
orthography-to-phonology mapping, *see* letter-sound correspondence
outside-in strategy   63

perception   42–43, 57, 72
Period for Integrated Studies, *see* PIS
phoneme manipulation, *see* manipulation
phoneme, definition of   16, 20
phoneme recognition and location test   90, 223
phoneme manipulation test   90, 223
phonemic awareness   18, 20–21, 59–60
phonic book reading   137
phonics   17
phonological awareness
    and early reading development   17, 23–25, 39
    definition of   16–17
    development of   21–22
    development by Japanese children   58–61
    developmental models of   21–22, 59–60
    difference in necessary levels across languages   46–48
    implicit level of   57
    importance of instruction   61–64
    importance of multi-level awareness in early English reading   48–50
    influence on L2 word reading   54–55
    influence on learning to read   23–27
    learnability of   178
    levels of   16–17, 22, 46
    multi-level awareness, importance of   4
    of Japanese children, characteristics of   34–39, 164–168
    rudimentary   28, 58, 68
    skills of, *quasi-parallel* relationship   27, 70
    teachability of   178
    unitary construct   22, 27, 46, 69
phonological awareness assessment
    delivery   175
    dispute   177
    number of phonemes   72
    position of target phonemes   73
    target levels   71
    task differences   71
    task difficulty   70–75
    teaching materials   176
    types of target phonemes   74–75
phonological awareness in L1, influence on L2 early reading   54–55
phonological awareness instruction
    controversial issues of   4–5
    effect / effectiveness of   65, 163
    length   68
    letter use   68
    skills taught   68–69
    target students   65
    unit of delivery   67, 69
    explicit instruction, importance of   61–63

phonological complexity, influence on transfer 52
phonological strategy 35
Piaget's theory of cognitive development 8
PIS 3-4
precursor 23-24, 29, 39, 48, 173, 184
production 71-72, 165
psycholinguistic grain size theory 46

readiness 6, 44, 61, 172, 184
reading by analogy, theory of 24, 49, 61, 68
reading experience in an alphabetic script 30-31
    influence on phonological awareness development 30-31
reading readiness approach 63
real word and non-word reading test 91, 224
recognition 72, 114, 124, 165
reflection sheets 160-161
rhyme awareness 17-18, 23-24, 59-60
rhyme, word-level 19
rime 19
Roma-ji 8
    influence on phonological awareness development 56-58
Romanisation of the Japanese language, see *Roma-ji*
rhythm
    language-specific, influence of 43
    moraic / mora-timed 39

school system of Japan 2
segmenting, *see also* speech segmentation 31, 70, 81, 165
shallow orthography 56
shiritori 41-42
short vowel 32, 84

silent *e* 92
small-unit hypothesis 24-25
sound categorisation 23
    test of 88, 222
speech segmentation
    influence of language rhythm 40
    influence of reading in an alphabetic script 40
    of Japanese children 39
    of Japanese speakers 41-42
split-grapheme rule 84
structured approach 83
substitution 70, 81
supplementary tools for oral communication 1-2, 7, 12, 85
syllabification principle 19
syllable awareness 18-19, 59-60
    shared importance of 48, 50
synthetic skills 72
systematic phoneme 21

tasks of phonological awareness, *also see* phonological awareness assessment 70, 72
transfer of phonological awareness, cross-linguistic 15-16, 51
    affecting factors 52-53
    evidence of 51-52
    negative, interference 16
    positive 16
transparency, *see* orthographic transparency

upper-case letter 1
unit size effect 72

writing system 47
    alphabetic 38, 40, 46
    kana 42, 46
    Roma-ji 56, 69, 85, 88

Introducing Phonological Awareness and Early Literacy Instruction
into Japanese Elementary School English Education
— Its Significance and Feasibility —

著作者　池　田　　周

発行者　武 村 哲 司

2015 年 1 月 25 日　第 1 版第 1 刷発行©

発行所　株式会社 開 拓 社　　〒113-0023 東京都文京区向丘 1-5-2
　　　　　　　　　　　　　　　電話　(03) 5842-8900 (代表)
　　　　　　　　　　　　　　　振替　00160-8-39587
　　　　　　　　　　　　　　　http://www.kaitakusha.co.jp

印刷　株式会社 あるむ　　　　ISBN978-4-7589-2206-7　C3082